The Soul Solution

The need for a theology of the earth

"Glacier Valley"
by Maggie Oliver

Praise for *The Soul Solution*

By living The Way as Teddy Goldsmith calls it, thoughtfully, lightly and with respect, the Harringtons show us the richness of lives lived filled with love and spirit. *The Soul Solution* is their critique of our dilemma and their uplifting vision of what can be.

DAVID SUZUKI

This book shares my own view that God is in everything, plants, animals, earth, water, air and sky.

ANDY RUSSELL Author: *GRIZZLY COUNTRY* and *LIFE OF A RIVER*

A work of exceeding vision, and profound sympathy, understanding and compassion for our world and for life in all its brilliance. This work illuminates a spiritual path which all of us must choose if we are to survive.

DAVID GORANSON M.D. Founder: RIVERS CANADA and THE GREY OWL FUND

A thoughtful discussion of humanity's place in the scheme of things…a gentle critique of our all-consuming focus on material things and lack of respect for Mother Nature. . .an alternative perspective to the normal push for progress and prosperity. A sophisticated and inspiring read. Highly recommended for senior high school libraries.

SCHOOL SUPPORT SERVICES
CALGARY BOARD OF EDUCATION

A spiritual journey illuminating the importance of the connectedness between all life forces. It is the author's belief that the rekindling of this soul force will save this planet. This book offers a positive pathway to a future where economics and nature become partners in achieving this solution.

"ANNOTATIONS" LIST OF RECOMMENDED TITLES FOR B.C. HIGH SCHOOL LIBRARIES
PRODUCED BY B.C. MIN. OF EDUCATION and ASSN. OF BOOK PUBLISHERS OF B.C.

I have just finished reading your book with great admiration. I was fully impressed with the depth and width of your insight as much as with the solid documentation of great thinkers of past and present and East and West. There is so much to meditate on and digest in your book! Your message is of vital importance.

DR. SHUKEI YAMAGUCHI
Author: *METAPHYSICS OF LIFE, YOU MIGHT MEET GOD,* and *ZEN AND BERGSON*

As always I marvel at your scholarship and knowledge of earlier thinkers that gives you the enviable ability to present the wisdom of the ages to your readers. I found your book useful in ways both educational and inspirational.

DR. J. STAN ROWE Author: *HOME PLACE*

The Soul Solution

The need for a theology of the earth

Bob Harrington
with
Linda Harrington

Foreword by
David T. Suzuki

hancock

house

ISBN-10: 0-88839-648-1
ISBN-13: 978-0-88839-648-8

Cataloging in Publication Data

Harrington, Robert F.
The soul solution : the need for a theology of the earth /
Bob Harrington ; with Linda Harrington ;
foreword by David T. Suzuki.

Includes bibliographical references and index.
ISBN 978-0-88839-648-8

1. Human ecology—Religious aspects. 2. Nature—Religious
aspects. 3. Environmental ethics. 4. Human ecology—Philosophy.
5. Philosophy of nature. I. Harrington, Linda II. Title.

BD311.H27 2008   201'.77   C2008-900758-1

Printed in Indonesia — TK PRINTING

Editor: Theresa Laviolette
Production: Kelly Parry & Mia Hancock
Cover design: Mia Hancock
Front cover: *Glacier Valley,* oil painting, Copyright Maggie Oliver 2007
Authors' photo: Paul Gagnier

*We acknowledge the financial support of the Government of Canada through the
Book Publishing Industry Development Program (BPIDP) for our publishing activities.*

Published simultaneously in Canada and the United States by

HANCOCK HOUSE PUBLISHERS LTD.
19313 Zero Avenue, Surrey, B.C. Canada V3S 9R9
(604) 538-1114 Fax (604) 538-2262

HANCOCK HOUSE PUBLISHERS
1431 Harrison Avenue, Blaine, WA U.S.A. 98230-5005
(604) 538-1114 Fax (604) 538-2262

Website: www.hancockhouse.com
Email: sales@hancockhouse.com

Contents

Dedication

To a new awareness of the health and stability of the planet

And so they grow richer and richer, and the more they think of making a fortune the less they think of virtue; for when riches and virtue are placed together in the scales of the balance, the one always rises as the other falls.

PLATO, *THE REPUBLIC, VIII*

Foreword

Echoing the 8th century Brahman philosopher Shankara, *The Soul Solution* suggests that the ecological impasse we are experiencing cannot be solved by logic, but by awakening spiritual insight. This requires the cleansing, enriching and deepening power of our souls. The book recommends that we adopt a theology of the earth, which involves becoming conscious of the earth as the essential part of our existence.

Biologists believe human beings evolved in Africa some 100,000 years ago. We can only surmise the incredible array of animals that must have inhabited the great plains that gave birth to us — the vast herds of wildebeest, elephants and gazelles on land, fish, crocodiles and hippos in the rivers, and birds of every colour in flight — while here and there in groups of three or four, were two-legged, upright, furless creatures that were our ancestors. We were not impressive in numbers, size, speed, strength or sensory acuity. There was little in our appearance to suggest the incredible fate of our species in less than a hundred millennia. Our biological advantage was hidden from view, a two-kilogram organ protected within our skulls.

The human brain is the most complex structure in the known universe and endowed us with an enormous memory, insatiable curiosity and impressive inventiveness and imagination, traits that were the key to our survival. That brain invented something unique, the concept of a future, and because of that, we alone of all species recognized that we could affect the future we arrive at by deliberately selecting from a variety of options in the present. Remembering past experience, we might consider a move to the right which should lead to edible plants while the path left leads to an area rich in predatory lions. In deciding to go where the food might be, we also avoided potential danger from predators. And it worked, taking us to the position of dominance we occupy today. The very definition of being human is to look ahead, recognize where the hazards and opportunities lie and then select the best avenue for survival.

It is strange that today, with all of the amplified brainpower represented by scientists, computers, engineers and telecommunications, we no longer seem able to do what our ancestors did to get us to where we are today. Ever since Rachel Carson raised the alarm about the unexpected consequences of modern technology — in her case, pesticides — environmental awareness grew with explosive speed. When *Silent Spring* was published in 1962, there wasn't a single Department of the Environment in any country on the planet. Rachel Carson put the environment on the agenda. Only ten years later, the movement had grown to such an extent that the United Nations convened a world conference on the environment in 1972 where scientists like Paul Ehrlich, Barry Commoner, Margaret Mead and Barbara Ward, were among the voices warning of problems from overpopulation to toxic pollution, species extinction and economic inequities. In the years following, we learned of ecological consequences of chemical spills in Seveso, Love Canal, Bhopal and Basel; nuclear accidents at Three Mile Island and Chernobyl; oil spills in the ocean that culminated in the *Exxon Valdez;* and new problems such as ozone depletion and global warming. It was leading scientists who were discovering the environmental consequences of much of human activity and technology. In 1987, the Brundtland Commission released *Our Common Future*, pointing out the hazardous degradation of the planet's life support system and invoking the target of "sustainable development." In 1988, public concern was so high, George Bush ran on the promise that if elected, he would be "an environmental President" and a conference of atmospheric scientists in Toronto was so alarmed by the threat of global warming that they called for a reduction of greenhouse gas emissions by 20% in 15 years. In 1992, the largest gathering of heads of state in human history, convened in Rio at the Earth Summit. Agenda 21 was a massive blueprint that could put humanity on to a sustainable path. In November, a document called "World Scientists' Warning to Humanity," signed by more than 1500 senior scientists, including more than half of all living Nobel prizewinners, was released. It began ominously:

Human beings and the natural world are on a collision course. Human activities inflict harsh and often irreversible damage on the environment and on critical resources. If not checked, many of our current practices put at serious risk the future we wish for human society...and may so alter the living world that it will be unable to support life in the manner that we know. Fundamental changes are urgent if we are to avoid the collision our present course will bring about.

The document then lists the areas endangered: atmosphere, oceans, water, soil, forests, species and population. At that point, the words grow even more bleak:

No more than one or a few decades remain before the chance to avert the threats we now confront will be lost and the prospects for humanity immeasurably diminished. We the undersigned, senior members of the world's scientific community, hereby warn all humanity of what lies ahead. A great change in our stewardship of the earth and the life on it is required, if vast human misery is to be avoided and our global home on this planet is not to be irretrievably mutilated.

The document ends with a suggestion of what has to be done in order to head off catastrophe.

The astonishing response was total indifference from the media. None of the major North American television networks bothered to report it, and both the *New York Times* and *Washington Post* rejected it as "not newsworthy." When leading scientists of the world make a profound pronouncement, this is not considered worthy of mention, but O.J. Simpson, Princess Diana, Bill and Monica, and Michael Jackson receive endless exposure for months and years. What will it take to take the observations of experts seriously? We have learned of the massive destruction of global forests, toxic pollution of air, water and soil, ozone depletion, changing climate, depletion of marine fishes, loss of topsoil, extinction of species — the list is long and frightening. In March 2005, the most extensive examination of the state of the planet's ecosystems and the "services" they perform, was released. At a cost of more than

$22 million, the Millennium Ecosystem Assessment involved some 1300 scientists from 91 countries and reinforced the warnings that had been made 13 years before. In Canada, the release of the report did not merit front page coverage in the national newspaper, the *Globe and Mail*, and disappeared from the media after one day, pushed out by the Pope's imminent death. What will it take to focus our attention on the warnings, and why can't we see the planetary holocaust? As *The Soul Solution* suggests, there is no greater time for introspection and a reawakening of the spiritual and ethical meaning of life.

The great French geneticist and Nobel laureate, Francois Jacob, suggests the human brain is "hardwired" to need order. When things happen around us that we don't understand, we find it frightening and attempt to make sense of it all. Our earliest ancestors recognized patterns and rhythms in nature — day/night, seasons, tides and lunar cycles, animal migration and plant succession — and their pre-dictability became a part of our strategy for survival. Human beings create "worldviews," the collective observations, insights, guesses, superstitions, stories, songs and prayers of a people. In a worldview, nothing exists in isolation or separate, everything is interconnected. I have been privileged to spend time with First Nations communi-ties in Canada and aboriginal people in other parts of the world where I have listened to their stories, songs and prayers. They tell us who they are and where they belong on this earth; they celebrate being part of the natural world and thank their Creator for nature's abundance and generosity; they acknowledge that as part of nature, they have responsibilities; and they promise to act properly to keep it all going. That's how it has been in countless cultures around the world.

But suddenly, we have shattered worldviews, living instead in a mosaic of disconnected fragments. We no longer recognize that every deliberate act has consequences, and therefore carries respon-sibilities. Examination of a newspaper reveals the rupture of per-spective — a flood in Bangladesh, hurricanes in the Caribbean, drought in Somalia, severe fires in British Columbia — each is reported separately as if it has nothing to do with any other story. Radio and television "news" is reported as snippets so devoid of context or history that we are blind to any possible solution. And now that we have undergone a transition from rural village living to large urban centres, we have become disconnected from the natural world, living in a human-created environment where the economy seems to be the source of all that matters. But as Bob Harrington reminds us, the fundamental economy is of the earth — a photosynthetic economy which produces 300 billion tons of sugars or precursors of sugar annually.

We no longer recognize that our most basic needs are served by the biosphere, the zone of air, water and land where life exists. As biological beings, we remain utterly dependent on clean air, water and soil, sunlight and the diverse web of living organisms that cleanse, create and replenish those basic needs. As social animals, we need love to be fully human, love that comes from strong families and supportive communities that have full employment, equity, security and justice and freedom from terror, war and genocide. As spiritual creatures, we need sacred places, an understanding that we emerged from nature and will return to it upon death, acceptance that there are forces impinging on us that are beyond understanding and control and knowledge that the planet is not simply a resource for our exclusive use.

The consequence of a shattered world is that we no longer recognize that when we shop in a Walmart rather than local merchants, purchase garments of cotton, wool, leather or rubber, buy computers, television sets and cars with metal parts, there are repercussions that reverberate around the world. Parents who rush their asthmatic children to emergency wards during smog alerts by driving to the hospital in SUVs clearly fail to recognize that their lifestyle is a part of the problem they are dealing with.

As the economy assumes greater importance in our lives and society, we sacrifice the very means whereby we live; we lose sight of the primacy of family and community, focusing instead on corporate priorities and consumption; we dismiss as primitive and backward, our need for spirit. Is our society's highest priority tax relief, the need for greater corporate competitiveness and profit, and more and more stuff? *The Soul Solution* proposes an alternative, that renunciation of the superfluous is an essential step in the restoration of our souls, our world and our peace of mind.

By elevating the economy and consumer products to the highest position in our lives, we assume a very destructive perspective on the world. And the values we cling to shape the way we perceive and treat the world. I accompanied the ethnobotanist, Wade Davis, to a village in the Andes Mountains of Peru where he has worked for more than fifteen years. He told me the children in the village are taught that the mountain behind the village is an apu which means "god." "That's not a symbol of god, it is a god," he told me. "You can imagine how respectfully they treat that mountain, and contrast that with a kid in Trail, BC who is told all his life 'those mountains are full of gold'." The way we view the world shapes the way we will treat it. Is a river a vein of the land or an opportunity for hydroelectric power and irrigation? Is a forest a sacred grove or merely timber and pulp? Is another species our biological kin or a resource? Is the soil a community of life forms or simply dirt? Is our house a home or just property?

My father was 85 when he died. I moved in to care for him through his last weeks. He was blessed with lucidity and absence of pain right up to his death and helped me write his obituary May 6, 1994:

Carr Kaoru Suzuki died peacefully on May 8th. He was eighty-five. His ashes will be spread on the winds of Quadra Island. He found great strength in the Japanese tradition of nature-worship. Shortly before he died, he said: "I will return to nature where I came from. I will be part of the fish, the trees, the birds — that's my reincarnation. I have had a rich and full life and have no regrets. I will live on in your memories of me and through my grandchildren.

Family gathered to say goodbye and as we talked and laughed, cried and reminisced, our time was not spent revelling in memories of closets full of designer clothes, big cars, a huge home or money. Our conversations were filled with the joy and pride of family, friends and community and the riches of experiences shared with them.

Bob Harrington has spent a lifetime pondering these matters, humanity's awesome duality, the capacity for love and compassion and our terrible destructiveness. By living "The Way" as Teddy Goldsmith calls it, thoughtfully, lightly and with respect, the

Harringtons show us the richness of lives lived filled with love and spirit. *The Soul Solution* is their critique of our dilemma and their uplifting vision of what can be. Written years ago, the wisdom suffused throughout this book was never more urgently needed, and offers us a different path to take.

David T. Suzuki

CHAPTER I

Soul: The Root of Life

*Can a single cell think? Can a subdivision of a cell experi-
ence a mental event? No one has proved it can or cannot. But
there is a good deal of advanced opinion holding to the concept of the nonexistence of any lower (or upper) limit to consciousness...*

Guy Murchie
The Seven Mysteries of Life

On weekends, Linda and I sometimes travel to explore
favorite places within our home terrain. One such weekend
we went up the relatively unvisited Incommapleux River valley,
locally known as the Fish River. Thus, on a particular Sunday we
were sitting with our backs against a log, eating our lunch. It was a
bright day, without a cloud in the blue sky and we were grateful for
the shade of a huge old cedar tree and a few surrounding hemlocks.
These trees, so far, had escaped the holocaust of industrial logging
that has reduced the land on both sides of the Fish River to a mas-
sively clear-cut area with only a few small islands of trees left standing. Some of the clear-cuts have been replanted, many of them to a
single species, spruce, which the human powers probably felt would
be the most desirable from an economic standpoint. The logging
industry has advanced slightly since then and now tends to plant two
or more species of seedlings to replace the centuries old giants that
have been cut. Just as monocultured wheat fields must seem to be
heaven on earth for chinch bugs, so single species of trees are an
open invitation for invasions and infestations of spruce budworms

or other opportunistic insects. Hopefully there will be other species reseeding naturally to help restore the earth.

Sitting in our tiny island of trees we talked about the likelihood of awareness existing in the trees around us. It has always seemed apparent to us that our own intelligence must have been derived from a greater intelligence than we possess. That awareness should exist in other life forms seems sensible.

If such an idea seems new, it really is not. It is interesting to note the thoughts of Gustav Fechner, a 19th century medical doctor and professor of physics at the University of Leipzig. Fechner transcended the scientific thought of his time in considering that spirit, or soul, permeates the universe, and is possessed by all things. All things thus are a manifestation of the *anima mundi*, which can be translated as "soul of the world" or as the spirit of the cosmos. Fechner maintained that the body and soul are but two different aspects of the same reality. Plants thus can be thought of as rooted souls, while animals better befit the title of wandering souls. "Plant people," contented in their rooted state, might well wonder at the frenzy in which other creatures hasten about the world and would likely be aghast at such an unintelligent way of life as one which thinks it is progress to breakfast on one continent and sup on another. "In addition to souls which run and shriek and devour, might there not be souls which bloom in stillness, exhale fragrance and satisfy their thirst with dew and their impulses by their burgeoning?"[1] He further suggested that just as the voice comes from inside a human, so scent comes from within a plant, and as we can recognize one another by voices, so plants can recognize one another, by day or night, through scent.

In the English translation of selections of Fechner's work by W. Lowrie, entitled *Religion of a Scientist* (New York, 1946), Lowrie attributes this thought to Fechner:

I stood once on a hot summer's day beside a pool and contemplated a water-lily which had spread its leaves evenly over the water and with an open blossom was basking in the sunlight. How exceptionally fortunate, thought I, must this lily be which above basks in the sunlight and below is plunged in the water — if only it might be capable of feeling the sun and the bath. And why not?

I asked myself. It seemed to me that nature surely would not have built a creature so beautiful, and so carefully designed for such conditions, merely to be an object of idle observation...I was inclined to think that nature had built it thus in order that all the pleasure which can be derived from bathing at once in sunlight and in water might be enjoyed by one creature in the fullest measure (pp. 176–177).

Two millennia earlier, Zeno of Citium (332–262 BC), a Greek philosopher and the founder of Stoicism, expressed a viewpoint favorably quoted by Cicero: "Nothing that is destitute of life and reason, can generate a being possessed of life and reason; but the world does generate beings possessed of life and reason; the world therefore is not itself destitute of life and reason." Sharing such thoughts ourselves, we conjectured that the ancient cedar and its younger comrades may have been agog at the havoc that took place around them when their comrades of many years were systematically slaughtered. They still seemed to echo the thought "unbelievable," and made us ashamed of the deeds of our own species.

The venerable cedar a few feet away from us was probably at least three or four centuries old. There is a possibility that its lengthy lifespan has given it sagacity far greater than we realize. Considering the selfish tyranny we impose upon other living organisms we may well have over-rated our own intelligence and under-rated that of other living beings.

During the cedar's tenure, grizzlies have pursued their unhurried way beneath its boughs. Wolverines, marten, and fishers very likely climbed among its branches. Woodland caribou fed on Usnea (beardmoss) hanging from its limbs; kinglets and chickadees sported in its foliage, whispering their secrets. Winter storms have roared through the valley and draped its boughs with snow; spring freshets resounded in the nearby river; summer warmth bathed its leafy arms, and lightning flashed all about it as thunder resounded from the hills. Autumn's mellowness has immersed it in lambent light and the first hard frosts have signalled the approaching quiet time of year.

Am I claiming sentience as a characteristic of this noble tree -

that it was aware of the forest denizens as they passed? Am I merely projecting wishes when I ascribe nobility to it? Am I playing with some transferred anthropomorphism and being utterly impractical? What I am doing is simply expressing my own agreement with the many great thinkers who have identified soul-force as present in all living things.

German philosopher, Friedrich Paulsen, in his *History of Philosophy*, spoke of "the obstinate dogmatism of popular opinion and of the physical conception of the universe" as being a "nightview" of the universe. He credited such a view as natural to a mechanized civilization in which people have lost the ability to notice and appreciate any quality that cannot be measured or calculated. Only lately have a few rays of light begun to slightly dispel the pitch blackness of this dark night of the human soul. One can only hope that the dawn of a new worldview will be embraced in time.

Nature, to my own comprehension, is the art form of the Great Workman. If man is "fallen," nature is not. It stands erect, and in spite of our frenzied "development," it still beckons us with beauty everywhere. It is a constant and conspicuous sign of works beyond our own capabilities. Because of our impetuous natures, we are engaged in a race between whatever insights we can garner about reality, and our own tendency to chop and change at a life-threatening pace. Yet nature always stands about us — grave, serene and just, although perhaps less patient. There are signs that we are at a crossroads, with insights at hand that could lead us to exchange our unreal aspirations for ones that will fit within the permissible parameters that the Earth affords. Contrast, for example, the reductionist goal we are blindly pursuing with a more holistic worldview we could adopt, one that would allow us to reattach ourselves to the sacred world in which we live and move and have our being. For clarity's sake, a few words about the reductionist outlook might be of value.

Contemporary society is repeatedly referred to as reductionist, as focused solely on materialistic, lucrative and prestigious goals in defiance of any wider perspective. This worldview rests precariously on thoughts espoused by Galileo (1564–1642) and Rene Descartes (1596–1650), who claimed that the aim of science was to reduce the laws of nature to mathematical relationships. Adoption of such thought as a central reality for the industrial juggernaut has been a convenience for the exploitation of nature and a disaster to planetary ecology. These beliefs included the view that animals were simply reactive machines without consciousness, and the very thought that there might be any consciousness among plants was beyond imagining. Focus on quantifiable data narrowed room for metaphysical speculation. Life became simplified. The role of the citizen became one of credulous consumerism; that of the entrepreneur became one of socially sanctioned exploitation; and the role of the earth was relegated to that of a mere stock pile of resources — a folly of incredible magnitude.

One of the darkest ages in history — the Dark Age of Rampant Technology — has been allowed to dominate the world until we stand today at the edge of an Armageddon of our own creation. Earth wisdom, which had been accumulating through the ages, was chucked aside as madcap progress blinded humanity to any other values or ideals. A vast social disease has resulted and is at a crisis point today.

The pagan understood that God provided all things. Modern religions permit the Deity to be removed from this world and leave divinity in outer space to rule from heaven, but not to interfere with progress here on earth. There is much that is obviously fallacious in our thoughts and actions. It is true, though, that there is a gradual awakening taking place, at the roots, but hardly at the pinnacle of the social structure. It has taken a number of centuries to partially crawl from beneath the mechanistic burden that wealth-seeking imposed on humanity.

Thoughtful analyses of our present condition have been made, but not popularized, because they are often obstacles in the economic stream of events. Yet individuals ranging from Plato to T.H. Huxley and Henry Thoreau provide beacons on our road to enlightenment. In his book *Physics and Microphysics* (1955), Nobel-prize-winning quantum physicist Louis de Broglie indicated his agreement with French philosopher Henri Bergson that humanity now had more fossil fuel, hydroelectric, and atomic power available than it could properly control.[2] Like Bergson, he saw that our mechanism demands a mysticism, lest it destroy us. De Broglie reiterated

Bergson's call for "a supplement of soul" that would enable us to control the tiger we have by the tail.

Although I profess no formal creed, I take heed of the fact that ancient sages we call prophets, men who roamed the hills and lived under the sun and stars as we no longer do, were much more closely attached to nature than we are. They were men whose internal world was in harmony with the external world.

I feel far more respect for the prophet Job than I do for today's titans of commerce, especially when I read thoughts of his that I have never heard seriously discussed by professional churchmen. In the 12th chapter of the Book of Job, he declares:

> But ask now the beasts, and they shall teach thee;
> and the fowls of the air, and they shall tell thee;
> Or speak to the earth, and it shall teach thee;
> and the fishes of the sea shall declare unto thee.
> Who knoweth not in all these that the hand of the LORD hath wrought this?
> In whose hand is the soul of every living thing, and the breath of all mankind.[3]

My intuition moves to accord with what Job wrote, and declares him a man of deep insight. I wonder why the pulpit has so long been silent on such a salient statement; for there are creeds, I understand, that believe every word in the Bible is literal truth. Such Christians could hardly be faulted for considering all other life forms as imbued with souls — intentionally. It is interesting to note that God chose to speak to Moses from a burning bush, and that Solomon in all his glory was not arrayed as lovely as the lilies of the field. How differently we would behave on earth if our civilization had allowed itself to realize that we humans are not the only creatures of importance in this living world!

As modern science peers beyond the limitations afforded by our unassisted senses, it repeatedly encounters vibrant complexity that calls its earlier assumptions into question. Mathematician, physicist, and astronomer Sir James Jeans came to see the world as closely resembling a "great idea." In his words:

The concept of the universe as a world of pure thought throws a new light on many of the situations we have encountered in our survey of modern physics...If the universe is a universe of thought, then its creation must have been an act of thought.

We are actually beginning to see the significance of ideas that have been emerging throughout the years. Hermann Lotze's words in *Mikrokosmus* (Vol.1, Leipzig 1856–1864), are an outgrowth of earlier thought and a predecessor to today's experimental knowledge:

> All motion of matter in space may be explained as a natural expression of the inner states of beings that seek or avoid one another with a feeling of their need... The whole of the world of sense...is but the veil of an infinite realm of mental life.[4]

This was apparently intuited by famous American scientist George Washington Carver (1864–1943), who referred to nature as an "unlimited broadcasting station which would speak to all who cared to listen."

Carver's own achievements lay in developing undreamed of uses for plants, particularly peanuts; although he also discovered 536 dyes extracted from roots, stems, leaves and fruits of various other plants. His work earned superlatives. Henry Ford named him "the greatest scientist living." Carver's analysis of his own ability was that living things talked to him and that, "I know by watching and loving everything." Although Thomas Edison espoused the belief that, "Carver is worth a fortune," Carver himself embraced the philosophy that since God did not "charge me or you" for making peanuts, "Why should I profit from their products?"[5] While skeptics might shrug and deny his views, his attainments suggest that he had an uncommon insight.

From the general view of mind permeating matter we can look more closely at the world of plants.

Much important work on plant sensitivity was carried on by physicist and plant physiologist Sir Jagadis Chandra Bose (1858–1937), professor at Presidency College, Calcutta from 1885–1915. Bose focused on the similarity between animal and plant responses and, through the development of precise instrumentation, which greatly magnified the effects of stimuli, he was able to show plant, leaf and stem reactions to be identical to nerve–muscle responses in humans. His work, which led to a knighthood from the British government in 1917, caused a French newspaper to quip that after learning of his discoveries one wonders when a woman is flirtatiously struck with a flower blossom, whether the woman or the blossom suffers more. Scientists who visited his laboratory and saw, through his delicate instruments, the twinging and wincing of plants reacting to mechanical manipulations or minute electrical shocks, were convinced that he had opened a field of research that was a milestone in scientific achievement. George Bernard Shaw, one of his visitors, dedicated his collected works to Bose with the inscription: "From the least to the greatest living biologist."

Bose's numerous and voluminous publications remain as an introduction to fields of research that are likely to discover much about relationships between all living things and about similarities between living things and the mineral kingdom as well.

More widely known are some of the research studies of Cleve Backster, especially since publication of a feature article on his experimentation in "National Wildlife" in February 1969. His studies were elaborated in *The Secret Life of Plants* (1973), written by Peter Tompkins and Christopher Bird. One of his experiments showed that monitored plants reacted "strongly and synchronously" to the death of brine shrimp in boiling water. Scientists studying the automated monitoring system concluded that the reactions were five to one against the possibility that they could have been caused by chance. Readers of the "National Wildlife" article were particularly intrigued at the thought that a tree might quake at the approach of a woodchopper, or a carrot quiver as a rabbit hopped toward it.

Thus, there is reasonable ground for us to consider that the cedar tree we visited was aware and greatly disturbed at the logging that had taken place around it, and that it was even aware of our presence and of the fact that we felt affection for it, and interest in having our lunch nearby.

Indeed, the world about us is apparently far more sentient than we realize, and we are not as separate from it as we think. After all, our bones are related to the mineral kingdom, our bodies have been nourished since conception, by the ingestion of food provided by the plant and animal kingdom. The idea that "all flesh is as grass" (1 Peter 1:24) and that it lives and withers away is a reality. And as for our minds, consciences, and souls, it is irresponsible to ignore the fact that they do not stand in isolation but are derived from the energy of the universe.

The fact that the sound and movement in motion pictures concur in time is called synchronization. People often comment on the occurrence in life of related incidents. Carl Jung (1875–1961), noted Swiss psychiatrist and founder of analytic psychology, defined the concept of synchronicity as coincidences of such a meaningful nature that they can hardly be attributed to chance alone.[6] Physicist Dr. F. David Peat (Queen's University) suggests that such incidents can be attributed to the holographic nature of the universe and that they reveal a much closer connection between our thought processes and the physical world than has been suspected.[7]

Jung's principle interest in synchronicity had to do with events that take place in response to concerns or questions in the human psyche. The scarab story told by Jung is an interesting example. He was treating a woman whose own rational convictions about life made her a constrained patient, one who found it difficult to respond to therapy. After a series of frustrating sessions, she told Jung about a dream that involved a scarab beetle. He was aware that in Egyptian mythology the scarab is associated with rebirth, and wondered if she was indicating subconsciously that she was on the verge of psychological rebirth. He was just starting to tell her about this association when he heard a tap on the window and looked out to see that a heavy-bodied, green-gold scarab beetle had landed on the outside of the glass, the only time he had seen such a thing happen. Jung opened the window and the beetle flew into the room as he interpreted the dream for his patient. The stunning synchronicity of the occurrence overcame the lady's resistance to treatment, and her response to therapy was vastly improved.

Another amusing coincidence to the writing of this incident was involved when I looked in a *New Age Encyclopedia* (1980) to find the dates of Jung's life. I noted quite accidentally that on the page facing the article about Jung, there is an article entitled "June Bug or June Beetle." My own interest in entomology caused me to take courses in that field, and I knew that a June Bug (common in

Canada) belongs to the family of scarab beetles. I looked to see if that was mentioned, and found the commentary identifying these beetles as being "of the scarab beetle family, Scarabaeidae." One could go overboard looking for apparent synchronicities or presume a jokester gremlin running around trying to awaken our attention to the existence of such phenomena. For example, when the encyclo-pedia is closed, the article on Jung and that on the June beetle, par-tially rest against one another; and I suppose that I could add that if I hadn't studied insect biology and learned the Latin names of bee-tle families, I wouldn't have checked to see if the word "scarab" was mentioned in the June beetle–June bug article. Just for the record, the June beetles are not bugs at all, since bugs, taxonomically, do not belong to any beetle family.

The foregoing incident is by way of introducing an odd experi-ence of synchronicity that took place only a few days after our pleasant lunch by the cedar tree. It is our habit in snow-free weath-er to spend two or three days of the week working on land that was privately logged by the previous owner, mainly clear-cut. We bought the land to reforest it and have planted 8,000 trees thus far and have also collected burlap bags of cones from various trees, shaken them out, and broadcast the seed from them on the land. We did this because we wanted to do something to restore the bared land to forest cover.

On that particular day, when we arrived there to work we found a pickup truck parked right in front of our gate. We had just begun to look for the owner of the vehicle when a dog appeared and a moment later an elderly gentleman, probably in his late seventies, came into sight. He was affable and knowledgeable and immediate-ly commented on the many trees he saw planted, and asked if this was our doing. Shortly afterward we were engaged with him in a general conversation about replanting and about the diverse species we are trying to grow. We told him that we transplant a lot of trees that are growing in roadside ditches, which would otherwise be mowed down by the road maintenance crews. Other trees are pur-chased from nurseries, but because we realize that the nurseries use seed from select stock, we like to encourage genetic diversity by planting ditch trees that are the result of random dispersion of seeds by indigenous species. We feel that there is a real likelihood that recessive genes may be very valuable in the struggle for survival resulting from increased ultraviolet radiation and from the greenhouse warming that is taking place. Other factors, such as depleted soils and increasing pollution, also indicate the need for preserving genetic traits that may be of vital importance.

As the conversation went on, we also spoke of the difficulty of getting all the roots when we dig trees from ditches where the soil is often very compacted and rocky. We have learned that it is much easier to get most of the roots from trees ten or twelve inches high than from other taller ones which we would prefer to transplant. Experience also seems to be teaching us that the smaller trees catch up with the larger ones in a year or two, probably because of less root damage done while transplanting.

At one point Linda commented on a chapter she had recently read in *The Secret Life of Plants,* which described experiments that involved attaching electrodes to plants and connecting them to a polygraph lie detector. She explained to the man that in one experiment a plant leaf was dunked in hot coffee without effect on the polygraph tracing, but when the researcher simply *thought* of holding a lighted match under the leaf there was a dramatic upward tracing made on the graph. The experimenter had commented that it seemed apparent that somehow the plant was "reading" his mind.

Our new-found friend responded by telling us that he had worked for a number of years for the forest service in Alberta. During some of this time he was employed in a greenhouse where experiments were being carried out with growing trees. When trees were dug for replanting, polygraph leads were attached to them. It was learned that when the roots were severed, the lines traced by the polygraph shot sharply upward, "as though the plants were screaming." This experiment led directly to planting the seedlings in Styrofoam cups to reduce transplanting shock, and later to planting in Styrofoam blocks that contain many cylindrical holes for individual trees. Seeds are now planted in a special rooting medium in each hole, and when it is time to transplant the seedlings the trees are simply lifted out of the holes with minimal root disturbance.

So we are left wondering if ours was a chance meeting or an "arranged encounter." It is the present vogue in our technocratic society to be disdainful of any sign of "intention" in the vast embrace of what we call nature. In our dismal pursuit of affluence, amidst the garbage dumps of our own creation, we engage in one sophisticated trivial pursuit after another. We are largely oblivious to the fact that quantum physicists are encountering the phenomenon of the ubiquity of consciousness. As Sir Arthur Eddington has explained, "the stuff of this world is mind-stuff," and the shadow behind reality is awareness. As he says: "The mind-stuff of the world is, of course, something more general than our individual conscious minds, but we may think of its nature as not altogether foreign to the feelings in our consciousness."[8]

My own certainty that there is sentience in nature is corroborated by a significant number of scholars at the leading edge of our sciences.

It is notable that Stephen Jay Gould, Harvard University palaeontologist, made some interesting comments in one of his regular columns in *Natural History* magazine.

Suggesting that it would be "enlightened self-interest" to adopt the golden rule as the major principle of our relationship to the Earth, he stated that to do so "would be a blessing for us, and an indulgence for Her." Reminding us that a bit of humility would be good for us he stated, "the planet holds all the cards," and suggested, "We had better sign the papers while she is still willing to make the deal."

While he did not address the matter of sentience directly, it is at least inferred in the observation that if we make an effort to change in such a manner, "earth will uphold her end of the bargain."

But, he continued, "If we scratch her, she will bleed, kick us out, bandage up, and go about her business at her planetary scale."[9]

It is urgent for us to realize that there is no health for us or our families, no future for us or our children, unless we understand that a healthy, cared for earth is the *sine qua non* (without which nothing) of our own existence. The earth is the primary consideration. Wealth, affluence, and all the things we presently value are secondary issues.

CHAPTER 2

What is Soul?

*The problem of restoring to the world original and eternal
beauty is solved by the redemption of the soul...The reason
why the world lacks unity, and lies broken and in heaps, is
because man is disunited with himself.*

Ralph Waldo Emerson

It started with a spontaneous question. "Do you believe in miracles?" I pondered for a moment. I knew that a trite answer wasn't appropriate. The question was asked in class by one of my biology students, and I knew by the intent expression on his face, that he expected a serious answer.

Silently I blessed the Latin teacher who had pounded into us, in my own high school days, the frequent importance of Latin in determining the root meaning of words in our own language. I knew that "miracle" was derived from a word pertaining to things that inspired one to wonder or to realize them as wonderful. I was more comfortable answering his question than I would have been if I were constrained by the theological idea that miracles refer to things that contradict known scientific laws.

"Yes," I replied, "I do believe in miracles and in fact, I'll bring one to class tomorrow, if you would like."

That pretty well took care of the last eight or ten minutes of the class period. A volley of hands shot up. I had to respond to questions such as: "You're not joking? Do you mean a real miracle?" "Is this something we will think is a miracle too?" "Is this going to be spooky?" And the class skeptic remarked, "I don't believe in miracles at all. You're just kidding; this is some sort of gimmick."

I assured them that I wasn't joking, that there really were miracles, and after tomorrow's class they would probably agree with me. I guaranteed them that I wasn't into "spooky" things, and I told them I thought miracles could be quite straightforward and convincing without much outside help.

Maybe teaching and prize fighting do have one little thing in common. Both offer situations in which one can be "saved by the bell."

When I thought about it after the morning class, I realized that this was one of those things that people call a teachable moment. When I was kidded at lunchtime in the staff room about having a miracle on the next day's agenda, I realized that the topic of miracles had people talking. This was confirmed just before the end of the day when I was asked by two students, who weren't even taking biology, if they might attend my class the next day provided they could get permission to be excused from study hall. As long as they had permission, I told them, I didn't mind at all.

The next morning when I walked into school I was immediately asked if I had remembered to bring the miracle. I think that I was expected to have a big package or something like that in my arms when I was asked, "Where is it?" I assured them I'd brought the miracle but declined to answer the question as to its location.

When class began there was expectation in the air with more questions about the miracle, and a groan was elicited when I said that first I was going to hand back some quiz papers.

Walking around, handing out papers, I could feel the anticipation grow — a rather nice feeling to have in a normally more prosaic atmosphere.

Returning to the front of the room, I responded to a spontaneous request, "How about that miracle now?" by hamming it up just a little, leaning to the left as though carrying nearly unbearable weight and saying, "Gosh, it's heavy!"

Because I'm not a very good thespian, that didn't seem to impress anyone.

I told them, first of all, that miracles were much more commonplace than people realized, explaining that the word miracle didn't necessarily refer to anything magical but actually referred to things that were wonderful. In other words, this meant things that a person would really wonder about if he or she thought carefully.

I then said that I had something in my pocket that could potentially weigh more than a million pounds. It seemed pretty wonderful to me, I told them, that something I could keep in my shirt pocket could eventually come to weigh that much. When I had leaned to the side, I told them, it was simply that I let myself imagine what an incredible potential weight I was carrying.

At this point I took a packet of seeds from my shirt pocket. "These are seeds of trees known as Giant Sequoias. I'm sure that many of you have heard of them and know that the Giant Sequoias are the biggest trees on earth and also the largest living things. I happen to have this package of seeds because I hope to sprout a few of them, and see if I can get them to grow on my own place."

I went on to tell them that I had counted the seeds in the packet and there were 48 of them. I explained that it was anybody's guess how many seeds might germinate, but I would be pleased if even a half-dozen of them did.

The wonderful thing, to me, I explained, is that a single sequoia the size of the General Sherman tree in California could grow from such a tiny thing as the individual seeds in the packet. At this point I put a number of the seeds in a Petri dish and passed them around.

"Just think! The General Sherman tree weighs 1,250 tons, or 2,500,000 pounds, and is 105 feet around at the base. It is still growing and is one of the oldest living things on earth. So, if forty of the seeds in this little packet were to attain their potential size, their weight could reach or surpass a hundred million pounds."

Not surprisingly, after discussion, the student consensus was that the phenomenon of all sorts of seeds, is a continuing miracle. So to speak, they ran with the ball once it was thrown to them.

Luckily, we were far enough ahead in our class work that they could mull over the issue and come up with ideas of all sorts of miracles, including ourselves, our eyes as part of ourselves, and a fact they had never before considered — that life itself is a miracle.

One student recalled that when we had been talking about recycling, I had pointed out that nature has been recycling ever since life began. She thought it miraculous that life could come from death, and brought out a laugh from the class when she exclaimed, "Maybe the brontosaurs are still here, but now we are wearing runners and taking notes!"

The following semester I could see that the idea of miracles was alive and well. In my chemistry class we were discussing the law of conservation of energy and matter, that neither matter nor energy can be created or destroyed but can be changed from one form to another with the total amount of mass-energy remaining constant. One of the students who had been in my biology class in the last semester piped up, "Isn't this a sort of miracle too? Seeing that we are made up of energy and matter, and you can't destroy either but only change them from one form to another, doesn't this sort of guarantee our immortality?"

"Maybe it does!" I said.

What exactly is the soul? Looking at some of the factors in the evolution of the idea of soul may help us find an answer.

Soul is considered to be the essence of life: the radix (lat.) or root of being. The word animal is derived from the Latin *anima*, which means soul. Soul is thus the life-giving characteristic, the animating principle. Many religions have deemed it to be immortal and separable from the body at the time of death, a fragment of divinity that exists in all beings. Life itself, and therefore its essence — soul, is vastly older than religions, and involves transitions from matter that are not entirely explicable. Wherever a religion might call for renunciation of the flesh or the earth, it is treading upon the basis of its own existence.

When omniscience, omnipotence, and omnipresence are spoken of as attributes of God, it is not illogical to expect a spillover of these attributes into the totality of creation. Consider, for instance, the almost incomprehensible energy revealed through nuclear fission; or at the opposite end of the scale, the wonders of the far-flung web of life that is suggested by the studies of the Hindu physicist Jagadis Chandra Bose, who in measuring plant sensitivities also discovered traces of similar sensitivities in metals. That "All is One" seems less elusive as a thought than it once was.

The Eleusinian Mysteries, most famous of the Greek mystery cults (ca. 600 BC or earlier), center on Demeter (the corn mother), and Persephone (the corn daughter), and give some insight into the antiquity of "soul" as a human concept. As part of the Lesser Mysteries, we are told that Persephone was picking flowers in a beautiful meadow when Earth opened and Pluto, the Lord of Death, emerged riding in a splendid chariot. He seized the struggling, screaming Persephone and carried her to his underworld palace where he forced her to become his queen. Demeter (Ceres) eventually appeared before Pluto and pleaded with him for the release of Persephone. Although he refused at first, he eventually compromised and agreed that she could return to the world of the living for six months of each year, but that she must return to spend the remaining six months of the year with him in the darkness of Hades.

As Dr. Manly Hall has pointed out, Persephone symbolizes "soul," and Pluto the "physical nature of man." The gloom of the Lesser Mysteries makes apparent the miseries of a spiritual soul deprived of expression because it is forced to live amidst the illusions and limitations of material concern. Part of the lesson afforded by the Eleusinian teaching, Hall says, is that if an individual does not grow beyond the quest for material possessions in this life, the same goal will go with him or her into invisible life and be a torment forever. Failure to surmount ignorance in mortal life will lead to wandering forever in eternity, repeating life's mistakes. We choose to live either by the insights of our living spirit or by the demands of mortal, physical personalities. Felicity is to be found only by freeing the spiritual nature from the bonds of the material nature.[1]

At the same time, while emphasizing that the soul is a spiritual entity, striving for higher worlds, the Eleusinian teaching stressed that suicide is a great evil to be followed by great sorrow. Life is not meant to be circumvented at will.

Nor were the Eleusinian Mysteries unique in their focus upon soul. Plato considered the soul as of a higher nature than the body, and referred to the body as the sepulchre of the soul. Socrates taught that soul was endowed with all knowledge prior to life, but became stupefied upon entering a mortal body. If exposed to a correct form of life, the soul could reawaken and gain its original knowledge. Socrates saw the aim of his teaching as being the contemplation of God and freeing of the soul from its corporeal limitations.

The Stoics, of more pantheistic inclination, maintained that since there is nothing better than the world, the world itself is God. Zeno contended that the reason of the world is diffused throughout it as seed, and defined nature as God mixed throughout world substance. Although various religious perspectives have their differences they also have similarities, and there would not seem to be serious disagreement between the Stoic view of God's omnipresence and St. Paul's observation to the Athenians that in the Lord "we live, and move, and have our being" (Acts 17:22–28). Cleanthes, a Stoic, in giving explicit meaning to life's "creative fire," pioneered the term *pneuma*, which is translated "spirit" and became the divine spirit that we refer to today.

Marcus Aurelius, Roman emperor and general, is perhaps the most notable Stoic, and his classic *Meditations* is still widely read. Some idea of the pertinency of his thoughts can be gained from these brief quotes:

> Nowhere can man find a quieter or more untroubled retreat than in his own soul; above all, he who possesses resources within himself, which he need only contemplate to secure immediate ease of mind — the ease that is only another word for a well-ordered spirit.

> Always think of the universe as one living organism, with a single substance and a single soul; observe how all things are submitted to the single perceptivity of this one whole, all are moved by its single impulse, and all play their part in the causation of every event that happens. Remark the intricacy of the skein, the complexity of the web.

> As a part, you inhere in the Whole. You will vanish into that which gave you birth; or rather, you will be transmuted once more into the creative Reason of the universe.[2]

It is interesting to me to note how one may be influenced in his own thought by something he has read and seemingly forgotten. Marcus Aurelius referred to the universe as "dear city of God," an expression that seemed right. I remember that one night when we took a late walk under a sky ablaze with stars, I mentioned to Linda that the stars are streetlights in the city of God. I still like to think of them in that way.

Avicenna (Abu Ali al-Husein ibn Sina) 980–1037, a Muslim doctor referred to as the outstanding Medieval philosopher, thought of God as the only being existing as a result of its own essence. God is therefore the First Cause of all things. As a result of his gift of life we are all aware of soul as our deepest internal perception. It is spiritual, and enables movement and growth in a body. Even the celestial spheres have souls and "the whole cosmos is the manifestation of a universal principle of life." Each soul possesses a measure of creative power and freedom because it is a product of the First Cause. Evil is not the product of First Cause but is derived from the measure of free will each soul possesses. The pure soul after death is reunited with the World Soul. To worship God with spiritual love, without fear or hope, is the highest achievement of mankind.[3]

St. Thomas Aquinas (1225–1274), known as "Prince of Scholastics" was both theologian and philosopher. His theological writings were utilized as a source of precise formulations of Christian beliefs by general councils of the Roman Catholic Church from Lyons (1274) to the Vatican Council (1869). Aquinas pointed out that our senses provide us with natural understanding that God exists. His majesty shines forth and is vividly displayed in the organization and wonders of the world. However, we are incapable of knowing His essence except through revelation. Being aware of such qualities as love, intelligence, freedom or truth in ourselves, we can comprehend by analogy that these qualities must also exist in man's creator in a corresponding proportion between ourselves and infinity. God is Being itself. The masculine pronoun, he says is used to signify God, but this is only a matter of convenience, because there is no sex in God or in the angels.[4]

Thomas considered the soul to be of a life-giving, form-creating nature, and indivisibly found in every part of the body, its inner energy. It is spiritual and infused in us by God, and is the vital force upon which all physical processes depend. The highest good is the acquisition of truth during life, and in afterlife to see this truth in God. Aquinas visualized that the greatest accomplishment and satisfaction of the soul would be "that on it should be inscribed the total order of the universe and its causes." This, to be sure, might be the greatest good to a person whose quest was knowledge, but other appetites might find peace and happiness in areas other than intellectual fulfilment. Considering the modern era, it is interesting to note that Aquinas thought of the pursuit of wealth beyond one's needs as sinful covetousness. In this respect, it is unfortunate that Christianity, which does focus on the development of the soul, has neglected to follow the teachings of one of its most distinguished philosophers; it has failed to assign greater value to simplicity and austerity than to the gaudy and demoralizing trappings of materialism. Aquinas also condemned outright attempts to profit at speculative trading and making gains from market fluctuations.

Throughout history, much attention has been given to the concept of soul, relating it to the inborn drive to live a life of meaningfulness. John Keats, in an 1819 letter to his brother and sister, commented that we all have some sort of electric fire that strives to purify within ourselves. He wrote, "Call the world if you Please 'The Vale of Soul-Making'...I say *Soul Making* — Soul as distinguished from Intelligence — There may be intelligences or sparks of the divinity in millions — but they are not Souls till they acquire identities, till each one is personally itself." He asks how each of these souls could gain an identity other than through "the medium of a world like this." Keats envisions this world as a school for all humans, who are as little children. Listing intelligence, the human heart, and the world as the raw materials for the formation of soul, he asks, "Do you not see how necessary a World of Pains and troubles is to school an Intelligence and make it a soul? A place where the heart must feel and suffer in a thousand diverse ways!"[5] The codependency of the material and immaterial suggests that we must have great respect for both.

Seeing as through a glass darkly, it is difficult to live life without making many errors. Philosopher Lewis Mumford compares life to a musical score that we cannot rehearse, but must play upon first sight. To make it more difficult, we are amateurs at the use of our instrument and find it hard to understand what the composer of the music of life intended. Additionally, the score that we attempt to read is incomplete and many improvisations, for which we are unprepared, must be made. Some of these improvisations are lengthy and are difficult particularly because of our own lack of experience. As he points out, it is not sufficient to stoutly deny our own errors, but it is essential that we transform and assimilate the errors and discordances so that we grow through them and somehow perform credibly in spite of our handicaps. If it was not for the fact that our forefathers have encountered similar difficulties, and that our racial memory helps us recall some of the notes and their sequences, Mumford says, "we might often give up in sheer despair."[6] The amazing thing, he continues, is not that there is so much chaos produced as that there is much harmony and progression in spite of the difficulties posed by life.

Our spiritual natures are often suppressed by a life filled with the illusions and limitations of material concerns. This is where the matter of individuality becomes very important. Compare, for instance, the often-heard cliché that "everybody has his price," with a more thoughtful statement that is seldom voiced, namely that, "the most difficult task in life is to remain an unpurchasable person." The claim that everyone has a price is further clarified by another expression — "money talks." It is obviously easier, and requires less willpower, to go along with the concept that there is a price that will get a job done. It is unfortunate that in our dream of civilization there are individuals not troubled by conscience, who are hireable for a wide range of deplorable deeds.

People do not think as much about the matter of being unpurchasable, but I did see this point called to the attention of an individual once. Hopefully it was an occasion that the student would not forget.

While teaching at a Catholic university I was appointed to a committee whose purpose was to conduct an oral examination for a student who was to receive a Bachelor of Science degree in chemistry. The "oral," as it was called, was a last hurdle on the way to earning the degree. Each of the half-dozen committee members would ask the student two questions: one as to his general knowledge, and the other in the field in which he was taking his degree. Unwittingly, I precipitated a memorable incident.

The student had achieved excellent grades in his courses, and breezed through the questions relating to his discipline. We had begun asking questions regarding his general knowledge. I asked him what his reaction would be if the company he worked for instructed him to help develop a product which he knew would be socially injurious or perhaps dangerously life threatening. Frankly, I was thinking of extremely toxic biocides that have been manufactured and even more of agents of warfare, which are almost endlessly profuse in modern society. I was, in short, asking him to consider a moral issue that confronts many people today.

His answer was unhesitating and quite decisive. He said that the company he worked for would pay his salary and he would do the job they assigned him.

The chairman of the panel was the university president, a Jesuit scholar. I believe that all of us on the panel and the student, will remember this long-geared, six foot six man, garbed in a brown robe, rising slowly to his feet and pointing a bony hand toward the student. "Do you mean to say," he growled, "that in four years at this institution you have not learned that you are morally responsible for every thing you do, and cannot simply say — as so many men have said — that I am 'simply carrying out orders'?"

The student of course, had made an unfortunate error, one which it is to be hoped also taught him something. A constructive discussion followed. He was granted his degree but, because of the questioning, perhaps gained new insight into his soul.

The student's automatic acceptance of the role he would play as obedient, unthinking servant of a company for which he worked, is indicative of a serious moral problem of society. It is reminiscent of Thoreau's reflection that the young person gathers his materials to build a bridge to the moon, or to pursue some other idealistic venture, while the middle-aged man eventually uses the same materials to build a woodshed. So the youth of the 1850 era started off with idealistic dreams, which often failed. But since the 1850s, as indicated by our graduate student, there is no longer even an idealistic dream and people expect little more than to be a cog in some faceless machine.

Now I think that the chairman of the oral exam performed a heroic service in reminding the student that we do have responsibility to morality, which in itself is the maintenance of an ideal. Idealism may be considered poppycock by devoted materialists, but idealism is the real hope of civilization, or perhaps for civilization. Economic sufficiency can be attained without the destruction of ideals but ever-increasing economic abundance, like a cancer, is a pathological rejection of the long-standing ideals of measure and balance, of the moderation of physical demands by spiritual intuition.

A particularly fetching title of a book by Father Murray Bodo called *The Journey and the Dream* merits thought because it is a compact description of what life should be. The book, which is about Francis of Assisi, suggests to the reader that life is indeed a journey, from the cradle to the grave. But the journey that takes place between birth and death needs a dream to make it worthwhile. The dream or ideal is that which gives life meaning. The dream need not be a spectacular thing. Not all people want to be a famous politician, war hero, or industrialist and have a statue erected in their memory, or a mountain, dam, lake or building named in their honor. St. Francis of Assisi was prescient in an unusual way as he tried to establish the brotherhood and sisterhood of all living things. His ideal is yet only on the horizon of thought, but is becoming more visible to the inner-eye of many individuals.

I have also often thought that the oral exam committee chairman's abrupt defence of moral responsibility in the workplace indicates the notoriety of unethical behavior common in our industrial society.

Even in the 1960s, Lewis Mumford envisioned these problems that are now rampant in society and stifle our souls. He foresaw over-organization and over-specialization that would destroy individuality, turning people into consumers who earned wages primarily to pay bills, and supporting economic aims that are fostered by the multiplication of superfluous wants. Such a society would tie itself into knots because it was no longer able to put first things first. Expansion of materialistic concern would entail a shriveling of spiritual insight. The protection of one's inner being, of soul, involves resistance to conformity, and must be rejected by an increased determination on the part of individuals to evaluate offerings, and to reject those that have no real meaning to one's inner being. Protecting individuality means that we should react to such overwhelming forces as those expressed through advertising by becoming more Spartan in our own behavior. We must protect our own souls by refusing to be bulldozed into the belief that the mere accumulation of material goods is the primary hallmark of a successful life. Mumford also predicted that the mere quantitative increase in information could produce its own form of ignorance and that the continual increase in goods would itself be productive of chronic dissatisfaction, and an eventual sense of living on a meaningless treadmill. "Simplicity," he advised, "does not avoid mechanical aids; it seeks only not to be victimized by them."[7]

In a fundamental sense, Mumford asks again the age-old question, "What profits it a man to gain the whole world and lose his own soul?" We are obviously out of balance, teetering on the very tips of our toes preliminary to a great fall. We can put our feet on the ground and regain our balance only when we reaffirm the spiritual, aesthetic, intellectual, and compassionate aspects of our being that have been surrendered to an ignoble, and perhaps Satanic, fascination with covetousness.

Throughout history it has been reiterated countless times that the soul of man is immortal and imperishable. This essence, this seed of being, was our call into life. By drifting aimlessly and by letting more autocratic individuals do our thinking for us, we have choked the wellspring of existence with accoutrements far beyond what is called for by necessity. Soul has been buried beneath a heap of rubble, beneath things that are desperately craved one moment, and immediately lose their importance as soon as they are acquired. Renunciation of the superfluous is an essential step on the pathway to restoration of the soul. Moderation is the silken string that connects all virtues, and its attainment, while certainly a challenge, is likely of first importance in maturation of Soul.

We have a tendency to simplify and organize, which may pose a special problem in relation to the fact that our own existence is a blend of spirit and matter, or of soul and body. We like to keep things simple, to keep bolts of one length and thread size in a certain container and those of another size in a different container. Our organizing ability blinds us to the disorder we create in disassembling the natural world prior to rearranging the products into patterns that will suit our particular needs. What we order for our own use often leaves irreparable chaos in its wake. This is often caused by the fact that we look inward to our own needs and wants, without consideration for the whole.

Dr. J. Stan Rowe, professor-emeritus in ecology, University of Saskatchewan, describes a modern day attitude toward soul that is worthy of consideration:

> I'm trying to use this "mind" of mine to look outward at the world not inward at my psyche, believing that the inward focus is a root cause of our disastrous behaviour in this world. Looking outward is of course one definition of ecology (as contrasted with physiology which is inherently inward looking and reductionist). Looking outward has another advantage, namely that of sanctioning teleology. It opens possibilities for anti-reductionism or holism, for finding the logic-of-things in their larger context, purposefully...the danger in "soul" (it seems to me) is in the definition that confers on it a *higher nature* than the body, making it "other than" our total being, which strikes me as masculine head-stuff. Women, living much in their bodies, have been stigmatized as more earthy, "closer to nature," "less spiritual," etc. They've suffered from this soul/body, mind/matter, higher/lower dichotomy. As you know it's a chief reason too that material Earth has been so easily desacrilized for plunder by men otherwise engrossed with higher, more spiritual matters — like saving their immortal souls. Perhaps "soul" could be "saved" by conceiving it as psyche attuned in a value-seeking way to Earth-body that is its source?[8]

It troubles me that soul is considered otherworldly, which leads to such ideas as the common one that earth is relatively unimportant or of no importance at all. Obviously we must exhibit serious concern for our home place before we render it unliveable. Thoreau realized long ago that owning a beautiful home wouldn't amount to much if we didn't have a decent planet to put it on. A cavalier attitude toward earth cannot be considered a favorable recommendation for an exalted future life. It seems much wiser to use soul force in this life to activate human conscience to the slovenly condition of the planet, which marks the presence of our species.

One way of thinking about soul is that it is a catalytic order of cosmic energy, infused in us by God — a spiritual given that "enables movement and growth in a body." It is essential to our being and is integrated with material of the created world that comprises our bodies. We are a combination of body and soul, not merely one or the other, and all of our actions are enhanced when they result from visionary co-operation of spirit and flesh. A balanced approach to life will always fully entail genuine respect for the material and the immaterial, for what is concrete and abstract, for things seen and things unseen. Janus-like, if we would be truly whole, we must look both outward and inward. I put them in that order because, except for reflex behavior, we look outward to detect and assess with our senses, and inward that we may reflect upon sensory data before we act. Only in such an apparently studious mode will we be able to dispense with innumerable hasty decisions which satisfy short-term goals and later produce overlooked long-term consequences. Our dependency in both directions, a matter of universal law probably rather than human law, establishes the certainty that we should honor the First Cause of our being, as well as the mundane but precious world of soil, rock, flesh, water, air and wood, these being the special and essential, although commonplace, things that sustain our existence.

CHAPTER 3

The Miracle of All Life

Possibly in our intuitive perception, which may be truer than our science and less impeded by words than our philosophies, we realize the indivisibility of the earth — its soils, mountains, rivers, forests, climate, plants, and animals, and respect it collectively not only as a useful servant, but as a living being.

Aldo Leopold
Conservation is a Moral Issue

Our relationship with earth is strangely superficial. Though it is our common ancestor, we largely ignore the possibility that it may be imbued with soul, intelligence, awareness and benevolence. This seems a glaring oversight since earth is the "Overparent" of all life forms, being a repository of all the attributes inherited by its diverse species.

Life force is a planetary characteristic vectored through generations of living organisms. Whether we speak of the Big Bang or of "Let there be light," the earth is a creation and it is an undeniable consideration that the Big Bang would have produced tremendous light. The fact that this creation, basking in indulgent rays from the sun, was delegated further creative energy is a matter of visible, living proof, much more convincing than fantasies devised by marketing forces in our industrial society, e.g., that the telephone or telegraph would make all people neighbors and thus bring peace on earth and goodwill toward all.

Indeed there is an urgent need that we refocus our trust from technological exploration to that of the intelligence and design of nature. This will be a positive benefit, *providing* that we can learn to adapt ourselves to the sensible limitations it imposes upon us, and *providing* that we can base our actions upon a vision of long-term benefits to all life rather than short-term benefits to a single, impatient generation of our species alone. As a long-lived model, nature has acted without haste. The hundreds of millions of years that elapsed between the reptilian, toothed birds of the Jurassic period, such as Archaeornis, and today's chickadees and nuthatches are indicative of a slower, perhaps more thoughtful pace than the period that elapsed between Model T Fords and what we consider today's high-tech vehicles.

It is imperative that we stop exploiting ecosystems in ways that are a threat to the creative energy of the earth. Our present behavior, particularly in the light of knowledge of ecology, resembles stubborn adherence to belief in a geocentric solar system long after it was proved that earth and all other planets were satellites of the sun. That Earth has the capability to bring forth organisms, particularly in spring, can be witnessed by everyone. It is not unreasonable to consider this an ability delegated by the cosmic soul which, as we are told, operates in mysterious ways. As our home place and our sustenance, Earth has first claim on our loyalty, respect and concern. Though we usually deny this home planet recognition in our courts, it no doubt has standing in a universal court that deals not with trifles, but with universal laws that are applied as impartially in judging a species or planet as in dealing with a meson or molecule.

Giving appropriate recognition to our planet does entail a different role for humanity, one in which it recognizes itself as part of nature, rather than as a chosen species given dominion over whatever is within present or future grasp. While such a radical change in thought seems improbable, especially in contrast to the puffed-with-power view we have of ourselves, it is nonetheless essential.

Sober respect for the earth is even more appropriate when we consider the innumerable times people over the ages have repeated the opening lines of the 24th Psalm: "The earth is the LORD'S, and the fullness thereof; the world, and they that dwell therein." Can we really believe that this majestic planet is human property?

The Hebrew Gates of Prayer also elucidates the matter of

respect thoroughly: "And God saw everything that was made, and found it very good. And God said: This is a beautiful world that I have given you. Take good care of it, do not ruin it." It goes on: "It is said that before the world was created, the Holy One kept creating worlds and destroying them. Finally God created this one and was satisfied. God said to Adam: 'This is the last world I shall make. I place it in your hands, hold it in trust. For if you defile it, there will be no one to set it right for you.'" We can also read of one of the Jewish values, "tikkun olam," which acknowledges the duty of repairing the world.

Close relationship to nature is equally an Eastern idea. In his foreword to Douglas and de J. Hart's *Forest Farming* (London: Watkins, 1976), E.F. Schumacher reminds us that one of the foremost teachers of India was the Buddha. The Buddha taught that it was an obligation of every devout Buddhist to plant and see established at least one tree every five years. Schumacher noted that as long as this obligation was observed, India had good forest cover, abundant water, freedom from dust, plus shade, building materials and quantities of food. This, he added, could be done without foreign aid or investment, and provided many of the basic essentials of life.

A change of worldview in which we recognized earth as the primal fact of our existence would offer a foothold in reality for new efforts on our part to extend an overdue measure of concern to our planet. She is essential to us and, as many scientists have pointed out, we are not a necessity to her. Ninety-nine percent of all the species that have been alive have passed into extinction, and one more species, even our own, would not interrupt the earth's existence.

Earth, according to geological records, has rolled in her airy bed more than once, and such an axial shift would send the rubble of our cities cascading across the surface of the planet. Intense solar radiation during the last decade has caused temporary decouplings of the core and mantle of the earth, and a shift of 1,000 km in the magnetic pole was noted as recently as 1992.[1] This wobbling of the magnetic pole has increased beyond the normal pattern of the past. It is not unlikely that these phenomena are related to atmospheric perturbations such as a thinning ozone veil, global warming, and perhaps also to runaway desertification. The onus for change on our part may be a requirement for the continued existence of our species. Retired Canadian ambassador James George suggests that whereas polar shifts and reversals are known to have occurred, it is "not impossible that these polar wobbles may presage a relatively imminent shift of the earth's magnetic pole."

Much biological evidence exists that points to polar migration causing the submergence of large continental masses at the close of the Paleozoic era. This polar shift was the reason for the "all but universal extinction of life, so that only the pelagic and deep-sea types of the oceans (especially of the Pacific) and the terrestrial types in the interior of the continents, remained unaffected."[2] These remnant populations were probably the source for repopulating the earth after the widespread extinction of life in shallow water and on the verges of the continents.

We and the earth are of a oneness. We emerge from the earth and, in due course, return to it. Our bodies are vectors for the life that is an implicit characteristic of the planet. The old adage that "a hen is an egg's way of making another egg," makes us realize that the "business" of life is the perpetuation of life, which speaks considerably of the *genius loci* of earth itself.

We are part of a continuing miracle, and while we seek all about us for myriad astonishing innovations pertaining to transportation, communication, governance, and other technological wonders, we rarely admit to the truly astounding miracle that is involved in simply BEING. When we hold our hands before our eyes to look at what we grasp between them, we scarcely realize that the truly amazing things are the hands that *can* grasp, the eyes that *can* see, the minds that *can* comprehend. Matters of extreme priority indicate that it is unwise to keep our heads so far in the clouds that we fail to keep our feet on the ground.

Our aspirations toward the outer cosmos should not blind us to the fact that the very dust beneath our feet has been alive and teems with life at every moment. From this dust, filled with the vestiges of ancestral life, and the fertility rendered to existent life, we reap our daily bread and draw our lifelong sustenance. As our friend Modesto Depretto once remarked, "When we are alive we eat the earth. When we die, it eats us." Earth and all life upon it, above it, and beneath its surface constitute a planetary whole. It is not insignificant that both the words "whole: and "holy" are derived from a common Anglo-Saxon root. Thus what is whole, healthy, holy, and hale constitutes a single unit and in spite of appearances is undivided. We also speak of what is whole and holy as being sacred.

Our arrival upon earth from the infinity of time, but also from earth itself, occurs at the moment male and female gametes unite to form the zygote that eventually becomes the consumer eagerly awaited by the business community, and the taxpayer avidly sought by government. Focusing our thoughts on material gain we sacrifice the miraculous to the mundane, the truly awesome matter of being alive to the measurement of life as a contributing part of the Gross National Product. Nature has not chosen to advertise, but if we do not have "made from earth" emblazoned on our foreheads, there is no doubt we should see this with the eyes of our minds.

Nothing will change the fact that the multigenerational roots of our existence spring from this terra firma on which we spend our lives. Returning to deep awareness of our planet is more vital than a fascination with space exploration and travel, or extending our mercenary aims throughout the universe. It is enough to be concerned about one world at a time. Before we earn heaven, or the heavens, it seems logical that we must first learn to deserve the earth. And therein, we have much to do.

In this book my intention is to celebrate earth by discussing its richness and diversity, and by reminding the reader of the possibility that earth itself, with all its abundance, is a living entity — an entity with soul and intelligence as described by ancient Greek philosophers. Tied as we are to a narrow concept of cellular life, we blind ourselves to the possibility that there may be a more immense form of life. Do we summarily reject the Old Testament's God who asked Job where he was, "When the morning stars sang together, and all the sons of God shouted for joy?" (Job 38:7). Should we merely dismiss this as metaphor or a bit of poetry? Or does it indicate that the mystery of the universe must be sought at the *level of the soul?*

There are reasonable grounds, which I will pursue, to suggest that nature watches us quite intently and intelligently. This is not an uncommon idea, and has been reiterated from earliest written thoughts to the present. As Herbert Wildon Carr pointed out in *The*

Monadology of Leibnitz (University of California, 1930), "There is nothing dead in nature. Everything in it is sentient, animated... There is neither birth nor death in the absolute meaning. There are only metamorphoses and transformation. Our souls are not created at the moment of conception nor are they destroyed at death."

Unfortunately we have largely rejected our kinship with all life, thereby cutting ourselves off from the true wonders of our universe. The richness of our lives is denied when the dragonfly, the beetle, the ant, even the strawberry we have for dessert no longer reminds us that we inhabit a living world. How grievous to think that we may have become the targets of the cosmic joke we are perpetrating in giving no importance to anything other than ourselves.

Fortunately, my wife Linda and I live in a relatively remote area and have frequent experiences that strengthen our own close ties with the world that we love.

For example, one wintry day we walked in the woods, as we do most days, and were accompanied as usual by a pair of ravens, a second generation pair that carries on a family tradition. It had snowed during the night and in the morning we saw the ravens flying across the lawn, with their wingtips brushing the snow. They usually land outside our dining room window in hopes (usually rewarded) of a piece of bread being tossed out for them. The wingtip brushing of the snow seems to be their way of determining whether or not the snow is too light and powdery to hold them up. They were prepared to escort us on our walk as soon as we went outside. As usual they flew ahead on our woodland trail, landed in trees, waited for us to catch up, flew ahead again, and repeated the process over and over. It is a daily ritual they seem to enjoy: accompanying us for a couple of miles and returning home with us. Yes, we do give them things to eat, and when they feel we need reminding, they land on snow-laden branches directly overhead and scatter snow upon us. Sometimes they tease the dogs by landing a short distance ahead to encourage them to give chase, a harmless pursuit that dogs and ravens both seem to fancy. Should we dismiss all this as conditioned mechanical responses lacking intelligence? I think not!

A couple of winters ago, a tough winter at that, we were regularly visited by a coyote that showed herself first peering from behind a small log cabin near the house. She next ventured to scavenge bread thrown to the ravens. Linda eased open the window one morning and scaled a pancake in her direction and in a few days she became The Coyote Who Caught Pancakes. Linda is not a major-league pancake scaler, but the coyote was a "natural" who would have made a spring-training coach jump with glee. Texas-leaguers or fence-busters made no difference, and were all handled with true snappy aplomb.

I mentioned the coyote to a friend who lives nearby. He advised, "Shoot it."

When I asked why, he replied, "It eats things."

I replied, "So do we."

He said with finality and a frown, "Shoot it."

We continued to feed her in the tough weather, but as soon as the days lengthened and warmed, she came less often until, with buds swelling, she came no more — probably moving on from a starvation period of life to one of satiated bliss.

On a special May 17th morning we were stunned to see a large grizzly bear rolling on its back in exuberance some twenty feet from our breakfast window. We were exhilarated when he rolled over onto his belly and we could see that the top of his head and back were snow white, and that a shaggy white cape extended halfway down his side. The rest of his body was chocolate brown. He contemplated us as we spoke to him through the window, and a moment later he turned and stared intently into the woods. In a few seconds we saw another grizzly, a brown female, appear and walk between cedars and hemlocks to join her companion. This was obviously the two weeks or so of the year that males and females travel together. He got up and the two bears sauntered across our rather informal lawn, then stood near a large birch tree and looked back toward us. We went out on the porch for a better look, and spoke to both of them. They were about fifty feet away. The female acted a bit jittery, and ready to bolt; but the large male, "wearing his dress suit" as we later said, watched us calmly, and silently spoke the message that he was not hostile. We urged the bears to watch out, for spring hunting season was underway; and they walked into the woods toward a small creek below. We felt blessed!

And then there was the July 4th grizzly, a blondish fellow, who showed up one morning in a little clearing just above one of our gardens. I had just started weeding, and glanced up to see the bear walk out of thick woods into the field. He looked at me, and I looked at him and then at the dogs — one watching entranced, the other starting to stalk in the bear's direction. I took both dogs by the collar and brought them to the house. I told Linda about the grizzly, and we both went out for a closer look. The bear, a citizen of nature, was eating huckleberries from a bush at the edge of the field. Experts would cry "folly!" but we followed the grizzly, staying about 100 feet back, as he meandered along, feeding on the abundance of berries that grew on the bushes that year. We walked along behind him on a trail to our small, upper field. The bear would glance our way now and then, but continued feasting on the delicious berries. His body language conveyed contentment. At one point we saw him eating while he sat on his rear, with both hind legs stretched forward. As he manipulated the bush, and stripped off berries, he would glance at us from time to time, with what I thought was an entirely jovial expression. This bear was a gentleman. When we all walked back down toward the house, the bear behind us — but taking his time — Linda thought of her camera. She went into the house for it, came out and took a few pictures, and then the bear, hearing a vehicle, rose on his hind legs, and she took an excellent picture of him in that posture. After an hour and a quarter we left the bear to resume our work, and in a half-hour or so he wandered off, perhaps to keep other appointments.

When we walk in the mountains, as we often do, we encounter other grizzlies from time to time; we are definitely aware of their potential for danger, and use reasonable caution. But the ones who came visiting somehow seemed benign, and of course we act according to our own intuitions. After all, we did elect to live in close daily communion with nature because that is somehow an essential part of what life means to us. We feel the truth in William Cullen Bryant's opening lines in *Thanatopsis:*

> To him who in the love of Nature holds
> Communion with her visible forms, she speaks
> A various language.

Yes, our home planet is a super-abundant place, and is riotous with vigor. It strews our woodland walks with white flowers of Queen's Cup, orchis, and bunchberry; with bluebells; with the purple and yellow of the orchid we call fairy slipper; and with erect pink flowers of wintergreen and Prince's Pine. Nature, as we see it, is never in undress and there is a quality of impeccability about even its random disorder. Its prodigality is amazing.

As snow begins to melt in March, its whiteness is speckled with the seeds of hemlock. Spring has been with us only a few weeks when the air is filled with seed-parachutists drifting down from balsam poplar. Any slight breeze will bounce them upward or change their direction. Bushes fill out with berries. Before long we are dodging cones severed from Douglas firs and white pine by industrious red squirrels, working overtime with non-union fervor. Seeds cascade to earth from myriad plants in inestimable numbers. They are dispatched in such quantities that even if millions fail to germinate, thousands will root themselves, to be eaten, trampled, crowded, girdled, parasitized, and otherwise stressed. Enough endure so that replacement numbers reach maturity.

Nature does not coddle her offspring. It is part of her strategy that healthy roots are needed to seek food, that vigorous branches hold leaves or needles aloft in the sun, that sturdy stems must compete for their place in the world. Life must be sought with all the energy a seedling possesses. This has been dubbed "survival of the fittest" and we understand it results in thriving fields and forests, and a healthy world. And, of course, luck (or fate) is involved, for a browsing animal may nip seedling x and y, but move along past seedling z.

Home is also an earth that many people recognize as being overstressed by human demands, fouled by our own greed and arrogance. This seems far more evident to ordinary people than to those whose focus is narrowed to a technological-industrial-economic form of tunnel vision. A neighbour of ours, sharing coffee with us one morning, reflected, "If we keep doing things the way we are, we just won't be around very long." He grinned and added, "It couldn't happen to a nicer bunch." Yet I know this man, blessedly unsophisticated, to be kind and compassionate and very aware. I remember talking to him in his garden one day, when he reached over and grabbed a double handful of soil and said to me, "This is what makes life, but the real world for most people now seems to be what happens on television and on the stock market." Another fellow I fished with one evening when trout were rising, summed up his own idea of the state of the world when we sat on a rock in the gathering twilight. "It's sure a beautiful world, but we're strangling it with corporate disease. Pretty clothes, flashy cars — living high on the hog won't amount to a tinker's dam in the long run."

In the reckless haste so productive of waste we have endeavored to harry the world into submission to the rule of technology, into obeisance to the dictates of narrowly focused experts unaware of the angels coming to and fro.

Centuries ago it was recognized that though the mills of the gods' grind exceedingly slowly, they grind exceedingly fine. As John Burroughs wrote, "The hand of time with its potent fingers of heat, frost, cloud, and air has passed slowly over the scene, and the miracle is done. The rocks turned to herbage, the fetid gases to the breath of flowers."3 Granite, limestone, and slaggy lava have become garden mold through the action of erosion and through the decomposition of generations of plants and animals. The life supported today on earth has sprung from the death and decay of ages past.

Knowing this, and being intelligent enough to recognize the wisdom of nature in fashioning the co-development of living organisms with enzymes that would enable their decay and make them part of the elemental wealth of the world, we could have slowly and carefully modeled our technology on this excellent example. But we wanted wealth and countless material possessions long before we knew enough to follow the wise model afforded by nature. Though the precedents and the laws that govern our economic impetus create the semblance of judicious decisions, they often speak defiance of laws that predate our existence.

Think how many millennia elapsed between the origin of our planet and emergence of the first primitive organisms! Aeons passed before enough soil existed to enable early types of vegetation to support substantial animal populations, and more ages passed before humans existed. Contrast the gradual changes of geological history with the pace at which we seek to redesign our planet. Does such haste really seem wise, or even sane?

It is plausible that the psalmists foresaw our plight in the lines, "Eyes have they but they see not. / They have ears but they hear not," (Psalm 135:16–17). We have forgotten to look back over our shoulders, failed to put our ear to the ground. If we seek a means of evaluating our technology, we have to look no farther than the world around us. Any field, meadow or forest; any living creature we encounter will suffice. *We* are high technology. The living things on earth and the integrated ecosystems of the planet, comprise the highest technology we are ever apt to see. Technology is defined as "applied science." We would not expect our computers or automobiles to "just happen" without benefit of a designer, but it miffs us mightily to concede the likelihood that there is an "applicator" with higher credentials than our own who designed this majestic universe. We would not expect a set of chairs to appreciate the artisan who made them; but we, especially because of our claim to wisdom (Homo sapiens), should have sufficient insight to appreciate the designer whose works surround and include us.

Do the following thoughts strike a responsive chord? Poet and printer Walt Whitman marveled at the world we live in and wrote:

I believe a blade of grass is no less than the journeywork of the stars,...
And the tree toad is a chef d'oeuvre for the highest.
...And the narrowest hinge in my hand puts to scorn all machinery,
And a mouse is miracle enough to stagger sextillions of infidels.[4]

The late philosopher Lewis Mumford, in his book *Technics and Civilization,* also argued that our machines at best "are lame counterfeits of living organisms." Our airplanes, he pointed out, "are crude uncertain approximations compared with a flying duck; our best electric lamps cannot compare in efficiency with the light of a firefly; our most complicated automatic telephone exchange is a childish contraption compared with the nervous system of the human body."[5]

Every aspect of our lives, from our mental and physical health, to the foundations of our greatest buildings and the genesis of every technology, is rooted in the earth. Our obdurate refusal to respect the earth is therefore nothing less than suicidal.

With all our enthusiastic loyalties for sports teams, clubs and other social groups, we are dangerously remiss in denying conscious and enduring loyalty to the earth, which makes existence of all the life we know a reality. Our broadly capable "high-technology thinking apparatus," like a malfunctioning phonograph record, is repeating over and over the refrain of economic single vision. Unless we jar it loose by our own volition, we are unlikely to hear the greater themes of the cosmic symphony that are yet to come.

In respecting nature more and in using it as a guide, we will, after all, be taking advantage of the clearly visible handwriting of the Maker of the Universe.

I believe that we can solve the staggering problems of our environment only by reactivating soul force. As philosopher-religionist, Martin Buber suggests, we have "grown blind to eternity" and must look again to the eternal values. He felt that the prime need of our times is for people to rescue their individuality from pressures to conform to mass behavior and popular social values. Why should one do a thing because it is advertised that "everyone is doing it," or that we will be behind the times if we don't behave in a certain way? Does everyone need a cell phone, a DVD player and access to the Internet?

Contrary to those who might advocate membership in a creed, Buber stressed the need for a personal, I–Thou, relation with the absolute. What he urged was that each person think for himself. He also felt that the deepest responsibility of the genuine educator is to encourage students to reject the collectivism that menaces selfhood.

CHAPTER 4

The Economy it is Death to Ignore

The great cities rest upon our broad and fertile prairies. Burn down your cities and leave our farms, and your cities will spring up again as if by magic; but destroy our farms and the grass will grow in the streets of every city in the country.

William Jennings Bryan
Speech given in 1896

From the serenity of his cabin at Walden Pond, Henry Thoreau pondered the meaning of life and realized that, "Most of the luxuries, and many of the so-called comforts of life, are not only not indispensable, but positive hindrances to the elevation of mankind." Although he was a religious non-conformist, he assigned a higher meaning to life and recognized the immortality of our essence: "So our human life but dies down to its root, and still puts forth its green blade to eternity." Unlike many of his contemporaries, he was not mesmerized by the economic impetus of his time. He concluded that people cluttered their lives with luxuries and heedless expenses because they lacked a worthy goal in life, and felt that the only cure for lives submerged in acquisition of unneeded goods would be a "rigid economy, a stern and more than Spartan simplicity of life and elevation of purpose." (Circa 1847).

In these days of asphyxiation by materialism, Thoreau's simplicity is a breath of fresh air, and offers a glimpse of economic sensibility. It is a first magnitude paradox that we burn the candle at both ends by exhausting the earth's resources to store up riches on earth. At the same time we live in a society that is generally considered Christian with a belief in the New Testament and the words of Jesus in which he advises that people store up their treasures in Heaven (Matthew 6:19–20). If the wealthy of the world were to "go and sell what thou hast, and give to the poor" (Matthew 19:24), many of the world's tensions would be alleviated and it would then be possible to try on still another ideal — the healing of the earth and the human spirit.

Modern economics, I suspect, is more of a religion than a science. Though it has a host of devotees, its god is a very junior god, one who probably holds a middle management role in the divine hierarchy, very likely in the Department of Short Term Affairs.

The human economy, in perspective, is itself quite junior. Often repeated comparisons between the age of our species, and the age of our planet when equated to a 24-hour day, indicate that our species arrived on the scene only some 30–35 seconds before midnight. Liberally, considering our Industrial Revolution to be between 250 and 500 years old, the modern economy can claim only 15–20 milliseconds of geological history. Given its lack of respect for the planet and the inflated sense of importance that humanity demands, it is highly questionable that the planet can tolerate our species for many more milliseconds.

Many references have been made to impending failure of the economic system we have developed, e.g. "Our lifetime may be the last that will be lived out in a technological society..." (Isaac Asimov); "I'd be astounded if this planet is still going by fifty years from now. I don't think we will reach 2,000. It would be miraculous..." (Alistair Cooke).

It is a bit difficult today for us to conceive of the simple fact that earth developed an economy of its own long before our species invented the word. This is only difficult because we have decided that the vibrant, exotic and erotic present is such an ideal world that it behooves us to ignore all forms of historical thought.

Plato, for example, would have had no problem accepting the idea of an earth-designed and earth-sustained economy. In the essay

"Timaeus," he wrote, "We may say that the world became a living creature truly endowed with soul and intelligence by the providence of God." In Plato's *Laws* (Ch.12), he expounded on the topic of souls: "No man can be a true worshipper of the Gods who does not know these two principles — that the soul is the eldest of all things which are born, and is immortal and rules over all bodies."

The idea of consciousness at all levels of being is a strong presence throughout history and into the present. C.H. Waddington, distinguished British geneticist, wrote: "Something must go on in the simplest inanimate things which can be described in the same language as would be used to describe our self-awareness."[1]

Of recent importance, James Lovelock's *Gaia, A New Look at Life on Earth*, postulates that the physical and chemical conditions of the earth surface, of the atmosphere, and of the oceans has been made fit for life by life itself: "The most important property of Gaia is the tendency to optimize conditions for all terrestrial life." Elsewhere he writes: "This brings us to the third property of Gaia, namely that she is a cybernetic system."[2] Norbert Wiener, American mathematician, first used this term (from Gr. *kubernetes* for steersman) to describe a branch of study concerned with "self-regulating systems of communication and of control in living organisms and machines."

Perhaps it would have been less difficult some years ago to suggest that the earth had a managed economy. More recently Western society has become very detached from the earth in our fascination with our own economic ambitions. John Ruskin's view that, "Technocrats constitute an ignorant bestiality," does have some merit. Intelligence suggests that we should expand our willingness to look at all aspects of life rather than contract them into an all-exclusive focus on the profitability of business.

Though most of our actions belie any sense of dependence on and integration with other life forms, our entry into life depended on such events as the emergence of blue green algae, some three billion years ago. The oxygen liberated by photosynthesis of early life forms over vast periods of time led to the sort of atmospheric conditions that would support life forms such as our own. We are still, as John Burroughs observed, "rooted to air through our lungs, and to soil through our stomachs."

When we release ozone-destroying chemicals into the air from our industries, and further ravage the ozone layer through nuclear explosions and space launches, we threaten the existence of all aerobic life. In fact, if oxygen liberated by photosynthesis had not given rise to an ozone veil that protects aerobic forms from shortwave radiation we now call ultraviolet B, neither higher organisms abundant on land or in surface waters could exist. Consulting an encyclopedia, one reads: "Prior to the formation of an ozone layer, primitive cells, including the early photosynthetic organisms, must have lived under about 10 meters of water to have received adequate protection from lethal ultraviolet radiation."[3]

Not surprisingly, when we look up the word "economy" in a dictionary, there are a number of definitions that have to do with management of personal, community, and business affairs. There is also a definition that refers to strict husbandry, which seems not at all a bad idea. The final definition of "economy" in my Webster's reads: "Theol. the Creator's plan; the design of Providence." To me that is the most sensible definition, one which I think of as God's economy.

I see much more intelligent design in it than I do in the air-water-soil-poisoning human economy. Consider merely the fact that the planet's ancient economy has been developing, growing and recycling completely for aeons, whereas the human economy that has been in full swing for only a century or thereabouts, is on the verge of destroying its own species and of doing disproportionate and possibly lethal damage to the entire planet.

Those whose predilections make them uncomfortable with the phrase "God's economy," might feel better referring to the original economy of the planet as "nature's economy." At any rate, everyone should recognize that there is a "planetary economy," and it is not too difficult to realize that our own economy has become dangerously parasitic on it.

Lest the word "parasitic" be construed as offensive, let me comment that one of the older meanings of the word is: "One who eats at the table of another, repaying him with flattery." Historically we seem to have been a bit more humble than is customary today — understanding that we were truly guests at the banquet of life. Emerson, for example, wrote: "We nestle in nature, and draw our living as parasites from her roots and grains." It may also be noted that Edward Hyams, in his highly regarded book, *Soil and Civilization*, subtitled the second section of his text "Man as a Parasite on Soil."

"Nature's economy," incidentally, is a highly productive economy, and teeming life is the result of its efficiency. It is obvious that we are all totally dependent on earth. One wonders then why religions have been reluctant to stress the fact that respect for the Creator would logically entail respect for the Creation. If we had recognized the wisdom of loving other things more and our own selves a bit less, our prognosis for survival would be better and our religions more convincing. To promote heaven and ignore earth is to put the cart before the horse.

Most of us learned a bit about the process of photosynthesis in school. That process might be looked upon as the "economic engine" that gives impetus to planetary affairs. It should help us to be more humble to realize that the world's most efficient factories are the leaves of plants. The human economy is utterly dependent on the fact that photosynthesis, powered by the energy of the sun and catalyzed by chlorophyll in plants, produces some 300 billion tons of sugar or precursors of sugar annually. The process takes place on land and sea. The raw material produced in this manner is further utilized in other important syntheses such as the formation of amino acids from which proteins are built. Our muscles, blood, bones and nervous systems are produced by food grown on the planet.

As the Hudson River naturalist John Burroughs stated: "We are walking trees and floating plants." Blood and chlorophyll are closely related. A molecule of hemoglobin contains 136 atoms of carbon, hydrogen, oxygen and nitrogen in an intricate arrangement around a central ring containing a single atom of iron. In a molecule of chlorophyll, the same number of atoms form the same arrangement around a single atom of magnesium.

There are about 1.5 million known species of organisms in existence. This figure is approximate because of the very close similarity between some species, and also because of the absence of a systematic accounting procedure. Although this number includes plants, animals, and microorganisms, there is agreement among evolutionary biologists that the figure given is probably only about a tenth of the number of species that actually exist in diverse habitats on earth. On the high side, estimates of the total number of species range from 30 to 100 million.

The wealth of diversity of life on the planet offers strong evidence that nature's economy is concerned with life itself as wealth. The fabric of nature is composed of interwoven and interdependent organisms. Both abundance and health spring from the mutual interdependency of the living fabric. Interdependence involves myriad complex feedback loops and alternative pathways that account for the dynamic stability of ecosystems. There are, of course, limits to endurance, and ecosystems that are over-stressed can collapse rapidly.

While Christians, sincerely or with tongue-in-cheek, insist that our species was given dominion over the earth and over all other beings, they do not remind one another of caveats that appear in other places in the Old Testament. For example, in Leviticus (25:23) we read: "for the land *is* mine; for ye *are* all strangers and sojourners with me." And, in even stronger terms, which call our illusion of importance into question, these words can be noted in Ecclesiastes (3:19), "For that which befalleth the sons of men befalleth the beasts; even one thing befalleth them; as the one dieth, so dieth the other; yea they have all one breath; so that a man hath no preeminence above a beast; for all is vanity."

Nature's economy is of such integrated complexity that we have neither been able to understand it fully or to discern our own place within this realm of overflowing generosity.

We seem at odds with all nature when we insist on being top dog, on being the most important organism in the universe. The first of the seven deadly sins is pride, and in our years of species self-flattery we have buried pride's opposite — humility — so deeply that it would be difficult to find if we should ever be tempted to search for it. Yet, Irish poet Thomas Moore recognized its true worth when he referred to humility as "that low sweet root, from which all heavenly virtues shoot." The word humility is derived from the Latin *humilis,* which means "on the ground." It is not unusual for someone to refer to a dependable individual as one who has her feet on the ground. Such a person is considered to be practical and without an inflated sense of importance. "Humus" and "human" originate from the same root, which implies to me that we were meant to be humble.

Actually we know enough about the indigenous economy of our planet to respect it far more than we do and to marvel at its creative energy. We know that life itself is humus forming and that the formation of soil results from the weathering of rock and from the decay of all forms of plant and animal life. The more death and decay has added to the soil, the more life it can bring forth. The photosynthetic engine that drives nature's economy uses a small fraction of the energy that is radiated from the sun. Throughout the aeons of geologic history, plants have taken in carbon dioxide from the air and produced oxygen — one reason why treed lands have earned distinction as healthful places. At night plants release carbon dioxide back to the air, as respiration utilizes the daytime increments of oxygen within their own bodies. Oxygen has increased in air over time because the oxygen produced during daylight hours exceeds the carbon dioxide released at night. Whether or not we choose to acknowledge the fact, it was a long time before the amount of oxygen in the air reached the present level of 21 percent, the amount that constitutes a healthy atmosphere for humans and other animals.

"All flesh *is* grass," wrote Isaiah (40:6), and just as grass and other forms of vegetation nourish the land animals, so the plant life of the oceans underwrites the fish of the sea. On land, of course, the soil lies at the base of the food pyramids, chains and webs; and soil, to be considered productive, houses a vast assemblage of plants and animals, and though in many cases microscopic, they are very much part of the web of life.

As pointed out earlier, life on land was not a possibility until the formation of an ozone layer. This layer is essentially opaque to wavelengths of solar radiation of 290 mμ (millimicrons) and downward, and reduces the burning effect of wavelengths up to 320 mμ. The ozone filter makes land life possible because wavelengths below 300 mμ are severely injurious to living organisms. The conditions for life on earth thus rest on the 1/535 billionth part of solar radiation that we receive and the protective veil of ozone which blocks out the harmful rays.

Just as an "eroded" ozone layer now poses a serious threat to the continuation of life and already offers serious threats to health, so the erosion of the soil that grows the vegetation on which food webs depend is a monumental assault upon life itself. Published studies state that soil erosion is measured in billions of tons annually. A Worldwatch Institute estimate in the mid 1980s was that 24.5 billion tons of topsoil are eroded worldwide each year.[4] Calculations made of the amount of food-growing topsoil on the planet indicate that it is being eroded at such a rate that in less than 150 years there will be none left. Add to this the poisoning of soil by pesticides and industrial fallout and it is obvious that soil conditions are such that they no longer display the health-giving characteristics they had when pristine.

Considering the pollution of ground water by similar toxins to those that affect soil, and the use of surface water to dilute other effluents, it is evident that while we may boast of a high-tech society we are making such claims without considering the cost to those most basic essentials required for the maintenance of life — soil, water and air.

The rapacious appetite of the forest industry offers an example of the economic blindness that classifies everything that can provide a dollar as "resources." The industry loudly proclaims a vast need for fibre, which is the popular term used for logs of all sorts. That much of the "need" is exaggerated may be easily demonstrated by the published statement in *Vital Signs 1994,* which points out: "Sixty percent of space in American magazines and newspapers is reserved for ads, while some 52 billion assorted advertising pieces — including 14 million mail-order catalogs that often go straight into the trash — clog up the U.S. post office every year."[5]

Dave McMillan of Nakusp, British Columbia, kept his junk mail in 1994 and weighed it at the end of the year. It came to 65 pounds. The millions of tons of living trees wasted in this process is blasphemous and suggests a great need for governance. One has but to walk into a post office and view overflowing waste containers full of unwanted junk mail to know that the public does not need or even wish to receive such material. Not only do politicians trapped in the pockets of business allow this waste, but the junk mail is sent at subsidized rates, paid for by the very public who discard it as useless junk the moment it is received. Add to this the waste of paper through the modern habit of passing photocopies of trivia to every-one, including students in schools whose lockers and notebooks bulge with such material, and one must ask how such copious waste can exist in a society that thinks highly of its intelligence. This is a true example of counter productivity. Junk mail, in particular, illus-trates a lowest use of modern psychology; a form of crude mes-merism intended to hypnotize the most gullible consumers into indulging their slightest wants. Of course, industry is always ready to trot out hired experts who will swear that this is sensible use of a resource.

At a time when any materials useful to humans are classified as "resources," it is important to understand that such a classification on our part does not take cognizance of the in situ value of such resources. Forests are an interesting example. Their importance to nature's economy lies in their role as essential life-supporting enti-ties. They play an important part in climate regulation through their influence on rainfall, humidity, temperature control, and wind movement. Their role in water conservation is highly significant. Bare soil may absorb up to 5,500 gallons of water per acre during each hour of moderate rainfall. Soil that has grass or low shrubs may take in nearly five times that much, about 25,500 gallons per hour per acre.[6] Forests are much more efficient at water storage and dur-ing a rainfall of about 0.4 inches per hour, act much like a sponge, and can absorb 100,000 gallons per acre. The carpet of leaf mold beneath trees, the porosity of forest soil, and interlaced roots allows forest land to *store* as much as 400,000 gallons, some seventeen inches of rain per acre. The aerial cover of leaves, needles, and branches retards evaporation and enables forests to be important storage reservoirs. The slow release of water from forested slopes recharges underground aquifers, produces springs and supplies streams with a steady water source. The combination of agricultur-al land below and forested slopes above provides good conditions for production of food crops. Whereas people concerned with their watersheds are assured that removal of forest provides more water, the water is dispensed as excess runoff due to lack of moisture hold-ing structure of the soil. Indeed, there might be more water for a short period of time in spring, washing away topsoil, eroding gul-lies, and causing flooding. When the season of rain is ended, earth will bake and become impervious to rain, making runoff and erosion a continuing problem. The removal of forests will also permit increased wind velocity, more baking of soil from the sun, reduced humidity, and changed precipitation patterns due to the reduction of transpiration.

The advantages of forests mentioned are merely some of the valuable roles they play in providing stability for nature's own economy. To these may be added habitat for many species of animals, birds, and other organisms; absorption of noise and of some air pollutants; and protection of biodiversity. They also have aesthetic and spiritual values, which receive almost no consideration as a result of our present worldview.

On the whole, forests tend to mitigate extremes of temperature, of drought and moisture. They are part of the equilibrium of nature, and it is this equilibrium that we are now seeing violated in devastating torrents and snowfalls, in unpleasant and dangerous temperatures, and in increasingly violent winds spawned from seasonal and unseasonable storms. It is an appropriate analogy that the human economy has "sown the wind" and is now in the process of "reaping the whirlwind."

In overlooking, quite intentionally, the cost to these foundation blocks of our physical being, we are demonstrating the illogical belief that we can disrupt the organization of our planet without suffering adverse affects. The truth of the matter is that all disruptions of our life-support system such as the erosion of soil or riddling the ozone layer with holes that permit the antibiotic effects of UV-B to increase, are equally unwise. What we must remember, as Robert Ingersoll, American lawyer and orator, pointed out, is that nature does not concern herself with rewards and punishments, but only with consequences. We are in great trouble because we covet things and do not realize that things have value only up to a certain point. Economics has to do with utility, with means and not ends. Forgetting this, we quarter our gross wants upon our starved spirits and wonder why we are frustrated.

Emerson was obviously prescient in saying, "The problem of restoring to the world original and eternal beauty is solved by the redemption of the soul." Redemption can only take place through renunciation of such idols of the marketplace as pride and greed.

And this can best come about when we turn our backs upon the blandishments of the media, which would have us brain-dead and unaware of our own consciences.

Business and economic interests dominate modern society. These interests, without interference from politicians who can rarely see beyond their own term of office, have come to own or control the newspapers, television, and other pertinent media. Dominated by self-interest, business forces have ignored the fact that we are all dependent or "parasitic" on the planet. In developing a consumer society, business has achieved the remarkable goal of becoming hyper-parasitic upon everyone, while convincing people that automation is an admirable goal. However, as a business analyst recently pointed out, the continuing emphasis upon higher profits and automation now amounts to the fact that through reduction of employees major corporations are, in effect, "firing their own customers."

The ominous problem we in the Western world have permitted to take precedence over all else, might be termed economic single-vision. We are thus enslaved to an idea that permits the destruction of all else in the pursuit of monetary affluence. To speak against this modern fetish is called "counter-productive," and to suggest the need to change our basic outlook is tantamount to modern heresy. We are not less religious than our predecessors, but have succumbed to an economic religion that does not make sense.

Well known essayist Wendell Berry observed sagely that, "If the Golden Rule were generally observed among us, the economy would not last a week. We have made our false economy a false god, and it has made blasphemy of the truth…Its principle is to waste and destroy the living substance of the world and the birthright of posterity for a monetary profit that is the most flimsy and useless of human artifacts."[7]

E.F. Schumacher, Rhodes scholar and economist with the British Coal Board, recognized that a thing might be immoral, degrading, soul-destroying or a threat to peace in the world. But as long as it was not *uneconomic*, it was considered worthy of manufacture for growth and profit.

In 1961 he asserted that Western economics is founded upon the basic error of failing to establish limits. These are his words:

Because Economics up to a point, can rightly claim universal validity, it has been accepted as possessing universal validity throughout. What do I mean by up to a point? The essence of materialism is not its concern with material wants, but the total absence of any idea of Limit or Measure. The materialist's idea of progress is an idea of progress without limit.[8]

Other economists agree with Schumacher's view that we are pursuing a dangerous path. When Herman Daly, then senior economist with the World Bank, and John Cobb Jr., theologian, combined forces to write *For the Common Good* (1989), they evaluated the economic trends with these words: "We human beings are being led to a dead end — all too literally. We are living by an ideology of death and accordingly we are destroying our own humanity and killing the planet."[9]

It is advantageous to present economic interests that we ignore history and live within the hectic pace of the present. We are encouraged to keep the sort of pace that the Red Queen recommended to Alice in Wonderland, "Now here, you see, it takes all the running you can do, to keep in the same place. If you want to get somewhere else, you must run at least twice as fast as that!"

It is sobering to contemplate that ancient Chinese society did not display particularly high regard for those who indulged in trade. "By custom the Chinese gave top rank to scholars, teachers, and officials, while placing farmers in the next class, artisans in the next, and merchants in the lowest, for they held that merchants made profits simply by trading the products of other people's labor."[10]

Christian Bovee, American editor and author (1820–1904), also contemplated the evolution of the business world and commented, "Formerly when great fortunes were only made in war, war was a business; but now when great fortunes are only made by business, business is war." There is another similarity in that all wars are eventually wars against the earth, and that business also thrives upon exploitation and degradation of the earth, de-developing the intricate ecosystems that support all life.

We in the affluent nations are also experiencing economic uncertainties, including severe unemployment, caused by our own unrelenting, blistering and unreflective pace. This may be a blessing in disguise as it might enable us to think more carefully about our true relationship to the wonderful world in which we live. The truly intelligent will see the wisdom of words written by George Perkins Marsh in 1864: "Man has too long forgotten that the earth was given to him for usufruct alone, not for consumption, still less for profligate waste." In this age of ostentatiously profligate waste, it is pertinent to know that Webster's New Twentieth Century Dictionary says, "Usufruct — in law the right of enjoying a thing which belongs to another and of deriving from it all the profit or benefit it may produce, *provided it be without altering or damaging the substance of the thing*" (emphasis added).

We are steadily decreasing our options as we choose short-term wealth for the few as a more desirable goal than long-term health and abundance for many generations. We are choosing the role of the beast, as spoken of by Renaissance scholar Giovanni Pico della Mirandola, who in his famous Oration had God tell Adam:

> Neither a fixed abode nor a form that is thine alone, nor any function peculiar to thyself have We given thee, Adam, to the end that according to thy judgment thou mayest have and possess what abode, what form, and what functions thou thyself shalt desire. Constrained by no limits, in accordance with thine own free will, in whose hand We have placed thee, thou shalt ordain for thyself the limits of thy nature…Thou shalt have the power to degenerate into the lower forms of life, which are brutish. Thou shalt have the power, out of thy soul's judgment, to be reborn into the higher forms, which are divine.[11]

Sunlight, chlorophyll, green leaves, soil, water and air! Life is a product of these real things that account for our Being and permit the secondary economy that has usurped our loyalty from our home planet.

Isn't it time we recognize our connectedness to everything else?

CHAPTER 5

The Great Chain of Being

Nor let the rich the lowliest slave disdain,
He's equally a link in nature's chain.

Samuel Richardson
in "Clarissa", 1748

From our earliest, dim history there have emerged thoughts of a totally powerful God, an *ens perfectissimum,* an immortal Being in command of all that has ever been or ever will be. The origin of this belief may be a bequeathed instinct or a reflective summation wherever sufficient consciousness exists. Let us explore the unfolding of one of the most interesting creation myths in the history of western civilization.

Plato (427–347 BC) expressed his Idea of the Good in *The Republic.* He envisaged that which was eternal, immutable, perfect, and ineffable in heaven, and proclaimed faith in a benevolent power who ruled over temporal affairs.

Qualities of this great Being were nicely summarized by the Neoplatonist Plotinus (205–270 AD): "The One is perfect because it seeks for nothing, and possesses nothing, and has need of nothing, and being perfect, it overflows, and thus its superabundance produces an Other."

From Plato's writing, particularly the *Timaeus,* grew an idea which people pondered upon for two millennia, an idea that reached full flowering in the 18th century. Development of the history of the idea was carried on by Professor Arthur O. Lovejoy of

John Hopkins University, and presented in the William James Lectures at Harvard University in 1933.

What Plato initiated was the idea of a Great Chain of Being, composed of links made up of every possible kind of living creature, from the very simplest organism possible to the Supreme Ruler of the cosmos. Though lowest to highest is inferred, it is also possible to think of ordinary chain composed of links of equal importance, each in its own place. This would fit well with the ecological niche idea of different kind of organisms filling a vital role in the web of life.

Plato used the term "Demiurge" (a now anglicized form of the Greek word for craftsman or artificer), to describe the Being who created order of initial chaos and transformed it into a cosmos. Just as a modern craftsman must work within the limitations of his materials, so the Demiurge had to employ reason to work with what was available and to contend with recalcitrant physical conditions that offered hindrance to its efforts. The first task of the Demiurge was to make other gods, for example, the world soul, which is the motivating force of the cosmos and the immortal part of the human soul. The gods that were created carried on the work the Demiurge initiated by devising other physical things, including human beings.

Plato expressed the attributes of the Demiurge. Such was its goodness that it was not jealous, and in lacking jealousy it wanted the world to lack nothing. If it lacked nothing it would be necessary that all-possible sorts of being should exist. As a result, living things progressing through infinite gradations were created, ranging from the most rudimentary to very complex forms. This numberless throng collectively formed the Great Chain of Being. The fascination of the concept still remains, and was termed "one of the most fertile yet neglected ideas in Western philosophy" by the authors of the *Encyclopedia of Philosophy* (1967), Vol.5 p.96.

The popularity of the idea of the Great Chain of Being rested on the widespread conviction that there is a rational Divine Power involved in every aspect of life. It does not seem illogical that goodness is an aspect of divinity. Most of us respect goodness and can appreciate it as an innate quality of a fully developed being. We can also comprehend the life-giving propensity such a being would possess. It is easy to surmise that a hierarchy of created beings, ranging from the simplest and most torpid, could expand upward far beyond our capacities into the realm of angels and other beings of light. Those who contemplated the Great Chain of Being conceived that each creature, in its own place, offered testimony to the infinite creativity of God and glorified its Maker through its own existence. Proponents of the idea of a Great Chain of Being, suggested a ladder-like progression through which one might move closer to the Divine Essence. The obvious tendency for human self-inflation should thus be tempered by the realization that ours is a place on the chain that advocates humility and recognition of the need for self-improvement. Our failure to display much evidence of humility flies in the face of long standing recognition that humility is an admirable and important virtue.

Professor Lovejoy, in writing of the history of this belief, stated that the very sort of world decreed by the Absolute in the Chain of Being involved all degrees of imperfections resulting from differences in species that displayed their own specializations and distinct limitations. Humans just happened to occupy a particular place in the Chain of Being, a place that could not be left vacant if the chain was to be complete.[1]

Thinkers in medieval times found the concept of a Chain of Being sound, although interpretations varied. Aquinas expressed the view that the multiplication of species adds more to the goodness of the universe than would the multiplication of numbers of individuals of a single species, and recognized that the universe needed diverse kinds and assorted grades of things. He also recognized a principle of continuity in the way one kind of organism grades into another, and spoke of "the wonderful linkage of beings" and of the way that a more complex genus (kind) will border closely upon the most advanced members of a less complex genus.

Averroes, the 12th century Moslem philosopher, asked why God created more than a single sort of vegetative or animal soul, and answered his own question by saying that the need for variety of species rested upon a *principle of completeness.*

It is interesting that present day ideas of the vastness of the universe were just entering people's minds a few hundred years ago. It wasn't until late in the 17th century that there was general acceptance that the fixed stars are suns like our own, with their own planetary systems. With broader knowledge and expanded imagination, the assumption grew that other planets in our solar system might have sentient and rational life; and the universe, as infinity with uncountable solar systems, became a mind-expanding and mind-boggling concept — even as it is today. To stand beneath the stars, and look and think, is a never-ending lesson in humility.

Of course there were prescient individuals who had surmised infinity even earlier. The mid-fifth century BC, Sicilian-Greek philosopher and mystic Empedocles had said that God is a circle whose centre is everywhere, and its circumference nowhere. And the Christian metaphysician Cardinal Nicholas Cusanus declared in *De docta ignorantia* (1440), "It is not within our power to understand the world, whose centre and circumference are God." Cusanus was firmly convinced of the wisdom of knowing that we do not know. This is reminiscent of the old tale that the Delphic Oracle pronounced Socrates the wisest of men, because when asked what he knew, he replied that he did not *know* anything. Cusanus also recognized that although we might be prejudiced and feel our own intellectual nature to be of a highest quality, it is quite possible that earth may be merely an assemblage of lesser beings that include us. That we have a long way to go, was obvious to him, and seems undeniable at present.

Giordano Bruno (1540–1600), Italian philosopher and poet, though burned at the stake by the fury of the Inquisition on February 17, 1600, had long contended, in a fashion not unlike some modern quantum physicists, "that all things are in the universe, and the universe in all things; we in that, that in us; and so all meet in one perfect unity." Consistent with his own pantheistic views, he saw in the Chain of Being that "there must be countless individuals such as are those great living beings of which our divine mother, the Earth, is one."[2]

It is interesting to note that the Cartesian influence often used to justify modern exploitation of earth is somewhat countered by Descartes' own conviction expressed in a letter to Princess Elizabeth in 1645. In it he mentions that as a guide in the conduct of life, we might utilize the concept that the universe is infinite. Meditation upon this, he said, should help us to become modest and "to detach our affections from the things of this world."

Today's greater understanding does suggest that his own words are nullified by his philosophical dualism that separates mind and matter.

As Pascal asked: "What is a man, in the midst of infinity?" The idea of all life being permeated by mind occupied a significant place in the thoughts of J.H. Lambert, whose pioneering work in scientific astronomy earned great recognition. Believing that the solar system had many habitable globes, he asked: "Could the world be the effect of an infinitely active Creator, unless in every part of its life and activity, thoughts and desires were found in the creatures?"[3]

Our own knowledge of the universe does not argue against habitable planets, but does make it apparent that not all planets in a solar system are likely to be inhabited by life forms as we think of them today. Distances from stars will affect the likelihood of temperatures suitable for life, as will the existence and nature of atmospheres. This was foreseen by philosopher Immanuel Kant in his speculations on these matters in the 1750s. Kant understood that not all places would be suitable for life, and asked: "Would it not be rather a sign of poverty than of superabundance in Nature, if she were so careful to exhibit all her riches at every point in space?"[4] Kant recognized that in an infinite universe there could still be infinite worlds that were inhabited. As he pointed out, a number would still be infinite even if a finite number was subtracted from it.

Two commonly known observations have been made that are pertinent in thinking about the Chain of Being. One is that the mills of the gods grind exceedingly fine, and the other is that we see as through a glass darkly. Professor Lovejoy comments that the 18th century marked the period when scientists, philosophers, poets, essayists, theologians, deists and others talked extensively of the Great Chain of Being. Agreement with the main principles was general, and wide rein was given to its implications. There were also dissenters: Voltaire and Dr. Johnson being notable in this respect. No matter how much the mills of human thought sought and sifted, it must be remembered that such effort was after the fact, and knowledge of essence lies behind the dark glass through which we must peer. What is truly remarkable is such proof of the genuine human effort "To strive, to seek, to find, and not to yield."[5] For our purposes I will highlight a bit more of this idea, and note how thought moved from the concept of the Great Chain of Being to that of Becoming.

The idea of the Chain of Being did bring into question the assumption that the world was made for the sake of our own species. That the world functioned primarily in service to mankind had been vouchsafed by Francis Bacon and was a favored theme of some religions. Such a purpose was challenged by the idea that the world was created to bring forth a vast series of forms, each of which had equal reason for being. Lovejoy refers to the assumption that everything was created for humanity's sake as "one of the most curious monuments of human imbecility."[6] It was reasonable to note gradations of species and to consider that amphibians represented a gradual change from organisms that lived in water to those that inhabited land; and although flying fish did not really fly it could be seen that they were able to leave the watery domain to glide briefly through the air. Credence was also lent to "infinite gradations" when one considered the many "moss animals" or zoophytes (plant-like animals). Less reasonable was the assumption that each organism, even those that we know live in the oceanic abysses, live only in thrall to human dominion and service.

Sir William Petty (1677) considered that it would do us much good to reflect upon the thought that there are in the universe millions of other beings superior to humans, many of which probably excel humans in manifold dimensions, to a greater extent perhaps than man might consider he excels the most insignificant insect.[7] Philosopher J.H.S. Formey commented how little right we have to exalt ourselves upon realization of the small pre-eminence we hold above irrational creatures, and reflected that these creatures often possess other advantages superior to our own.[8]

Consideration of superior beings does have a tendency to deflate presumptuousness, which in itself is not altogether a call to sensibility. Some thinkers pointed to the fact that we have obvious limitations, and it should be a cheering thought to look forward to more advanced states in which present weaknesses would give way to superior insights and modes of being.

Viscount Henry Bolingbroke (1678–1751) understood the Great

Chain of Being to be evidence of the true *raison d'être* of the universe, and felt it possible to have more faith in the universe when we realize that somewhere there may exist species with a higher rationality than our own. He felt it foolish to lament that we are a less important species than we would like to be. The best part of wisdom, he thought, was to accept things as they were meant to be.[9] After all, we know that there are insect sounds pitched beyond our range of hearing, orders of colors we cannot identify, and energy frequencies, such as X-rays, that our senses will not detect.

It remained for Immanuel Kant to suggest that humans occupy a middle rung on the Scale of Being. We are, upon consideration, a creature that must necessarily exist, one in which purely instinctual behavior has sporadically begun to be modified by the development of individual personality and resultant value decisions; a being torn by conflict within its own nature, one whose aspirations oscillate between the selfish and the noble, a creature living at this time in two worlds, neither of which it fits adequately.

It is a long wade through steadily deepening water to peruse, let alone study, the many things that have been considered in the Great Chain of Being. It may be traumatic to many people to think of themselves as only one of a mind-boggling number of creatures, all of which have value and standing in a universe-embracing throng. While it may give comfort to think of having pre-eminence above a vast number of more limited beings, it is probably equally disturbing to reflect upon the possibility of a multitude of superior intelligences. Alexander Pope's "Essay on Man," Epistle I, which focused on the idea of the Great Chain of Being, concludes with the summation, "One truth is clear, WHATEVER IS, IS RIGHT." It is difficult to imagine any better conclusion to a divine organizational scheme that might account for our very existence.

Bolingbroke offered the idea that the infinite number of suns and planets in the universe makes it unreasonable to doubt that many of them are inhabited by creatures that are adapted to their particular conditions. In consideration of such abundance of life it is vain and "impertinent" for us to believe that we are "foremost among created living beings." He felt that it was obvious that our intelligence is limited or finite, and it made sense to postulate that there may exist beings so distant from us and so far above our own intellectual, emotional and aesthetic capabilities that they are beyond even the limits of our imaginations. Think again of Giordano Bruno's conviction that "our Divine Mother, the Earth is a great, living Being."

In comparing human qualities to those of other inhabitants of our planet, Soame Jenyns (1757) offered the thought that, "The superiority of man to other terrestrial animals is as inconsiderable, in proportion to the immense plan of universal existence, as the difference of climate between the north and south end of the paper I now write upon, with regard to the heat and distance of the sun."[10] It is indeed a sobering thought that what seems to us like a huge gradation between ourselves and some other earth inhabitants, may be only a necessary but unique gradation between the highest levels of instinctual behavior and the lowest level of deliberated individual choice — a tearing experience in which rule of the flesh is sundered by a wavering certainty that spiritual growth should lead us toward concern for everything within our comprehension.

The essential duality of human nature was aptly described by Alexander Pope in the opening lines of Epistle II of the *Essay on Man*. It might be noted that in Pope's time, formal ecological concern was yet unborn. The proper study of mankind, at this time, is the ecology of the planet of which we are but a part.

> Know then thyself, presume not God to scan;
> The proper study of Mankind is Man.
> Plac'd on this isthmus of a middle state,
> A Being darkly wise, and rudely great:
> With too much knowledge for the Skeptic side,
> With too much weakness for the Stoic's pride,
> He hangs between; in doubt to act, or rest;
> In doubt to deem himself a God, or Beast;
> In doubt his Mind or Body to prefer;
> Born but to die, and reasoning but to err;
> Alike in ignorance, his reason such,
> Whether he thinks too little, or too much:
> Chaos of Thought and Passion, all confus'd;
> Still by himself abus'd, or disabus'd:
> Created half to rise, and half to fall;

Great lord of all things, yet a prey to all;
Sole judge of Truth, in endless Error hurl'd;
The glory, jest, and riddle of the world!

The limitations of the particular niche in which our lives take place
suggested to Pope the extent of our labors in the vineyard of life:

Say first of God above, or Man below,
What can we reason, but from what we know?
Of Man, what see we but his station here,
From which to reason, or to which refer?
Thro' worlds unnumber'd tho' the God be known,
'T is ours to trace him only in our own.

When we complain of our lot, and lament that we have no higher
talent than we possess, the poet reminds us that we could have been
born lower on the Chain of Being, and argues that our position is
just what it should be in relation to all other beings. Even though we
strive for perfection and seem to fall short always, " 'T is but a part
we see, and not a whole."

Then say not Man's imperfect, Heav'n in fault,
Say rather, Man's as perfect as he ought:

One of Pope's most quoted couplets refers to the frustration experienced in pondering upon life, and offers the thought that the blessing of hope is given us as surcease from sorrow:

Hope springs eternal in the human breast:
Man never Is, but always To be blest:

and goes on to say:

The soul, uneasy and confin'd from home,
Rests and expatiates in a life to come.

He observed that the Indian, unspoiled by education, sees God in
everything and finds heaven in the thought of a safer natural world

where he can simply BE, in freedom from the torment and avidity of those who seek to dispossess him. His life, close to nature has suited him well enough that he does not long for wings of an angel or other signs of steps toward divinity.

Daniel Defoe (1660–1731), prolific English author of more than 400 works including the very famous *Robinson Crusoe*, once identified pride as "first peer and president of hell." Pride was also assigned first rank among the seven deadly sins proclaimed by Pope Gregory the Great. It is not surprising that Pope identified pride as our central problem in seeking higher status than that assigned us in the Great Chain of Being:

> In Pride, in reas'ning Pride, our error lies;
> All quit their sphere, and rush into the skies,
> Pride still is aiming at the blest abodes,
> Men would be Angels, Angels would be Gods.
> Aspiring to be Gods, if Angels fell,
> Aspiring to be Angels, Men rebel:
> And who but wishes to invert the laws
> Or ORDER, sins against th' Eternal Cause.

In the foregoing lines can be sensed a problem about the very nature of pride, about the pros and cons of a characteristic that in some instances can be a virtue, and in others a vice. We all have a degree of pride, but it is when it becomes excessive that our problems begin. Superficial or avaricious pride can make an individual harsh, demanding, and intolerable. Since Pope wrote the "Essay on Man," a quarter-millennium has passed, and we, as a species, have made ourselves victims of the over-weening pride and arrogance called hubris. In Greek history one finds reference to "hybris" and sees additional meaning given the term as "insolent prosperity," "insolent presumption," or "irreverent pride." At all times hybris invited the attention of Nemesis, who meted out good and evil to men, and dispensed disaster to those guilty of hybris. And standing in the wings were the powerful Erinnyes, the Furies, who left no wrong unavenged. The pantheon of Greek gods also contained the mesmerism of Folly. In Homer's *Iliad*, Agamemnon describes "Folly, eldest of Jove's (Jupiter's) daughters, (who) shuts men's eyes to their destruction. She walks delicately, not on the solid earth, but hovers over the heads of men to make them stumble or to ensnare them." It might be quipped that we are the natural inheritors of Folly, because at one time she tricked her own father, who became enraged and "caught Folly by the hair and swore a great oath that never should she again invade starry heaven and Olympus, for she was the bane of all." Jove threw her from heaven so that she was cast upon the fields of mortal man.[11]

Irreverent pride! There is virtually nothing that we have not changed. We are phylogenetically and ontogenetically adapted to the self-regulating, therefore stable, ecosphere that made our lives possible. Yet, in countless ways we have taken apart the ecosphere to provide "resources" for a technosphere, a surrogate world in which the symbol for resources, which we call money, is theorized to have higher value than the resources themselves. Alas, every accretion to the technosphere is at the expense of a diminution of the health and stability of the biosphere.

This brings up a new, but necessary thought about the Great Chain of Being when considered as a creative plan in an infinite universe. Our own earth can be used as an example. The long history of our planet considered, our integrated ecosphere was basically life-supporting and life-sustaining before a species with as many strengths and weaknesses as ours arrived. Surely, if there is life on an infinite number of planets, there may be planets where an unhappy uniqueness of the occupying species may lead to disaster. Therefore it would seem that all species must be found on a number of planets, in different ranges of scale, so that a destroyed planet will not leave the Chain of Being bereft of any species. An accident resulting from such a cause as "irreverent pride" would be nullified by the presence of all the species that might be involved in more than one place and in various arrangements. The possibility of our own planet coming to grief has been suggested by a number of people. Note, for example, in Rachel Carson's *Silent Spring*, there is a dedication page that states: "To Albert Schweitzer who said, 'Man has lost the capacity to foresee and to forestall. He will end by destroying the earth.'" *Silent Spring,* in discussing the effects of pesticides, offers one example of "how" we might destroy all living things on earth. Biocides are, after all, killers of life.

The possibility of a collapse of the Chain of Being by breaking links of the chain until the whole chain collapsed was seen by Pope, although, in the accumulated literature encountered on this subject, I have not seen mention of the possibility that species of the chain exist in more than one place in the universe in order that a local tragedy might not lead to a hiatus in universal Becoming. Certainly though, upon consideration of the relentless pursuit of what we call progress, we may be rendering enough species extinct to threaten survival of this planetary chain. With enough ecological wisdom, we would see that it is essential to curb our rapid eradication of biodiversity. Pope, in this instance, offers a dire prophecy:

> Vast chain of Being! from which God began,
> Natures ethereal, human, angel, man,
> Beast, bird, fish, insect, what no eye can see,
> No glass can reach; from Infinite to thee,
> From thee to Nothing — On superior pow'rs
> Were we to press, inferior might on ours;
> Or in the full creation leave a void,
> Where, one step broken, the great scale's destroy'd;
> From Nature's chain whatever link you strike,
> Tenth or ten thousandth, breaks the chain alike.
> And, if each system in gradation roll
> Alike essential to th' amazing Whole,
> The least confusion but in one, not all
> That system only, but the Whole must fall.

Pope closes his Epistle I with a remarkable conclusion that makes much sense in a universe governed by an intelligence whose centre and circumference are ubiquitous.

> All Nature is but Art, unknown to thee;
> All Chance, Direction, which thou canst not see;
> All Discord, Harmony not understood;
> All partial Evil, universal Good:
> And spite of Pride, in erring Reason's spite,
> One truth is clear, WHATEVER IS, IS RIGHT.

While steady reiteration of the idea of keeping one's place within the Chain of Being can be readily criticized as productive of deliberate mediocrity, or of a sense of futility, this need not be the case at all. Within the concept of our theologies are such observations as that of dominion given to us by a God who has among other characteristics that of love. Upon reflection, our own dominion would have to be a dominion of love, since emulation of His characteristics would be an asset in moving up the ladder of existence. There is also an ideal that we hear from the time of childhood, one of peace and good will upon the earth; and there is the ideal much touted, particularly during periodic political campaigns, of good, honest, ethical government. We have also been told of the need of avoiding the seven deadly sins: pride, greed, envy, anger, lust, gluttony and sloth. Help in curbing these sins can be had by cultivating the seven cardinal virtues: four of them adopted from pagan times, praised alike by Pythagoras and Plato, the natural virtues of wisdom (prudence), courage, justice, and temperance; and three of them "theological" virtues — faith, hope, and charity.

Dr. J. Stan Rowe, makes the interesting observation that sloth, or laziness, for Homo sapiens, might be a virtue. Such an attribute would certainly slow down our destruction of the planet.[12] It would be refreshing to find a modern business shut down, with a sign "Gone Fishing" on the door.

Counting our real blessings would help us. As an example of a positive outlook toward life, there is the wise admonition of the Koran: "Don't complain that the rose bush has thorns; rejoice that the thorn bush bears roses." Also, within our consciousness there is the realization that on the broad scale of affairs, our battle is not to subdue nature but to subdue ourselves. Whatever control of nature is necessary will be achieved by loving insight when we have learned to control ourselves.

In other words, we have a long, arduous path to follow in adapting to our place in the Great Chain of Being. We might also help other beings, not so fortunately placed, toward their own perfection by understanding that all creatures on the path to improvement would live best by holding hands, by a communion of spirit.

If this is idealism, it is perhaps time we learn that idealism is realism responsive to an altruistic ideal. The ready use of the word "counterproductive" to disparage any move toward idealism, indicates that the status quo we strive to protect is the absolute antithesis to such concepts as "peace on earth," or of living in harmony with the planet. On the other hand, by embracing the humility required "to dress and keep the earth," we might well become civilized.

Pope spoke of the Great Chain of Being collapsing by removal of a single link, an unlikely happening in a universe presided over by an omniscient creator. But, what about the possible effect upon the universe of a species of a middle state, that elevated itself sufficiently to produce the nearest approximation to paradise within its grasp? Would not such a happening reverberate throughout the universe and become an inspired model for higher beings to marvel at and emulate with their own greater talent? In so doing, would not the human species move all the more rapidly toward its own cherished goal? Putting this into terms within our immediate frame of reference, imagine a species earning the "Order of the Universe" or being dubbed "Universarian." But, if we had achieved what we could within our own limitations, we would no longer need ostentatious honors. The reward would be the doing.

It really does seem that doing the very best we can do within the limitations we have is the challenge that must be met. Awareness of limitations suggests that we must consciously employ the different aspects of our beings, and use reason to its fullest to see that we function as wholes, not ignoring the mental, physical, aesthetic, emotional, or spiritual components of our selves. Only in this way can we be rid of such fanaticism as is now displayed in the concept that the business of the world is business. Consider the spiritual atrophy of a statement by a government minister in the 1980s: "There's one underlying motive in business shared by all — it's greed. We support it whenever it happens."[13] How Nemesis must smile to hear such words!

Like many ideas subjected to significant thought, change was in the offing in the late 18th and 19th centuries. The Great Chain of Being, which began as a purely speculative assumption that every form of life was established from the beginning and continued without change throughout time, became subject to a growing idea of Becoming.

The idea that all possible beings had already been created,

gave way to a realization, that with infinite time at his disposal the Demiurge need not hurry, need not bring every possible kind of organism into existence at the same instant. Certain forms of life might exist at one time and then disappear or become embodied in other organisms which persist. Still other organisms may not yet have arrived because their time is not yet, or the conditions of life are not suitable for their existence. The *principle of plenitude* was no longer to be seen as providing a "full household" of species at any moment of time, but as a principle that displays its diversity over its span of existence.

Not only did gradual unfolding reiterate the old idea proclaimed by Heraclitus (circa 510 BC) that, "There is nothing permanent except change," but this concept fit more closely with the observed scheme of nature. If all things had to be here at once and forever, where then were those ancient three-lobed crustaceans, the trilobites, and why had the dinosaurs given way if they were not a stage in the unfolding of the Chain of Being?

And there was the matter of hope. As Voltaire had pointed out, the permanently complete Chain of Being left no room for hope. Consider that if all partial evil is universal good, and perfect good is a characteristic of the universe that has always existed and will continue to exist, then everything is locked into a situation in which improvement is denied.[14]

Thinking back to the Demiurge's need to combat severe obstacles in the form of circumstances that impeded its labors, it seems reasonable that a living, functioning world had to be created, which over vast lengths of time might move itself toward perfection. Through our dark viewing glass we can gather only a distorted image, but the seeds of perfection might well lie in the unfolding of life, in the unfolding of mind, and particularly in the growing insight of soul, which would act as a guiding force throughout time. This is not inconsistent with the often voiced conclusion that life itself has brought out more and more favorable conditions for its own expansion, and that the interdependencies forged by developing life create a dynamic stability for its own perpetuation.

And, with the development of life, as thinkers pointed out, there would be a gradual emergence of intelligence. It was proposed, quite in keeping with the idea of modern quantum physicists, that there is mind everywhere, that even the least atom might possess intelligence "in a degree and of a quality suitable to it." (J.B. Robinet).[15] Infinite gradations were not likely to be confined to matter alone.

A significant thought on the route to an expanding view of the Chain of Being was invoked by the German poet, dramatist, and philosopher Friedrich von Schiller (1759–1805), who provided the Swiss national drama in writing *Wilhelm Tell* (1804). He argued that "the great Householder" of this world "who leaves no crevice uninhabited where life may be enjoyed" would want not only every kind of creature to exist, but would also expect every thought, emotion, and even error to be expressed, to be utilized in fulfillment of his great design.[16]

Schiller comprehended the essential difference between the two versions of the divine power presented by Plato. One is that of unchanging, self-sufficient absoluteness, and the other is the creative dynamism of the Demiurge, which through continuity and plenitude would permit all possible beings to exist through the unfolding of time. These two forms, one unchanging and the other with change as its essence, are part of the duality of being human: the one part being a drive toward unity with that which is pure and endless, and the rational aspect of life; and the other a drive toward that which is gratifying to the senses, is creative and expansive, which fulfils expression of the uniqueness of each individual. This latter form is the emotional aspect of life seeking change as expressive of life force itself.

In a sort of "Act well your part, therein the honor lies" decision, Schiller argued that it was better for us to try to be creative in our own right, within our limitations, than to idly speculate about a greatness that is beyond present comprehension. Given nobility of character we can find both materials and opportunity to climb steadily in the Chain of Being, with each fresh foothold upward providing a bit more vision, forging new understandings as the upward progression augments not only our scope, but comprehension as well. The ultimate, if it is ever to be attained, will draw nearer only through bursts of effort following each new understanding. Though he does not express the idea specifically, he intimates that sincerity of purpose will provide a guide to each striving soul.

The upshot of many centuries of pondering and comment on The Great Chain was a reversal of Plato's thought. The completely formed inevitability of creation, with its immutable scheme of progression upward had been transformed into a process of Becoming. Realization that the Demiurge had been handicapped by constraints brought about the idea that a less than perfect world had been a matter of necessity. The ultimate perfection of the universe would depend upon growth and progress of the entities that composed it. The idea that all possibilities would ultimately be realized still persisted, but the unfolding of these possibilities would only occur as successive grades of life forms produced conditions that enabled a higher scheme of life to unfold. God was envisioned as involved in a process of continuous creation. From this view has come the idea that individuals can be co-creators with God, through their own adherence to higher choices. Each individual is part of the future of a universe to be built from the bedrock upward rather than an insignificant part of a whole commanded to function from the top downward. That "partial evil" is a part of "universal good" can now be looked at differently, in the sense that as universal good commences to become a reality, partial evil will be eliminated.

One of the founders of German idealism, the philosopher F.W.J. von Schelling (1775–1854), contended that mind and nature are necessary to each other and are both manifestations of an absolute that lies beyond the scope of our reasoning ability. He expressed the view that God is both Alpha and Omega, the first and the last; but as Alpha He is not what the fully realized God will be at Omega. In a sense his comparison between the Alpha state, *(Deus implicitus)* and the Omega state *(Deus explicitus)* is somewhat like the comparison between a child who has not developed his potential, and an adult who has blossomed by attaining that potential.[17]

The idea of Becoming is expressed frequently by those of religious persuasion, non-denominational as well as denominational. I recall a summer in the 1970s when I taught an ecology course for the University of Calgary at its Kananaskis Environmental Research Centre. One of the friends I made, and walked and talked with on numerous occasions, was a "post-doctoral fellow: in physics, doing research at the centre. One day he told me of his own conception of fate and free will. It was his belief that each individual human is intentionally created (fated) with unique strengths and weaknesses and is to experience life from the vantage of talents and shortcomings thus provided. Free will operates within the parameters assigned a particular individual and choice of response to life situations enables that person to work toward more or less noble goals. The upshot of the matter is that when the soul returns to its Maker, its personal choices and actions become part of the Becoming of God. In the convictions of my friend, we are indeed part of the unfolding of the universe, for if, in the main, we choose to be good or evil, we impart these characteristics to the Divine Being. In this sense our own actions become part of the eternal order, which is continually manifested in the temporal order.

With a bit of a roguish glint in his eye, the exponent of this view concluded, "How could there be a finer democracy than one in which we each equally affect all eternity?"

CHAPTER 6

The Question of Being

Consider today's society: it gratifies and satisfies every need
— except for one — the need for meaning.

Viktor Frankl
The Unheard Cry for Meaning

Thoreau spoke of times when he ceased to live and began to be. This apparent paradox is one that does describe precious moments in which we are overwhelmed by the innate significance of life. At such times we temporarily transcend the limitations of mundane life and are transported into a feeling of complete satisfaction that is usually beyond expectation. We may be happily invigorated with a sensation of completeness, or a conviction of having undertaken a worthwhile task. Or we may be struck with wonder at an understanding never before grasped. Reflecting upon such moments, it seems that they are often a conclusion to an action done without regard to any expectation of reward. Needless to say, since we are all distinct individuals, such experiences are tailored to or from our own uniqueness. By sharing an experience of my own, perhaps it will be possible for you to think back to moments of unique fulfillment in your own life.

For years I have lived with a conclusion, gained from both intuitive knowledge and extensive study, that we imperil and shame ourselves by our lackadaisical and disdainful regard for the earth. We continually display an attitude of exploitation coupled with a refusal of responsibility toward the greater home that provides us with our individual homes. What usually happens is that things considered to be everybody's responsibility instead wind up being ignored by everyone.

I had been through the gamut of working at all sorts of odd jobs as a young man, and later as a geologist, and a teacher, while also giving lectures, and writing articles about our abuse of the environment. Now I felt that I wanted the visible satisfaction of working with my hands, of trying within the fragmented knowledge we all possess, to heal or mend the bludgeoning to which some small piece of our bleeding earth has been subjected.

Linda and I are both earth-oriented, and we found a logged-over acreage, for the most part clear-cut of trees, and bought it with the view of restoring it as a forest.

One of the first things we did was to walk the land and determine just how we were going to go about this mammoth task. Our attention focused first of all on an attractive mountain stream that flowed through it: a stream choked with tree-tops, broken logs, a few stumps, and a large number of branches. We counted eight places in which the creek was dammed or partially blocked, and two places in which it periodically overflowed its banks. At one spot the overflowing water had cut a ditch that was as much as several feet deep in places. At another place where it had inundated the adjacent land there were a number of small trees still standing and much of the ground cover was still intact. Where the land was thus moderately protected, the water had spread out without cutting a channel. On the ground a layer of silt several inches thick had been deposited. But, once the flow of water continued into an area from which all cover had been removed, the water had converged, cut deeply and washed away the soil.

When we talked with the man who owned the adjoining property, we learned that kokanee, a species of small salmonid that normally spawned in the creek each year, had been unable to swim up and lay their eggs the previous year because of the debris in the creek. We felt that clearing the dams from the creek would be an important undertaking that first summer, since spawning fish would be moving into the creek by mid-August. Accordingly, we decided to plant trees and begin clean up in spring, and later to start working on the creek as soon as it dropped in volume after the main runoff period. We estimated that we would have a month to work before it was time for the fish to spawn.

By mid-July we were able to begin our efforts in the stream with chainsaw, axes, a six-foot long crowbar and a come-along, and found that we had our work cut out for us. The usual procedure was that I would get in the creek with the saw and cut the larger debris into pieces that we could handle. It was a time-consuming process and, not being used to standing on slippery rocks while using a chainsaw, it was necessary to proceed with caution. One major dam, the one that had caused the destructive ditching, was quite large and had produced a waterfall that fish wouldn't be able to ascend or circumvent. We removed large limbs and smaller debris by hand, piling it on the creek banks; while the larger pieces of logs had to be winched from the creek with the come-along. Linda and a friend, Marilyn Taylor who taught school in Revelstoke, worked with the come-along, and when they got the water-soaked logs to the edge of the creek I would lift them out, or get the bar under them until they could be skidded out on the bank and then rolled or carried to a pile. We noted that the creek helped in that as the dam was removed, the accumulated silt was washed along by the water, reducing the quantity of material that had enabled the flooding to occur.

We proceeded slowly, allowing the silt to clear without making the water excessively dirty, and there was satisfaction at every fresh and noticeable improvement. The women were particularly excited and pleased each time they were able to winch a large log out of the dam so that I could cut it into smaller pieces.

It so happened that we began to remove the last downstream dam that blocked the fish at the very time when kokanee were gathering in the pool below, and jumping in vain to try to get above the dam. I worked on the downstream side, cutting material away, and Linda pulled the debris from the creek as I freed it. When a channel made it possible for the fish to get through, they started up between my legs and found themselves free to undertake the culmination of their life's drive toward reproducing themselves.

We felt elated, of course, when the kokanee started moving upstream, and as we had worked through the morning and into the afternoon that day, we were ready to eat our lunch. We decided to walk upstream to a pleasant spot that was partially shaded by some of the remaining trees and see if the fish made it that far while we were eating. Since we had worked for about ten days at cleaning

the creek, we wanted to make sure that the fish weren't being held
back anywhere by material we had left in the creek as cover for fish
and protection for the stream banks. Fish of course work on their
own fishy schedules, and we had just about finished lunch when
Linda spotted several kokanee, red in their spawning color, poking
their way around a bend and coming into view beneath where we
sat on a knoll a few feet above the water. Within a few more minutes there were 15–20 fish scattered along the stretch of stream
within our sight.

It was just natural to grin and feel that something really wonderful had taken place. Mind you, we knew it was nothing momen-
tous in the affairs of the world, nothing earth shaking, but still something that really should have been done. Here we were, sitting sort
of in the middle of nowhere; at least we thought most people would
look at the place as rather insignificant. But, on the other hand, we
had done something on the side of life; something that would enable
the normal affairs of the world to be carried on as they should be.
And, at that moment the thought appeared in my mind and I said to
Linda: "Do you know?...It seems to me as if, somehow, what we
have done here may be the most important thing we have ever done
in our lives." To both of us it was one of those times when we felt
very close to everything that exists: to the earth, to the immense
intelligence that stands alert behind every action that is taken, to the
sky, water, trees, shrubs, and grasses that are living parts of the vast
and pleasant land about us. Our spirits were infused with the understanding that we are parts of an intelligent order beyond our descriptive powers. It seemed apparent to us that with the use of reason and
the action it inspires, we could dress and keep the earth and gain in
self-respect from every deed, however humble, that we perform
from deepest sincerity.

Our whole experience with cleaning up the creek and seeing the
fish swimming upstream to spawn led to that pinnacle moment
beside the stream when we were unequivocally positive that we had
done a thing that we were meant to do. In Thoreau's terms it enabled
us to surpass the mundane events of ordinary living and to suddenly realize BEING, a sense of cherished membership in the community of everything that was, is, and will be. Although our bodies
might no longer be able to jump in the air and click their heels

together a couple of times while still aloft, our spirits felt elated enough to do just that.

Oh yes, I pondered the progression that led to that moment. We bought the land, even though we realized that in spite of the human laws to the contrary, the land actually owns us more than we will ever own it. We are convinced that everything belongs to a power beyond our ken. We bought it because we felt intuitively that we should do so in order to mitigate some of the havoc to which it had been subjected. When we first walked by the side of the water and saw the impediments presented to fish, we quailed at the thought of how much work was needed to make it passable enough for spawning. We began the work with uncertainty that we could succeed or sustain the effort needed. But the stream murmured to us as we worked, the dappled light filtering through small streamside trees encouraged us, and perhaps recognizing that reason is often inadequate without the impetus of emotion, our hearts sang with enthusiasm (lit., the God within) as we worked. Nice little things happened: a bald eagle sat on a cottonwood branch and surveyed the countryside for a few minutes, a black bear wandered through with its head turned in our direction, and a trio of mule deer peered at us inquisitively one afternoon. And the more we achieved, the more eager we were to get back to the task.

And then, suddenly it seemed, we were done with the work on the creek, and were even surprised that no more needed doing for the time being. The realization grew upon us that we were privileged to have been able to do the job; that only patience, caring, and not unpleasant manual work had been required. We knew that we had learned something indefinable and that the equally indefinable reward to our inner selves was greater by far than the work expended. Oh yes, we realized a cynic might make mileage of such thoughts, but only in the form of non-doing required by cynicism. I am reminded that Oscar Wilde once defined a cynic as "a man who knows the price of everything and the value of nothing." And we felt that our action, though it might not add to the GNP, had value of its own.

The whole matter of being is far simpler, I suspect, than it is made out to be. It seems connected with doing things that need or should be done, but yet are left as matters of free choice subject to our own decisions. But it also consists of non-doing and being responsive to quiet insights and impressions that come to us when we let ourselves be sensitized to the vastness about us.

I remember, years ago, listening to reminiscences of a man who had spent considerable time in Nepal as a graduate student from a California university. He recounted tales of the way a belief in karma affected the lives of ordinary people in Nepal. He spoke of a laboring man who had spent his life saving money that he might buy a female of the domestic yak species (I remember that he called the female of the species a dri or dree) and release that animal to a free life in the hills. By doing this he would gain karma, or reward for a good deed. It was this man's belief that good karma would be of help to him in the next cycle of his life. The animal that was released, I was told, was marked in such a fashion that no one else would interfere with it. He also spoke of poorer individuals who might buy a bucket of frogs or similar small, edible organisms, and release them in a river for the same purpose. These are acts "on the side of life" undertaken for karmic reasons, but with the welfare of other beings in mind.

It was shortly after hearing this story that I was walking toward a restaurant in MacKenzie, B.C., with Cliff and Linda Wood. We were sauntering along a narrow road and heard a car approaching at a distance behind us. Linda noticed a large toad sitting in the middle of the road, cupped her hands, picked it up and released it safely some distance from the menace of being crushed beneath the wheels of the oncoming vehicle. I couldn't help but tell her that she had gained positive karma by her action, and then recounted the tale of my friend from Nepal.

The point is that although we do not know all there is to know about this condition of existence in which we find ourselves, there seems to be an innate comprehension and compassion that drives many people to concerns and actions that go beyond the selfish preoccupation with getting and spending. It seems to me that instinctual compassion arises from seeds of religiousness buried deep within us. Furthermore, these are seeds of the oneness of all life. Today's focus on self-love and materialism tends to shrive us, I believe, of nobler feelings that are buried daily beneath the unending wants of trained consumerism. Because of the fact that our lives are measured in decades rather than in centuries, we are mostly unaware of the modern litany of unending wants that has helped estrange us from the world in which we have our being. We will suffer defeat so long as we play the inconclusive game of want. As Ralph Waldo Emerson saw many years ago, "Want is a growing giant and Have could never cut a coat large enough to cover him."

If we look back into history we can find without difficulty that the idea of human mortality was alien to primitive religious thought. Ernst Cassirer expressed the view in his "Essay on Man" that, "Primitive religion is perhaps the strongest and most energetic affirmation of life that we find in human culture." We might think about what intuitions we have lost when we read that primitive people have in their racial histories, beliefs that humans once conversed with the gods and had the ability to communicate with birds, mammals, and even with insects. It is sometimes contended that we are too sophisticated for such pagan beliefs; but is also humorous to find among the definitions of sophistication that it is "false wisdom." In earlier times our forefathers claimed that human consciousness was not confined to its present narrow range, but enabled movement into the spiritual dimension and the animal world. This had to do with the idea of human descent from superior beings, and was a reminder to all of the value of living in a sacramental manner in order to stay in touch with our spiritual roots.

Less than a half century ago we would have scoffed at this idea. We would have contented ourselves with the thought that primitive people are basically gullible children. We would have had to do this from a tongue-in-cheek sense of superiority because we lack in almost every way the toughness of fibre that enabled primitives to survive and to hand on their genetic inheritance to us. We would have been highly dubious of their illusions that the world was alive in every dimension. Fifty years ago we were probably at the peak of complacency, sure beyond doubt that we knew exactly what we were doing and were on the road to a life of comfort, where mechanical servants of all sorts would perform the distasteful work. Now we are not so sure. We are experiencing the backlash of overzealous industrial production. We are witnessing problems with garbage, pollution, radiation, and the appearance of toxic chemicals in the bodies of all living things.

The last few centuries have been marked by a steady move toward the secularization of society. The idea that there is an intelligent Author of the Universe has been determinedly, but not quite successfully, moved into the wings of this stage upon which life takes place. When we hear for example of primitive tribesmen running for hours, and then sitting down to wait for their souls to catch up with them, we are conditioned to consider such behavior a quaint anthropological fact, and probably nothing more...but we are not quite so sure.

We have been taught to believe that problems are best submitted to scientific inquiry and then solved by utilizing technical knowledge. We have been lulled to a considerable extent, by the multiplicity of scientific gadgets that call for our attention. But there is a counterforce operating, a nagging reminder that no matter how many technological diagnoses of problems are made, with various solutions recommended, the problems continue to multiply. We are learning that age-old questions, such as: Who am I? What is the meaning of life? How can I become what I should become?, are not answered through pragmatic or empirical methods. Tranquilization of major concerns into a fuzzy world of indifference does not constitute either a short- or long-term solution. While the modern world knows something about matter and energy, it knows relatively little about self or mind. Through a steady barrage of mind numbing "communication," the ontological dimension of life has been stifled. The question of Being, which stems from ontology, has been ignored and many of the frustrations, anxieties, disorders, and rebellions we experience today are rooted in growing realization that the goals of modern life are at best only partially meaningful, and at worst entirely banal.

Within each person there is a sanctuary, an interiority, a private place of reflection: this is the supreme court of our Being, within which our soul's judgments can best be made. The world's busyness would have us run with its discord, and make its hasty conclusions our own. Today's problems will only be resolved when we reinhabit our souls and formulate our ideas from the bedrock of our being.

Emerson expressed well the idea that the battle for the integrity of the soul must be fought daily:

God offers to every mind its choice between truth and repose. Take which you please — you can never have both. Between these, as a pendulum, man oscillates. He in whom love of repose dominates will accept the first creed, the first philosophy, the first political party he meets...He gets rest, commodity and reputation; but he shuts the door of truth. He who in the love of truth predominates will keep himself aloof from all moorings, and afloat. He will abstain from dogmatism, and recognize all the opposite negations between which, as walls, his being is swung. He submits to the inconvenience of suspense and imperfect opinion, but he is a candidate for truth, as the other is not, and respects the highest law of his being.[1]

An impression of the direction being taken by 20th century society was recorded by G. Lowe Dickinson, who taught at Cambridge University in England. After a visit to the United States in 1909, he wrote of his conviction that religion was becoming a part of practical business in the U.S. "This conversion of religion into business is interesting enough. But even more striking is the conversion of business into religion. Business is sometimes so serious that it sometimes assumes the shrill tone of revivalist propaganda." Think of his evaluation, given so early in the century, when you watch the ads on television or peruse your way through a Sunday paper. The domination of business as a pre-eminent goal in society is without precedent in history and may well hamper the unfolding of more important dimensions of the human psyche. Even before Calvin Coolidge's term of office as U.S. president (1923–1929), business had dominated U.S. affairs. His official policy of "more business in government and less government in business" was re-echoed even more emphatically by Canada's Mulroney government with its view that "the business of Canada is business." When it is soberly considered, this is a statement so sterile as to be shocking.

Another instance of Thoreau's thought seems to fit into the matter of Being, and also into the matter of *doing* that emanates from Being. Among his reflective comments is one that I remember from the time my Dad first plopped a copy of *Walden* in front of me when I was fourteen years old and said, "Here! Read something good for your mind." A comment of Thoreau's that puzzled me at the time, and that returns to me often as I think about the modern quagmire of junk mail, was his observation that we can be certain that the person who gets the most mail when he goes to the post office, hasn't heard from himself in a long while.

It returns to me again when I think of the overwhelming bombardment of stimuli via the various forms of media that befuddled people are subjected to today. I am happy to recognize Thoreau's influence on me in the fact that I have never owned or wanted a television, listen to the radio infrequently, and read newspapers with ever-increasing reservations. Considering the way in which newspapers are regularly gobbled up by large interests, it is obvious that what passes for truth is filtered and selected fact, fed as approved diet for manipulated minds.

As far as the idea of Being is concerned, it is a condition that we understand by experiencing life, but not a condition that can be easily verbalized. Being, after all, encompasses and antedates our best descriptive powers, and is an innate characteristic of the Universal Ocean of Life. Graciously or ungraciously, it is a condition we can only accept and hopefully appreciate. It is not difficult to agree with Spinoza's implied view that there is no proper definition of Being. In his *Ethics* (I, Ax.4) Being is divided into that which is "in itself" and "in another." He defines God as "Being absolutely infinite" and it seems to me that we, individually, can at least feel the spark of the Divine within us. We also recognize our duality in feeling one impetus that causes us to want to strive and improve, and another in the power of self-love, which urges us to grasp and gather, to "have a blast while we last." It seems logical to me that our respect for the spark within should be sufficient cause for us to also respect the Creation — the magnificent setting in which we are allowed to live, and move and have our Being. Reflection challenges us not to be distracted by every leaf that drops across our path, but to always keep in mind the path which leads to the "Being absolutely infinite."

Most of my life has been spent in rural places, because I prefer the greater serenity of nature to the hubbub and haste that seems to be a characteristic of urban life. This choice on my own part has enabled me to become acquainted with many farmers. Among them I have found individuals who have been remarkably sensitized to the wholeness of nature and to a great depth of meaning that lies behind the surface aspects of life.

Wherever I have lived, I have done a great amount of walking. Without a few miles of roaming around outside each day there seemed to be something important missing from my life. Usually, I have set off walking toward wooded places.

One such place where my daily after-work walk took me led past a small mixed farm. It was a remarkably well-tended place where I often saw the farmer, a man in his fifties, who was working in the evening hours. He usually raised his arm in a silent salutation to which I would wave in response. One evening at dusk when I was returning, he was standing by his fence. He told me his name was Ira and said that he was waiting for me and invited me to stop in for a piece of pie and a cup of coffee. This pleasant interlude marked the beginning of a long friendship.

We hit it off. Ira told me that he had noted my habit of walking and suspected that we must have something in common. We talked about casual things, about the land, crops and life in general. It was a parrying but enjoyable conversation. His wife was very pleasant, said little and crocheted steadily.

As I got to know him it became obvious that he was a happy man — a person who was in the right niche. Husbandry was his calling and one could be sure that land entrusted to his care was a responsibility he accepted with joy.

When I got to know him I realized the wisdom of the old adage that the best fertilizer is the footsteps of the farmer. He visited the farthest nooks of his farm with regularity. Ira and his wife had 160 acres, several fields of two or three acres in crops that would bring cash, larger acreages in hayfield and pasture, and something on the order of fifty acres in woodlot. There was also a patch of about ten or fifteen acres that he said "belongs to God." This was a bit of natural forest, quite majestic, which he "calculated shouldn't be touched but should be left the way He made it to be."

I helped him from time to time. Together we repaired the roofs on a pair of small buildings and built log cribbing that we filled with rocks and gravel to keep a good-sized stream from eating into his pasture. As I came to know him better I admired his ability to repair things, to improvise and do whatever was required to keep the farm in tip-top shape. I learned that his simple directness was coupled with fastidiousness. Ira was a man who was always thinking and had a natural devoutness and remarkable ability to sense the core of his being.

He told me one day that he realized he wasn't a very important man but was happy that he could live as he did. "I've learned," Ira told me, "that we need to work at something bigger than ourselves in order to be happy. I've run into a lot of people who say there's no purpose in life, but that's not true. I get along without a lot of fancy tools, and I don't make very much money, but by working with what I've got, I don't need as much money as most people do. I figured out that the most important thing we have is time, and we don't know how much of that we have. But I also figured out that the cost of everything is time, and if I don't want something or can get along without it, I have more time to do what I want. Suppose I wanted a tractor instead of using the team of horses I have. I'd have to give up something else in order to have the tractor — maybe even God's trees, and I think it's just as important to tithe part of the place as it is to give money." He paused and mused. "There's no overtime in life you know. It doesn't work that way." I could see that he was laboring for words. "I guess that I'm a religious man, though I don't go to church. My way of thinking of it is that, though I live here and own the place free and clear, I should respect it and not make too many demands on it, and should always leave some of it to be the way that it's meant to be. I read in the Bible that it's God's earth and we are sojourners here. I looked that word up and it means we are just passing through life and through this world — I've no argument with that. It seems true enough to me. But I'm comfortable here. It's beautiful and I love it and I know there's a lot more to this life than we realize."

Ira had idiosyncrasies, as we all do. Over the years I knew him, we walked back into the woods for considerable distances, often to go fishing in remote streams or ponds. He told me, the first time we went, that he would like it if we didn't talk on the way into the pond where we were headed. That is, we wouldn't talk unless we saw something the other fellow should know about. His reason, he said, was that he liked to be silent part of the time. He liked time to think and to look, and time to let the country "soak into" him. That way, he said, a fellow has all the advantages of being alone, but can yet enjoy company.

I also learned of a peculiar habit adapted to his and his wife's deliberate life of frugality. He carried his money in a sort of thin, leather sack that he stuffed in his trouser pocket. The sack was fastened with a rawhide drawstring that was knotted a dozen or more times. When I was with him in town on occasion, I would sometimes see him looking at some item through a showcase window. He might then take the sack from his pocket and begin untying knots. Often, he would get half the knots out of the cord and then retie it. After I'd known him for quite a while, Ira said one day that he guessed I probably wondered why he had that sack with all the knots in it. "That's my conscience in a way," he told me. "If I want something real bad, I buy it. But most of the time, I think I want something, and while I'm untying the knots I realize I don't really need it." To that he added his view that advertising and display tried to make out that things that were really luxuries were necessary in order to be happy. "Shucks," he commented, "I don't have much but I don't even need a lot of what I have already, and I'm plenty happy with my life."

As I write these words and think about this simple man and his enduring commitment to the farm that was his life, I am reminded of an Oriental proverb: "God will not enquire of thy birth, nor will He ask thy creed. Alone He will ask: 'What hast thou done with the land I loaned thee for a season?'"

Our society today is a busy one, too busy keeping up to have time for reflection. It is as though someone years ago said, "Run," with the result that people began dutifully running and haven't stopped since. We are like the rabbit in Alice's Wonderland who declares, "I have no time to say hello. Goodbye, goodbye, I'm late!" This constant doing has outdistanced us from our inner selves, from reflection about the meaning that life holds for us as individuals. We become evermore the tools of our tools. Whereas in the past we worried about becoming slaves, we must now worry about becoming robots.

Eternal vigilance is surely the price of more than one kind of liberty.

It may be surprising that the mesmerism of machines was

commented on as early as the 4th century BC. In his writings the Chinese philosopher Chwang-tse tells the story of a pupil of Confucius who watched a gardener repeatedly going to a spring with his bucket in order to water his flower beds. The pupil asked the gardener if he would not like to get water without undergoing such labor. "How can I do that?" asked the gardener. "Use a piece of wood as a lever," said the pupil of Confucius, "weighted behind but light in front and use it to dip water. The water will come up with very little effort. This is called a draw-well." The gardener thought about this for a few moments and being somewhat of a philosopher, answered: "I have heard my teacher say, 'If a man uses machines, he carries on all the affairs of life like a machine; whoever carries on his affairs like a machine gets a machine-like heart; and when anyone has a machine-like heart in his breast, he loses true simplicity."[2]

I realize that my farmer friend, with his daily diligence and his knotted money-sack had seen the threatening clouds of voluntary robotism on the horizon, and was determined to live out his life close to the land, close to the Divine Author of Creation, and close to the guidance of his own soul. Though he sometimes referred to himself as a "simple farmer," his faith in things unseen also made him a visionary.

Gandhi's disciple Vinoba Bhave made the following observation in an essay on education: "In the Upanishads, the praises of ignorance are sung side by side with the praises of knowledge. Man needs not only knowledge but ignorance, too. Knowledge alone, or ignorance alone, leads him into darkness. But the union of fitting knowledge with fitting ignorance is the nectar of eternity."[3]

Recognizing this relationship between knowledge and ignorance would be useful to help us realize that the partial knowledge of our experts may appear as ultimate truth to the naivety of our collective ignorance. Sometimes, it must be understood that the informal intuition possessed by the less informed must serve as a counterforce to the narrow-vision of expertise, which, while it is focused, like a long focus lens leaves the foreground and background blurred.

A "simple farmer," Ira called himself, but he had not lost his perspective. He did not do his work totally preoccupied with his immediate task and immediate goal. He looked around himself thoughtfully and never forgot that he himself was a miracle, abiding in a far greater miracle that is utterly beyond comprehension. He gratefully applied the knowledge gleaned from science to his diligent husbandry of his land, but was not misled enough to believe that our science is anything more than a superficial film that rests on a boundless ocean of impenetrable nescience that is beyond either our tools or talents to comprehend.

"I may drive a truck and have some of these modern conveniences," Ira mused one day, "but I've read a bit about how much peasants knew about the land in olden times, and I think I'm a peasant at heart, and happy to be one." He reminded me that Oliver Goldsmith in *The Deserted Village* (1770) had talked of the value of peasantry, and that night I looked and found these lines:

Ill fares the land, to hastening ills a prey,
Where wealth accumulates and men decay;
Princes and lords may flourish or may fade;
A breath can make them, as a breath has made;
But a bold peasantry, their country's pride,
When once destroy'd, can never be supplied.

I took the book along with me the next time I visited Ira and read the lines and others to him, twice as a matter of fact because he wanted to hear them again. After listening both times quite attentively, he simply said, "My, didn't he know a lot — and so long ago too!"

And a decade or so ago, when I came across an article Henry Beston had written about how the peasant civilization of Europe had survived centuries of massacres, pillage, invasions, and burnings and somehow restored itself through the fertility of the land, only to begin succumbing to "a social revolution whose intellectual origins are entirely urban," I reflected upon the land wisdom Ira had accrued. It becomes increasingly evident that Beston's worse fears are materializing rapidly:

To this new order ancient customs are so much ignorant nonsense;
and a brutal and "efficient" mechanizing of all farm life is the

answer of the planners to all farm problems. The protagonists of this mechanized and industrialized agriculture apparently do not see that the old farming could face almost anything and carry on, while gasoline agriculture must live or die with the machine age.[4]

As Thomas Carlyle wrote, "This world, after all our science and sciences, is still a miracle; wonderful, inscrutable, magical and more, to whosoever will think of it."[5] It is this ancient world, as reflection upon the very history of our species will indicate, that we are related to most closely. If there is a peace that lies deeply beyond understanding, it is not merely a cessation of hostilities, a truce amidst the hectic activities undergone in pursuit of wealth, status, and strategic acquisition. Spiritual values can be directly derivative from the natural world that is our sponsor in the puzzling quality of Being that we are experiencing. Peace will embrace us when we realize that we truly have a place in this entire world, that most of what we pursue in daily life is symbolism, and that true comfort can attend us when we finally realize that we are at home in all that is about us. In fact there is no other home — and all about us there is an unsolicited grandeur that links our natural being to all that is divine. Heaven is under our feet as well as over our heads.

We are gradually recognizing the seduction of spirit in which we are entrapped. Yet this entrapment was pointed out long ago, which is perhaps a reason why we are urged to live a contemporary life, and to reject the insights that are available to us through history and philosophy. Consider these words written by a 19th century thinker, the Swiss diarist Henri-Frédéric Amiel, in 1852:

Every despotism has a specially keen and hostile instinct for whatever keeps up human dignity, and independence. And it is curious to see scientific and realist teaching used everywhere as a means of stifling all freedom of investigation as addressed to moral questions under a dead weight of facts. Materialism is the auxiliary doctrine of every tyranny, whether of the one or of the masses. To crush what is spiritual, moral, human so to speak, in man, by specializing him: to form mere wheels of the great social machine, instead of perfect individuals; to make society and not conscience the center of life, to enslave the soul to things, to depersonalize man, this is the dominant drift of our epoch. Everywhere you may see a tendency to substitute the laws of dead matter (number, mass) for the laws of moral nature (persuasion, adhesion, faith); equality, the principle of mediocrity, becoming a dogma; unity aimed at through uniformity; number doing duty for argument; negative liberty, which has no law in itself, and recognizes no limit except in force, everywhere taking the place of positive liberty, which means action guided by an inner law and curbed by a moral authority...

Materialism coarsens and petrifies everything; makes everything vulgar and every truth false. And there is a religious and political materialism which spoils all that it touches, liberty, equality, individuality. So that there are two ways of understanding democracy.

Surely the remedy consists in everywhere insisting upon the truth which democracy systemically forgets,...on the inequalities of talent, of virtue and merit, and on the respect due to age, to capacity, to services rendered,...and when the institutions of a country lay stress only on the rights of the individual, it is the business of the citizen to lay all the more stress on duty. There must be a constant effort to correct the prevailing tendency of things.

We know that the prevailing tendency today is degrading both the physical world and our own souls. We have to reach deeply into our spirits and bring forth an absolute determination to correct the moral deficiencies that are leading us towards disaster.

CHAPTER 7

The Problem of Separation

Detached, separated! I say there is no such separation: Nothing hitherto was ever stranded, cast aside; but all, were it only a withered leaf, works together with all; is borne forward on the bottomless, shoreless flood of Action, and lives through perpetual metamorphoses... Rightly viewed no meanest object is insignificant; all objects are as windows, through which the philosophic eye looks into Infinitude itself.

Thomas Carlyle
Sartor Resartus

He was a grizzled old-timer whose eighty years had bowed him surprisingly little. Our paths had crossed often over the years and we both seemed to like the ruminative encounters that marked each meeting. Although he lived by choice 'far from the madding crowd,' his perception of modern affairs was marked by great concern, and as he often said, "by great sorrow." His mind had remained unfettered by the modern chase after status, and was singularly analytic. He taught me afresh that though our society has a rather hasty tendency to write off such people as senile, the wisdom of our elders merits much respect. One day we had roamed past a seldom visited woodland pond, a gem of a place where loons periodically uttered their eerie wailing cries; and where fox sparrows kept the air alive with music from their alder and willow bowers. We settled on a log that offered a good view over the pond and enjoyed the just-right temperature afforded by motes of sunshine filtering through breeze rippled leaves.

I had never heard his views expressed on modern mobility. In fact, I wouldn't have guessed that he thought very much about such a thing, since he was remarkably comfortable in his immediate surroundings and seldom ventured elsewhere. But his thoughts do have a bearing on our lives today.

"It used to be," he reflected, "that when I went to town, it took three days each way. Now there's a gravel road right down at the end of the lane. I'm not saying that the road isn't a pretty nice convenience, and that it isn't handy to be able to get to town in just a couple hours. But, it seems to me, that for everything we gain, we lose something else.

"As for myself, I don't have the St. Vitus dance that most people seem to suffer from nowadays. I don't feel that I have to be going somewhere all the time. It sometime seems to me when I see people tearing along the roads, that they're either trying to run away from themselves, or else maybe looking for themselves.

"However it works I guess I really don't know. But I'll tell you Bob, that since we've got all this progress, people just can't sit still anymore. Now I'll grant you that I'm getting along in years and I might be thought of as pretty old fashioned. But, somehow I think we've become victims of the way we live. As far as anything making sense, it seems a lot more natural to saddle up a horse and ride off in the bush instead of chasing our tails down one of these highways. A lot of people don't seem to have the faintest idea any more how much there is to learn and how much beauty there is, just within walking distance of where they live. They would rather scoot into one of these modern four-wheeled broncs and take off clear across the nation — and I often think they really don't know what they are looking for, because even if they are trying to find themselves they keep so busy chasing around that they never have time enough to learn who they are. It scares me to see people becoming part of their machines. The Good Lord gave us legs instead of wheels, but we don't seem to savvy the difference.

"I've got a grandson," he continued, "who has hitchhiked across Canada and back — not once but twice. He has seen all this country that can be seen from a highway; but he has never wanted to walk over to Ptarmigan Spring against the mountainside, because he can't tolerate the flies and mosquitoes. I guess I'll never understand a chap who is happy going eighty miles an hour in a piece of tin, preferring to play Russian roulette on wheels, than have to swat a few bugs away now and then. Besides that, I believe that the faster you go the less you really see, and the less you know.

"Along with all this mobility, we've lost our sense of home. I've lived in this country for over sixty years, and could be set down almost anywhere within forty or fifty miles in any direction, and know pretty well where I was standing. But the ability to trot all over the country in hardly any time at all has destroyed our identification with the place we live. We need roots as bad as any tree does. This great nature all around us is what keeps us going and it's become pretty grim when there's no love left for the place where we live. We've become coast-to-coast tumbleweeds and have divorced ourselves from the good earth."

I know my friend would have nodded his head sagely in agreement with words of Chief Luther Standing Bear of the Oglala Sioux: "We did not think of the great open plains, the beautiful rolling hills, and winding streams as wild. Only to the white man was nature a wilderness and only to him was the land infested with wild animals and savage people. To us it was tame. Earth was bountiful and we were surrounded with blessings of the Great Mystery."[1]

In years long past there was awareness of a form of sin that lay at the very heart of all other sins. This sin, "attavada," is known as separation or dualism. It is derived from the Sanskrit word *Ahimsa*, an ethical principle of non-injury that was subscribed to by most Hindus. Ahimsa involved recognition of all living beings as kin and therefore forbade the taking of life. Because of this, no animal food was eaten and warfare was rejected. The principle also led to behavior such as that of Jainists who swept paths before them that they might refrain from crushing even insects, and who strained water to remove minute beings.

Although we would for the most part reject the food habits dictated by such an ethical stance, we are aware of mounting scientific evidence disclosing the close relationship between all life forms. While it once would have seemed ludicrous to ask if a cell can think, advanced opinion admits that consciousness exists at many levels. It may be that there is no lower or upper limit to consciousness and that perhaps awareness and life are synonymous. It is therefore comprehensible that the root of all sin or error can thus be traced, as Ahimsa suggests, to the underlying cause variously named duality, separation, or attavada as it was called by Jainists and Buddhists.[2] Indeed, application of the Golden Rule to all life, thus having respect as the core of our behavior toward all beings, would be a source of wholeness we do not yet enjoy.

Although a society of trained consumers might automatically harbor suspicion toward the asceticism of Ahimsa, many of us do recognize the brotherhood and sisterhood of all life. In fact many are troubled by reports of scientists that express concern over the reckless behavior that assails the interdependencies involved in the web of life.

Awareness of the concept of separation, combined with scrutiny of our own attitudes, could serve as a root for renewal and a foundation for reawakening of the soul. In almost every problem manifest in the world today, we can see tendrils that directly connect it with the idea of separation.

Since we all live on the planet earth, and draw sustenance and health from it, the most insidious form of separation is that which has blinded us to our utter dependence upon Terra.

A word picture of the human being, given in Shakespeare's *Measure for Measure*, graphically describes the hard exterior, or glassy essence, which acts as a barrier around the human soul and enables us to believe that destroying the earth for profit is a perquisite of business:

> But man, proud man,
> Dressed in a little brief authority,
> Most ignorant of what he's most assured,
> His glassy essence, like an angry ape,
> Plays such fantastic tricks before high heaven,
> As makes the angels weep.

Most of us have heard of the Twelve Labors of Hercules and of the prodigious strength of that individual. Among the stories about this hero of mythology, there is one that offers an analogy illustrating the importance of connection with the earth. It is the tale of Hercules' encounter with Antaeus.

On his journeys, Hercules passed through the land of the Pygmies who, in their fear of his prowess, employed as their defender the giant Antaeus, the son of Terra, the Earth. Antaeus was famed as a wrestler, and he insisted that all strangers wrestle with him. A renowned bout took place between Antaeus and Hercules, and although the strength of Hercules was prodigious, he could not subdue his opponent. The battle raged and Hercules finally noticed that each time Antaeus contacted the earth he arose with increased strength. Hercules finally succeeded in raising Antaeus aloft and keeping him from contact with the earth until his vigor diminished. Hercules thus won the match. The weakening and collapse of Antaeus was due to his loss of contact with his parent, with the basic reality that gave him his strength. In a similar manner our own separation and estrangement from the earth, our ancestral parent, has resulted in a weakened species no longer bursting with glowing energy and rich in health. This is a classic example of separation.

In these days when we are so taken with the records of attainments of athletes, there is an interesting and pertinent fact that is worth some thought. While men of earlier Olympic days were shorter than at present, 1.55 meters or less being average height as indicated by the length of bathtubs and tombs, they were not weaker. The strength of the Bronze Age athletes is confirmed by the weights and dumb-bells in the museum at Olympus. As a single example, there is a stone there that weighs 143.5 kilograms (316 lbs.).[3] This stone was raised above his head with one hand by Bybon, in the 6th century BC — a feat that has not yet been equalled. Bybon did not receive a gold medal, but a laurel wreath, which was the trophy adopted for the Olympic games.

Or consider that Milo of Crotona, a Pythagorean student and necessarily a vegetarian because of his membership in the Pythagorean school, became the strongest man in Greece. His remarkable strength came from "the calf that became a bull in his arms." History recounts that he lifted and carried a calf a certain distance every day of its life until it became a fully grown bull. Six-time winner in both the Olympic and Pythian games in the 6th century BC, he was enormously popular for his tricks and his amiability. He could hold a pomegranate in his fist so firmly that no one could take it from him and the fruit would not be injured. Or, in another test of strength, he would stand upon an oiled quoit and resist all efforts to remove him from his stance.[4]

It is truly remarkable how often an awareness of the fundamental unhealthiness of separation from the earth appears in the literary musings of people esteemed for their contributions to thought. In Emerson's famous essay "Self-Reliance," which has as its theme the divine sufficiency that can be attained by communion with one's soul, he considers our increasing remoteness from nature in these words:

> Society acquires new arts and loses old instincts. What a contrast between the well-clad, reading, writing, thinking American, with a watch, a pencil and a bill of exchange in his pocket, and the naked New Zealander, whose property is a club, a spear, a mat and an undivided twentieth of a shed to sleep under! But compare the health of the two men and you shall see that the white man has lost his aboriginal strength. If the traveler tell us truly, strike the savage with a broad-axe and in a day or two the flesh shall unite and heal as if you struck the blow into soft pitch, and the same blow shall send the white to his grave.

> The civilized man has built a coach, but has lost the use of his feet. He is supported on crutches, but lacks so much support of muscle. He has a fine Geneva watch, but he fails of the skill to tell the hour by the sun. A Greenwich nautical almanac he has, and so being sure of the information when he wants it, the man in the street does not know a star in the sky. The solstice he does not observe; the equinox he knows as little; and the whole bright calendar of the year is without a dial in his mind. His note-books impair his memory; his libraries overload his wits; the insurance-office increases the number of accidents; and it may be a question whether machinery does not encumber; whether we have not lost by refinement some energy, by a Christianity, entrenched in establishments and forms, some vigor of wild virtue. For every Stoic was a Stoic; but in Christendom where is the Christian?

Actually we need men like Emerson, Thoreau, Tolstoy, and Carlyle back in our curricula, men who thought for themselves and were not afraid to challenge the ideas of their times. They all believed that as long as people made mechanization and business their priority, they would run into patient resistance from God and nature. Emerson likened us to ships heading down a river toward the sea. There are obstacles on every side but one. When we are on the right course, the path of the soul, the ship "sweaps serenely over a deepening channel into an infinite sea." Olympian at times in his thoughts he suggested that books are needed for inspiration, but should not be used for crutches; that common individuals are capable of great thoughts, that we should not hide our heads in sand like an ostrich but should act responsibly in rejecting evil law or unadmirable practices. His own religious training did not alter his view that, "I like the silent church before the service begins, better than any preaching," and he believed that, "Men in all ways are better than they seem."

Henry Geiger, in his publication *Manas*, repeatedly expressed his admiration for Emerson's ability to shift from his private thought to public thought, and of his skill in tying them together. He spoke of this double consciousness as a talent such as circus equestrians have, to jump nimbly from the back of one horse to another, or to stand with one foot on the back of one of the horses and the other foot on the back of the other horse.[5]

Religions, which should be a unifying and calming force in human affairs, have on many occasions increased separation among people and helped estrange them from the planet. Like Tennyson's view of nature, religions have too often been red in tooth and claw.

History offers numerous examples of persecutions carried on in the name of religion, of various holy wars among which the Crusades are notable, of missionary attempts to convert "heathens" to "true" religious beliefs. It has been the habit to label people as heathens or as heretics from self-assurance that those doing the labelling have privileged access to the one true faith. It can also be noted in history that such theologians as Michael Wigglesworth referred to the newly settled continent of North America as a devil-infested, howling wilderness; and in 1662 this individual spoke of the unsettled portions of the continent as inhabited by none "but hellish fiends and brutal men." Thus we can see the justification of Luther Standing Bear's thoughts mentioned here earlier. Cotton Mather, a New England clergyman, identified the native American people as "not merely heathens but as active disciples of the devil."[6] It was not until the late 17th and 18th centuries, in the west, that a new view espoused by poets and other writers began to emerge, a view that was more respectful of the idea of divinity in all things. Many people began to realize that God was present in His creation and that one walked in God's temple in the wilderness.

Today most people can see the need for religions to make peace with one another, if for no other reason than to set an example for a world that is still riddled with a divisiveness that threatens all life.

Gandhi offered a valuable contribution to the idea of separation when he explained his belief in the universality of God. "I consider myself a Hindu, Christian, Moslem, Jew, Buddhist, and Confucian." In *Young India*, September 1924, he was quoted: "I believe in the absolute oneness of God and, therefore, of humanity. What though we have many bodies? We have but one soul. The rays of the sun are many through refraction. But they have the same source. I cannot, therefore detach myself from the wickedest soul nor may I be denied identity with the most virtuous."

Will and Ariel Durant, in their summary volume *The Lessons of History*, spoke of the need for religion, especially when laws become feeble and social order depends upon the power of morality. They also point to the lack of significant historic examples of a society maintaining moral laws without the help of religion.[7]

Realizing that academic procedures are unsuited to the study of mysticism, the Durants wisely did not speculate upon the matter of belief in God other than to say that if any theological view is supported by history it would be that of a "good and evil spirit battling for control of the universe and men's souls." They did comment on the "creative vitality of nature," a force that is extremely significant in causing thoughts of a supreme being to arise.[8]

Religions themselves, it seems, are locked in battles of defending and trying to extend their turf, and should consider the matter of "becoming" in increasing their tolerance and realizing that the search for meaning is the true mark of religiousness.

If we look closely at the world we live in, we can see that there is a group of people, very powerful and very self-centered, who form a dominant elite that is dedicated to its own protection. Its outstanding and easily recognizable tools are technologism and corporatism. These separative forces are succeeding in relegating many people to the role of second class citizens. Automation, as a single example, has succeeded in separating thousands of people from meaningful work, or from any work at all. It is acceptable to this wealthy elite that uncountable numbers of people will be bereft of employment and will be unable to find a dependable means of earning enough to have their own homes, or to have even adequate means of assuring that there is food on the table or sufficient income to afford health care and other basic needs. The prognosis afforded is dire in its implication for tyranny, violence and unrest. While greed is exemplified and sanctified, we may see such extreme chaos as to signify the likelihood of social collapse. Income inequality grows steadily in the world. With 6.4 billion presently alive, 1.3 billion people live on less than $1 U.S. per day. But, "The world's richest three people have more assets than the combined gross domestic products of the world's 48 poorest countries."[9]

In separation of rich from poor, one is reminded of the cynical comment of the Wobblies era that the law, in its pretenses to justice, prohibited both the rich and poor from sleeping on park benches. And the prevalence of violence toward women is proof that barbarism is still a hallmark of our society; as long as women must strive for equal wages for equal work, and for control over their own reproductive systems, we will not have not arrived at real civilization.

Once the idea of separation begins to permeate our consciousness, it can be detected in all sorts of human activities, extending from serious to pleasurable pursuits. Though undertaken for recreation and for healthful activity, sports events often result in animosity and belligerence. Riots and crowd tramplings are not uncommon outcomes of both minor and major hockey, football and soccer games. Reflect also upon frequent reports of over-zealous parents displaying poor sportsmanship at Little League games. One can dismiss such incidents as people merely being "carried away" by enthusiasm, but duality is, after all, a shallow matter of seeing oneself as a very special and privileged individual, and others as lesser individuals who have the temerity to think they are *as important as I am.*

Another allusion to the somnambulistic behavior of our times was made in the mid-eighties by George Kennan, former U.S. Ambassador to Russia, in speaking of the nuclear arms race: "We have done all this helplessly, almost involuntarily like the victims of some sort of hypnotism, like men in a dream, like lemmings heading for the sea, like the children of Hamelin marching blithely along behind their Pied Piper."

Although literature abounds with illustrations of the problem of separation, such ideas rarely surface in modern education. Studies in humanities have yielded to the demands of technologism and its focus on science and mathematics. In this respect, educational institutions have lost sight of the need to educate "whole" people, ignoring the fact that a narrow focus in studies may develop more and more expertise only through the sacrifice of general knowledge. Nicholas Murray Butler's definition of an expert as "a man who knows more and more about less and less," is a reminder of this fact.

A perusal of the creative efforts of William Blake (1757–1827) offers interesting perspective on the rent-asunder nature of humankind.

Blake considered original sin to be "Selfhood," which he saw as the effort of an isolated fragment of life to be self-sufficient. This resulted in alienation from one's self, from the world, and from fellow humans; and unless we wished to proceed toward apocalypse, we must elect recovery via the process of reintegration. In order to be healed, Blake felt we must regain a view of nature in which nature becomes humanized, and is therefore a place where all individuals may become reunited as cooperative humankind in a realized Creation. War, strife and greed are no longer tenable.

Blake elaborated not upon the fall of man, but on the falling *apart* of man into four distinct units. The resurrection of the species entails reuniting of these units into a peaceful fusion represented by the lion lying down with the lamb — a reconciliation of the opposing forces that normally tear us apart.

In his poetry he identified the four separations, calling them the four Zoas. These are Urizen, the cold and scientific aspect, which is the Zoa of Reason; Luvah, the pitying and weeping aspect, which is the Zoa of Energy, Passion and Feeling; Los, the fierce far-seeing boy, which comprises the Zoa of Prophetic Power; and Tharmes, or parent power, which is the Zoa of Spirit.

Each of these aspects is but a part of the wholeness of humankind, which is presently blinded by the narrowness of its worldview, and is starving for reintegration. Simply put, Blake felt that life tempted one to a narrow focus, to single vision. What else might be expected from an age of specialization and a reductionist form of education?

In his poem *Mock on, Voltaire, Rousseau*, Blake provided an example of his reasoning. He compared the single vision of Newton, and his scientific perception of the world, to a single grain of sand. Lying in its proper place on the beach, among its companion grains, it is a "particle of light," but when taken as the central meaning of life, it is as but a single grain of sand blown into the observing eye, blinding it to perception of the whole.

If we ponder the matter of the grain of sand separated from its context, removed from its wholeness, we can see that there resides in today's emphasis on greed and power — in what has been referred to as the "me generation" — an innate selfishness that wanders utterly alone in a world where true friendship and intimacy have been sacrificed for self-aggrandizement.

Traditional religions, with their inability to offer the expected quick solutions to problems of the modern age, have largely been abandoned. Possibly they have surrendered too much of the "higher ground" that needs defending. In their place is the modern priesthood of the medical consultant's office and the quick, if inadequate, chemical fix of mood altering drugs.

There are stanzas in William Wordsworth's poems that directly apply to our times, and show recognition that even at the beginning of the 19th century the human soul was assaulted by the rapidity of change. This one from his *Ode on Intimations of Immortality* is an example:

> There was a time when meadow, grove and stream,
> The earth, and every common sight,

To me did seem
Appareled in celestial light,
The glory and freshness of a dream.
It is not now as it hath been of yore –
Turn whereso'er I may,
By night or day,
The things which I have seen I now can see nor more.

Also, in his *Preface to Lyrical Ballads* he shows recognition of the opposing forces in life, which tend to separate us from underlying reality:

For a multitude of causes, unknown to former times, are now acting with a combined force to blunt the discriminating powers of the mind and unfitting it for all voluntary exertion, to reduce it to a state of almost savage torpor. The most effective of these causes are the great national events which are daily taking place, and the increasing accumulation of men in cities, where the uniformity of their occupations produces a craving for extraordinary incident, which the rapid communication of intelligence hourly gratifies.

Wordsworth spoke apologetically of the "feeble effort" of his own work to counteract this trend, and said that the "magnitude of general evil" was such that he would be utterly oppressed but for his deep faith that "the time is approaching when the evil will be systematically opposed."

Although it is more difficult in today's urbanized and denaturalized world to wander freely in natural settings, my own deep and abiding faith in nature, the earth, and the solemn meaning or source behind it all, has made me appreciate the poets and their visionary gleams. In Wordsworth's *The Tables Turned,* he offers an unsurpassable anodyne for the barren sterility of a world in which intellectual pursuit has smothered our soul force:

Up! up! my friend, and quit your books,
Or surely you'll grow double;
Up! up! my friend, and clear your looks;
Why all this toil and trouble?...

And hark! how blithe the throstle sings!
He, too, is no mean preacher:
Come forth into the light of things,
Let Nature be your teacher...

One impulse from a vernal wood
May teach you more of man,
Of moral evil and of good,
Than all the sages can.

Sweet is the lore which Nature brings;
Our meddling intellect
Misshapes the beauteous forms of things -
We murder to dissect.

Enough of Science and of Art;
Close up those barren leaves;
Come forth, and bring with you a heart
That watches and receives.

Echoing the Durants' conclusion that history best supports a theological view of good and evil forces contending for control of the universe and of human souls, a theologian of my acquaintance repeatedly points to the remarkable insight afforded by the Biblical observation: "For we wrestle not against flesh and blood, but against principalities, against powers, against the rulers of the darkness of this world, against spiritual wickedness in high places." (Ephesians 6:12). The decisions of powerful groups have always favored the rich over the poor. Consider as a single example that the English Parliament, which was controlled by propertied classes, passed nearly 5,000 acts between the 13th and 19th centuries, which in effect transferred land from the peasantry to wealthy landowners. It is not surprising that some unidentified wag summarized these acts by saying: "The law locks up the thief who steals the goose from off the common, but leaves at large the larger thief who steals the common from the goose."

While it is truly frustrating to face the magnitude of changes that need to be made, the onus does rest upon individuals —

whether they live in an urban high-rise, or in some sleepy backwater that is well off the beaten path. It is necessary out of our soul's wisdom, and out of the deepest intuitions we can muster, that we bring the strength of our individuality to have more force upon the somnambulistic activities of society than we permit them to have upon us.

There is widespread comprehension that the status quo of the present era is wrong as wrong can be. But there is also widespread rationalization, which takes many forms: "What can I do about it, I'm only one person?" "I know I should do something, but I'm just too busy." "What's the use of trying, it's too late anyway?"

Renewal of individual selves, a matter of personal determination, is essential if the whole is to be affected. The first step on the right path is the most difficult.

There is a sacred verse of the Hindus called the Gayatari that is used in initiation of the Brahman. It reflects the ancient view that we are immersed in the immensity of God and truth. We cannot recognize the whole because we are a separated particle. We cannot find the eternal as long as we allow ourselves to be enslaved in the transitory things of the material world. The challenge of life for pope or peon is to wash away evil deeds and thoughts, re-enter tranquility and to dwell within the ocean of soul from which we have our becoming.

> That which provideth sustenance to the Universe and to ourselves,
> From which all doth proceed, unto which all must return,
> THAT THOU ART.
> In the golden vase of thine earthly body
> May the pure light of the spiritual Sun shine forth,
> That thou may'st know the truth,
> and so do thy whole duty
> On thy journey back to the Sacred Seat.

Buddhism, since its inception about 500 BC, has accepted "The Wheel of Rebirth" and the laws of Karma as part of its creed. Buddha taught that a worthwhile goal in life is the extinction of individual desire, which is rewarded by being enabled to escape from the wheel of rebirth. It is an opposite sort of faith to the highly individualistic Christian disciplines that see heaven as the culmination of life. The Buddhist goal is simply return to the whole. Birth is the beginning of evil, and Nirvana — the final absorption of self — is the beginning of peace, of all that can be attained. Of the major religions, Buddhism is the only one that is biophilic in essence.

There is much to be said for Buddhistic belief. The economic view it offers stresses simplicity and non-violence. Saintliness and contentment stem from selfless and kindly behavior. Conduct is more significant than ritual or worship. Benevolence to all creatures is vital. The middle way between abject poverty and saturation with materialism can help one find the means of "Right Livelihood." Spiritual values definitely have priority over economic growth.

It is sometimes alleged that Buddha was an atheist, however, he did affirm that there is a "further shore;" but he insisted that human terminology is inadequate to describe metaphysical reality. He believed, however, that most people could find it for themselves by living morally. Nirvana was given as a distant reality; but Dharma, or right living, was the immediate reality available to anyone.[10]

A different outlook on the matter of transmigration was taken by Plato. He did not consider this existence an ordeal, a Star Chamber, or a potpourri of unassimilable events, for, presiding over each of our lives was an immortal soul. Plato and Plotinus both held the view that the soul pre-existed this life and had many voyages in this world, in many forms. The soul, it could be said, ebbed and flowed with the rhythms and cycles of nature. Prior to its current pilgrimage, the soul rested in the universe of Being. Released from its previous incarnation, it indulged in communion with itself, thinking upon and assimilating its previous experiences. "Alone with the alone" it became refreshed and invigorated until ready for greater knowledge of the universe, and for companionship with former friends. The soul was then ready for animation in another form with which to enter the swelling tide of Becoming.

The classic example of the illusion under which humanity toils was presented by Plato in the seventh book of *The Republic*. Plato's fame has earned many approbations, such as British philosopher Alfred North Whitehead's comment that, "All subsequent philosophy is but footnotes to Plato." In *The Republic,* Plato, speaking through the voice of Socrates, depicts the human situation as one lived within a cave where we are focusing upon an unreal shadow world that guides the senses to a false interpretation of life.

In Socrates' words:

> Behold! human beings living in an underground cave, which has a mouth open towards the light and stretching all along the den; here they have been from their childhood, and have their legs and necks chained so that they cannot move, and can only see before them, being prevented by the chains from turning round their heads. Above and behind them a fire is blazing at a distance, and between the fire and the prisoners there is a raised way, and you will see if you look, a low wall built along the way, like the screen which marionette players have in front of them, over which they show their puppets.[11]

Socrates goes on to speak of the people passing behind the low wall, carrying all sorts of things such as vessels, statues, animal figures, and various other items that project above the wall. The fettered people in the cave see only their own shadows, and the shadows of the things that are being carried by the people behind the low wall. They also hear, echoing from the wall in front of them, those things that are said by the passers-by.

To these people, Socrates said, "The truth would be nothing but the shadow of the images."

Socrates goes on to say that if a prisoner is suddenly released and compelled to leave the cave and look toward the light, he will first be blinded by the glare and will be unable to realize that what he is now seeing is reality rather than illusion. He will be perplexed and will prefer, after only a cursory look at things in the light, to feel that reality exists in the shadow world of the cave. As Socrates points out, it will take time for an individual to become accustomed to the sight of the upper world, or to be able to emerge into the light of the sun and to withstand its brightness.

Eventually though, the freed individual would see things clearly in sunlight and would think with pity of those still in the cave. He might return, especially if asked, to try to help those in the cave to understand their true situation.

And Plato has Socrates explain what the attitude of the people in the cave would be upon the return of their would-be guide.

> Now if he should be required to contend with these perpetual prisoners in "evaluating" these shadows while his vision was still dim and before his eyes were accustomed to the dark — and the time required for habituation would not be very short — would he not provoke laughter, and would it not be said of him that he had returned from his journey aloft with his eyes ruined and that it was not worth while even to attempt the ascent? And if it were possible to lay hands on and to kill the man who tried to release them and lead them up, would they not kill him?

Obviously Plato saw humans as individuals entrapped by their passions and desires. Though the seeds of godhood lie dormant within all of us, and show signs of germination in finer moments, they are suppressed by handy rationalizations that permit the short-term joy of sense gratification, while muting the patient, small voice within. It is only when the mind detaches itself from the world of senses long enough to fully explore some chink in the facade of illusion that the zephyr of reflection may bring dewy warmth to help germinate the seeds of truth that lie in the soil of the mind.

For Plato, true opinion is derived from *anamnesis*, the inward soul-memory, which resides within us. This is the memory of a life of immortal spirit prior to its imprisonment in fleshly bodies. True vision is rare in mortal life, because the soul is imprisoned in flesh and can only be freed by individual efforts to emerge into the light of truth.

Scholar Robert Cushman in *Therapeia* (Greenwood Press, 1976), points out that Plato foresaw the coming of the present, with its claim that knowledge is power, and virtue the use of power to satisfy our desires and further our intents. He states that Plato long ago emphatically proclaimed the superiority of *philosophia* to *techne*. But modern choice has rendered techne ascendant over philosophia, and has thus subordinated wisdom to science. Looking at the contemporary situation, we have devised numerous means by which we may destroy ourselves: thermonuclear; biological, or even cyber wars; chemical poisoning of air, water and soil with resulting damage to immune systems; or destruction of the ozone shield, to offer some examples.

As Cushman says: "If we allow Plato to speak, he will suggest that the question before us is whether we shall shrivel on the positivist vine or, with him, plumb the resources of the human soul and so recover, it may be, faith in the dignity of man."

It is possible that, with effort, the ultimate reality may be awakened in the human soul and utilized as a guide to life.

In his prose-poem *The Prophet* (1923), Kahlil Gibran spoke of the dismaying effect of separation:

> Your reason and your passion are the rudder and the sails of your seafaring soul.
> If either your sails or your rudder be broken, you can but toss and drift, or else be held at a standstill in mid-seas.

The paradoxes of our age are legion, and offer incontrovertible evidence of a foundering civilization. While mercy efforts for a single ailing child are admirable and justly lauded, we are also obsessed with a never-ending arms race that produces one horrible weapon after another, and profit-takers become enriched by worldwide trade in weaponry. All segments of society have greater certainty of their rights than of their responsibilities. In sports, power and prowess are dominant and the importance of sportsmanship is muted. Education, which was once considered to begin with the teaching of virtue, is now focused on the needs of a technological society, rather than on helping individuals grow out of the cave and into the light of a spiritual comprehension of the meaning of life.

The reintegration of individuals and individual souls is a concept whose time has come for implementation. As G.W.F. Hegel, German philosopher, noted some 200 years ago, the owl of Minerva, the symbol of wisdom, does not rise from its perch until the sun of empire has set, and it becomes steadily more apparent that a downward spiral persists in over-organized society.

A mere inkling of the extent to which we are controlled by things was given by Neil Postman in his keynote address at the

Frankfurt Book Fair in October 1984. Referring to Huxley's view *(Brave New World)* that people "will come to love their oppression, to adore the technologies that undo their capacities to think," Postman quoted the 1983 Nielsen Report on Television. This report indicated that the average American home has its television set on for seven hours a day and that an American who has reached the age of forty will have viewed more than one million television commercials and will see another million ads before retirement.

Television is a marketing device. It exists not for entertainment, but for profit. The outcome of kneeling in devotion to TV is that we will have both pockets picked before we get back on our feet.

We must draw strength from our spirits to turn once again toward the ideal of a true civilization. The alternative is that if we continue to draw our worldview from the media and the idols of the marketplace, we will go down with them into chaos. We must learn to think for ourselves rather than let the machine think for us.

CHAPTER 8

Self Restraint

No conflict is so severe as his who labors to subdue himself.

Thomas à Kempis

It has often been stated that the peril of ignoring history is that it forces us to repeat the mistakes of our past. The actual circumstances of today's involvement with technology are, insofar as we know, unique in these times. However, the fact that we amuse ourselves to death with mechanized mobility, with round-the-clock entertainment via television, and with other trivial activities, has historical precedence. Could it be intentional, one wonders, that only the blandest sort of history is mixed into the weak educational broth that is labeled social studies in modern schools?

As an example of one of the lessons that we have failed to learn from history, I came across these words written by the 16th century poet Etienne de la Boetie. They were set down in reference to the far-seeing policies of Cyrus, the Persian king of the 1st century BC.

When news was brought to him that the people of Sardis had rebelled, it would have been easy for him to reduce them by force; but being unwilling either to sack such a fine city or to maintain an army there to police it, he thought of an unusual expedient for reducing it. He established in it brothels, taverns, and public games, and issued the proclamation that the inhabitants were to enjoy them. He found this type of garrison so effective that he never again had to draw the sword against the Lydians.

Truly it is a marvelous thing that they let themselves be caught so quickly at the slightest tickling of their fancy. Plays, farces, spectacles, gladiators, strange beasts, medals, pictures and other such opiates, these were for ancient peoples the bait toward slavery, the price of their liberty, the instruments of their tyranny.[1]

No doubt if Cyrus had waged war against their rebellion, the Lydians would have fought bravely and sacrificed their lives against the Persian armies, but they succumbed without a murmur to the subtle seductions that he engineered. Lacking self-restraint they became willing slaves, and devotees of hedonism.

The world of enticement that Cyrus created for the Lydians is prodigiously magnified today. Mass advertising keeps us informed of worldwide pleasures to suit every taste and to fit the dimensions of every pocketbook. The "tempter" of history has been glossily packaged and made available on a 24-hour basis. Advertising is not the process of keeping people informed, but is temptation itself. And for individuals, as English poet John Dryden wrote, it would be far "better to shun the bait than struggle in the snare," for what snare is so deadly as the "play now, pay later" way by which individuals mortgage their futures and their freedom. Without a measure of astuteness and developed willpower we may be aware of the hook without being able to resist nibbling at the bait.

British scientist Thomas Henry Huxley, a serious champion of Darwinism in the years following publication of the *Origin of Species*, revised his views substantially in later years. He publicly declared in the famous Romanes Lecture "Evolution and Ethics," given at Oxford University in 1894, that humankind needed to defy the laws of a mechanical nature which he himself had once considered to be completely sufficient.

In his lecture he stated that goodness or virtue, that which is ethically best, involves conduct opposite to that which leads to what we commonly call success. Success, he felt, was achieved by ruthless assertion of one's own self-interest, but truly ethical behavior is dependent on acting with self-restraint. He saw the ethical progress of society as the outgrowth of resistance to self-aggrandizement, combined with active concern for the survival of other people.

Two years before expressing these views he had published an

essay in which he suggested that what people call "the supernatural" might be better regarded as a more inclusive extension of the natural. He had criticized the "impertinent" assumption that there is no greater intelligence than man's to be found throughout the universe. As he expressed it, "Without stepping beyond the analogy of that which is known, it is easy to people the cosmos with entities, in ascending scale, until we reach something practically indistinguishable from omnipotence, omnipresence and omniscience."[2]

In essence, Huxley's views concurred with those so well-stated by Robert Bridges, English physician and poet (1844–1930): "Man is a spiritual being, the proper work of his mind is to interpret the world according to his highest nature, to conquer the material aspects of the world so as to bring them into subjugation to the spirit."

It is difficult to say what inner experience made Huxley reverse views he had held for years and arrive at the conclusion that mechanical laws and the manifestations of them were not an adequate focus for life. While we can ask whether he was prompted by some guiding spirit or by reflection alone, we cannot say more than that in his "weighing of the world," factors came together that convinced him that the meaning of life lay deeper than the mere preoccupation with things and their manipulation.

A change in our essential viewpoint of life may in fact be a mark of great spiritual growth.

A seminal paragraph by Ralph Waldo Emerson in his essay "Self-Reliance" offers inspiration to many an individual who attains a clearer vision of life but hesitates to express this greater understanding:

A foolish consistency is the hobgoblin of little minds, adored by little statesmen and philosophers and divines. With consistency a great soul has simply nothing to do. He may as well concern himself with his shadow on the wall. Speak what you think now in hard words and tomorrow speak what tomorrow thinks in hard words again, though it contradict every thing you said today. "Ah, so you shall be sure to be misunderstood." Is it so bad then to be misunderstood? Pythagoras was misunderstood, and Socrates and Jesus, and Luther, and Copernicus, and Galileo, and Newton, and every pure and wise spirit that ever took flesh. To be great is to be misunderstood.[3]

And the sober tone of Thoreau's writing indicates that for him there was something of irrefutable subjective reality that assisted in the guidance of his thoughts: "However intense my experience, I am conscious of the presence and criticism of a part of me, which, as it were is not a part of me, but a spectator, sharing no experience, but taking note of it, and that is no more I than it is you."

Huxley, like many of us, probably found that an initial thought, when left on the back burner of the mind, will stew and simmer, mix with other ideas, and be thoroughly modified. His rejection of an earlier full acceptance of mechanism must have proceeded from a realization that a mechanical theory of life failed to answer the great questions that confront us all: the meaning of life, our place in the universal order, and the all-pervading importance of ethical principles. He may have heard from his own soul.

The acquisition of gadgetry that permits a convenient and simplified approach to life does not sustain itself, as many people are seeing today. Perhaps as William James suggested in his *Psychology: Briefer Course*, the brain may be a transmitter, and a cosmos of the mind-stuff lies behind the objective matter before our eyes. As we open ourselves to ideas by pondering upon them, our seeking emptiness is rewarded by a flow of ideas to meet our needs. This is not very far removed from the ancient Vedantic idea that there is a void from which all things emanate and a non-void in which we live. By seeking, we shall find; by asking, we shall receive; and by opening ourselves to the void, we shall be filled. Taking this a step farther, by utilizing self-restraint, and by reducing our fascination with the chase after material goods, we tune ourselves to an unfailing spring from which less perishable things of real value flow with undiminished vigor.

For a great many years the focus of society has been on the acquisition of things. This was observed in Wordsworth's poem, *The World Is Too Much With Us,* written in 1806:

The world is too much with us; late and soon,
Getting and spending, we lay waste our powers;
Little we see in Nature that is ours.

Of course there is no question that some material needs have utility, and these are not the sort of things to which Wordsworth was referring. Just as Scripture points out that, "The love of money is the root of all evil," (Timothy 6:10), so we can see that the love of goods may have a negative effect on our character. Wisdom of the ages has consistently warned that there are things of the spirit that are vastly more important than myriad material objects that may elicit our fascination and devotion.

The Mahabharata — the longest epic poem ever written (in Sanskrit) — product of a hundred poets and a thousand singers, a 100,000 stanza saga called "the greatest work of imagination Asia has ever produced," offers a vivid example that humankind has not always idolized material possessions as we do today.

Embedded in the narrative is the tale of a demon that inhabited a pool deep in the woods. Those who visited the pool were asked by the demon to give answers to five riddles. Failure to answer the riddles correctly sent the travellers into a deep sleep. These are the riddles together with their answers.

1. What makes the sun rise and set?
ANSWER: Eternal Law

2. On what depends the state of the Brahmin (the holy man)?
ANSWER: Not on knowledge of the law, but on Conduct alone.

3. What is it that, the surrender of which makes one rich?
ANSWER: Greed

4. What is real knowledge?
ANSWER: Comprehension of the ultimate reality.

5. What is compassion?
ANSWER: The desire to do good to all.

Trapped in our materialistic passions, we would be hard pressed today to come up with the answers to these questions, and may indeed be locked within a deep sleep of our own making.

To those who unhesitatingly accept the creed espoused by bumper stickers that advise, "The fellow who dies with the most toys WINS," or, "Let it All Hang Out," the idea of implementing self-restraint may seem to be a form of heresy. However, if we had sufficient self-restraint, many laws that act as restraints today would be unnecessary. Speed limits offer a single example. Back in the days when early vehicles were called "stink buggies," the speed of 15 or 20 miles an hour was considered outrageous. Today such speeds are considered an imposition, and to some individuals any limit on speed is taken as a form of persecution to be resisted as often as possible. Seat belts, air bags, roll bars, guard-rails, and warning signs are all forms of restraints aimed at protecting people from themselves and from their lack of self-restraint. Likewise, banisters on stairs, life-jackets, locks, burglar alarms, warning lights, and noise bylaws are among many necessary improvisations to protect individuals from their own carelessness, or excess, or from the anti-social behavior of others.

While self-restraint is obviously an individual matter, there is a cumulative effect to its absence, which is extremely serious.

In Harold Goddard's authoritative text on *The Meaning of Shakespeare*, he wrote a musing comment on the cause of war, which indicates the effect of greed unmitigated by self-restraint. Pointing out that, "War is not the supreme tragedy of men and nations," he goes on to say that once war ceases, the pursuit of hedonistic activities on the parts of many, and the pursuit of money, intrigue, and political chicanery on the part of others, result in the establishment of conditions that set the stage for future armed conflicts. Both the focus on dissipative pleasures or on hard selfishness have the same outcome. They till the soil of unrest and dissatisfaction to produce the crop of animosity that leads to new social conflagrations.

When sufficient imagination allows people to cherish life for the sake of life, and thus leads to the offering of friendship to all, we will have reached a level of maturity and social concern that will permit the scourge of war to be abandoned.

Further interesting thoughts on the search for underlying truth were given by Dr. Albert Einstein in a series of interviews with William Hermanns, a German-born sociologist and poet. The first of four interviews took place in Germany in 1930 and the others in the United States. It was Einstein's conviction that, "Intuition, not intellect, is the 'open sesame' of yourself." Intuition obviously cannot act effectively in a mind that is focused continually on the accumulation of material objects and has no time for more reflective behavior. Einstein explained to Dr. Hermanns that he had never been "attracted by specialization," but had always been drawn by the mystery of life and "wanted to know nature, creation itself." His religion, he stated, was to use his own ability to think as much as it was possible. It was his conclusion that, far more than studying or gathering facts, "Intuition is the prime factor in our achievement." He felt that, "If we want to honor God," we should use this intuition to understand as much as we can to "grasp the laws which form the basis of a perfect mechanism." It is easily deduced that he felt we are a part of a creation far greater than ourselves.

It is also interesting and saddening to know that Einstein was appalled at the use that governments had made of his mathematical discoveries — the creation of nuclear weapons. "Dr. Hermanns," he said, "if you want to do something for me, tell the world that if I had foreseen Hiroshima and Nagasaki, I would have torn up my formula in 1905."[4]

Peace, of course, is the alternative to war. Thomas à Kempis (1380–1471), author of the *Imitation of Christ*, noted that, "All men desire peace," and that, "Few men desire those things that make for peace." While it is difficult in many situations to establish the relationship between causes and effects, it is more evident in this instance to realize that when people compete for the material things and associated power and glory that lead to the causes of war, there is unlikely to be peace. Thus the importance of controlling oneself and one's desires can be seen to be positive action that, if widely followed, might indeed lead to the long-treasured ideal of peace on earth. As Confucius noted in *Analects*, "He that requires much from himself and little from others will keep himself from being the object of resentment."

It is not too far-fetched to consider Thomas à Kempis' statement about peace in terms of the health of the human body...everyone desires health but few will live in such a manner as to encourage it. While most people are aware of the wisdom of simple diets, regular exercise and fresh air; few are willing to give up the elusive chase for wealth and status that virtually demands habits of unhealthful living. Indeed, very few will take time out from their daily pursuits to stand firm on such issues as the importance of clean water and air, or healthful soil in which to grow food.

Nor will many people read, study or actively take time out to think for the sake of the expansion of their own minds and spirits. A great mental passivity has settled over a society camped before its television sets each night (and often day). This did not elude the attention of Arthur Michael Ramsey, Archbishop of Canterbury, who said in his enthronement speech in 1962: "I often think the doctrines of fasting in Lent and having meatless days are old-fashioned. It might be better to give up television. That would be a more meaningful self-denial in this day and age."

And to restrain oneself does mean self-denial, if we prefer to call it that. Commonly we find self-denial difficult in matters both large and small. I recall a peppery middle-aged lady talking caustically about her dietary habits and increasing girth. "When you get to be like me," she said, "it shouldn't be called a waist line anymore. It should be spelled w-a-s-t-e line. I know what my problem is: I call it an inflammation of the cupboard gland! I've always made cookies but now I can't pass by the cupboard without helping myself to one. 'Where's your willpower Hilda?' I ask myself, and to be honest I can say I've got lots of willpower about some things, but not enough about that."

If we dip back into late Medieval history, we encounter the name of Paracelsus, a Swiss physician who founded iatrochemistry, the merging of chemistry and medicine. His work was referred to in a late medical history as the precursor of chemical pharmacology and therapeutics.

Paracelsus, who lived between 1493 and 1541, is also referred to as "the Luther of physicians," his medical reforms bridging the gap between old procedures and modern medical practice. He was one of the first individuals to recognize that obsession by an idea can diminish the health of persons and societies. It was his view that the mind is superior to the body and if sufficiently undisciplined will lead to illnesses that do not arise as much from the body as from intemperances of the intellect. Dr. Manly Hall comments that only a "slight change in terminology" is needed "to reconcile the views of Paracelsus with the modern findings of Freud and Adler."[5]

If we consider the strong focus of individuals and society today on material acquisition and other symbols of wealth, and the lack of self-restraint involved in gratifying every wish — something we are constantly encouraged to do by advertising techniques — it seems that intemperances of the intellect are a profound problem in great need of being curbed. Serious reflection upon the effect of advertising on our lives should indicate the degree to which individuality and personal sovereignty has been sacrificed to the myth that economic aspirations are the most important goals of life.

People are constantly buffeted by external stimuli. As consumers they are unceasingly cajoled to buy one thing or another. This cajoling goes on night and day. Advertisers shriek from places of business, from billboards, newspapers, magazines, flyers, radios, and television. Consumers must not forget their role. Goods unto garbage: Wastemakers of the world unite!

Thoreau reminded his readers that if the head monkey in Paris wore a purple shawl, all the monkeys in North America would want one too.

But is style so good, so necessary, so indispensable? There is a tale told by a man who was an assistant professor in a western university. After 15 years with his university, the gods smiled upon him and he was promoted to associate professor. As he told the story, people (associate professors and full professors) who had never noticed him before, began to speak to him. He felt that he had arrived. At a meeting at the faculty club, he was taken off in a corner and urged to build or buy a home in an area of town where associate and full professors lived. He glowed in the attention he received, but was a cautious man, and had a cautious wife. They stayed in the part of town where they had lived for 15 years. "We know its natural to want to keep up with the Joneses and we actually discussed how we could afford a new home, and then," they both smiled at the memory, "and then we realized that by staying down where we presently live, on a bit higher salary, we had suddenly become Jones!"

It is a characteristic of these times that we assume we can discard the accumulated wisdom of the ages, while continually emphasizing that modern knowledge and insight are far superior to any thoughts held by people of other times. For the Biblical caution that people "do not live by bread alone" we have scoffingly referred to money as "bread" and unquestioningly subscribed to the idea that it is desirable to devote our energies to attaining as much "bread" as possible. The ancient maxim "nothing overmuch" is paid little heed in a world wherein flamboyant possession signals higher status than contentment with moderation.

In considering the matter of correcting "intemperances" it is worth remembering that temperance ranked from centuries ago as one of the four cardinal virtues. The essence of temperance was moderation, and a virtuous life was considered to be one in which an individual did not overindulge in the pursuit of pleasure. Often this virtue was felt to be synonymous with chastity, but we must remember that intemperance is also associated with things such as gluttony, greed, and drunkenness.

A particular important form of moderation today might be the reduction of average highway speeds and of the number of drivers under the influence of alcohol. I noted a statistic given in the 1994 issue of *Vital Signs* which stated that in the 100 countries that report the number of highway fatalities each year, 350,000 people died in accidents in 1993. It added that 90 countries do not report such statistics, and it is conservatively estimated that deaths on highways in these other nations would bring the total deaths from driving to half a million people. Add to this that 3.6 million are injured (some very seriously) in cars each year in the U.S. alone (1.5% of the population) and there is a strong argument for change in the direction of moderation. Indicating that the problem is worldwide, the article cited Belgium as having 88,000 people injured by cars each year, and in Germany almost a half million people are hurt annually. Even more alarming statistics are presented in *State of the World 1999* (p.143), which states that traffic accidents worldwide kill about 885,000 people each year, equivalent to 10 jumbo jet crashes daily. In addition vehicle exhaust is the leading toxin in city air pollution and is estimated to kill at least three million people worldwide, yearly. The solution that lies at the heart of this problem is the design of a society that is far less dependent on vehicles, less in need to be constantly on the move. Certainly, if the automotive industry, broadly speaking, was not so powerful, it would be imperative to make major changes because of these deaths and injuries. The foregoing is but a single example of habits that are ripe for moderation.[6]

As Lewis Mumford pointed out in *The Myth of the Machine*, there is a lethal flaw in the reasoning of those who call for unabridged mechanization. It is that, unlike organic systems, technological systems lack an innate method of controlling their own growth. Living organisms necessarily work toward dynamic equilibria, which favor life and growth. Leaders in science and technology, driven as they are by the modern economic system, look upon quantitative productivity as a *good* in itself. They recognize no desirable limits to the production of material goods. The single purpose goal — profit — like any obsession, blinds those who are its adherents to such things as chaotic climate events and other ecological signs that humanity must re-evaluate its goals and behaviors. With the age-old story of Humpty Dumpty to reflect upon, the value of restoring balance before we take a great fall should be obvious.

It isn't fair to propose self-restraint as a step along the path to solution of modern problems without giving consideration as to why it might be effective. Nor would it be honest to ignore the fact that others have considered the idea of self-restraint and rejected it as inadequate. Garrett Hardin, for example, in his well known article "Tragedy of the Commons" (Science, Dec. 13, 1968), argues in the latter part of his article that appeals to conscience do not work, and that those who respond to the problems of the world by enacting self-restraint on their own part simply make a contribution to other individuals who will not be moved by conscience to moderate their own behavior.

It seems far more important and constructive for an awakened individual to use self-restraint to begin resettlement of the frontiers of his or her own soul, and thus initiate the process of getting back into peak moral trim. And speaking of moral trim reminds me of our physical trim and the attention given to all sorts of mechanical gadgets, purchasable of course, to restore the body beautiful. The ridiculousness of rowing or hiking one's way to health via pulleys and ropes has apparently not yet impacted upon our conscience. And, if exercising in one's own home, in proper uniforms, is partially justified by the deplorable fact that urban streets are too dangerous, or the air too offensive to breathe deeply, we are saying much about conditions that should long ago have been rectified. We can wait forever for some mechanical gadget that will lead down an effortless path, thereby eliminating individual responsibility. The longer we wait, the more we play into the hands of those who would reduce all human behavior to the lowest common denominator.

Many people, whether or not they are familiar with Garrett Hardin's often quoted work, will recognize his contention that we have "created an industrial monster," which, lured by the smell of money, "continues at will to devour rapidly vanishing, virgin landscapes, excreting progress in the process." Through our own worship of business and our lack of thoughtful civic responsibility, the industrial monster has amassed most of the world's wealth and blatantly refuses to moderate its rapaciousness. As long as we devote our own lives to getting and spending, we simply nourish the bloated excesses of the monster and starve our self-sovereignty.

Self-restraint is active refutation of the lame excuse often hidden behind, that an individual is powerless and can do nothing about the way the world is going. We must realize that we vote far more actively with our pocketbooks than with the casting of a slip of paper into a ballot box. As to the importance of voting, Thoreau suggested that the vote one drops into a ballot box is of much less significance than the kind of a person who descends from one's chamber into the street each day.

It has always seemed to me that there is a remarkable bit of wisdom in the first short phrase written in the Gospel according to St. John. That phrase, familiar to most, is: "In the beginning was the Word..." Translating "Word" as the original idea that begets an action, the remarkable stimulus for self-restraint may be the idea of becoming more independent and giving more conscious direction to your own life. It may also be the thoughtful realization that something has to be done to get personal debts under control. One does eventually get tired of constant encouragement through advertising to become one of the world's great spenders. It is easy to see that we are living in a society that is trying to burn the candle at both ends.

Thoreau pointed out one time that a person is rich in proportion to the number of things he can get along *without*. It is also pertinent to realize that the price of everything you buy is the amount of time you have to work in order to pay for it. A new car may mean four or five years of regular payments that reduce your options to do other things that may be far more meaningful to you. Just think of the reduction of individual stress that exists when you don't owe a single cent. Unfortunately many people never experience that freedom. The idea of self-restraint really has to do with the establishment of control over one's own life. Our society is one in which there has been a steady corralling of the wealth and power of the world into fewer and fewer pockets. The ordinary individual has become a trained consumer; an individual kept in his place by the titillation of wants and by the burden of debt that renders him impotent. Such is the mania for money and power, that we now live within a world that has lost all sense of proportion and drives itself toward some unspeakable catastrophe — a world in which we have lost the sense of balance that depends upon the redemptive qualities of character and of the soul. It has been said that the poor will always be with us, but it is no less true that the rich and greedy will always be with us. Unbeknown to these latter and fewer individuals, their own hope for survival rests upon qualities not yet lost by many ordinary people.

Rather than those who know better, simply trying to emulate the obsession of endless accumulation that is displayed by the world's leaders, there needs to be a counter-movement by individuals aware of higher laws than those given observance today. Much as it is said that religion has lost its grip on people and is guilty of omissions and spurious commissions on its own part, one must realize that there are gems of truth in the world's religions, but that they also need to winnow the seed ideas from the chaff of poor habits.

Approved social consciousness today involves humble obeisance to the ideology of technological progress. Such obeisance is regularly encouraged by conventional media owned outright or controlled by business interests. It is not surprising that agriculturist-philosopher Wendell Berry suggested that getting rid of one's television might be an effective first step in breaking free of its paralyzing influence on minds. He cautioned that it wouldn't be fair to merely give away one's TV, but recommended instead that it be disassembled, preferably with a blunt instrument. Of course, disposing of the television may entail the old awareness that when the false gods depart the true gods arrive. This is not necessarily so, of course. Dispensing with TV, or greatly curtailing its use, is only a deed of value if something more worthwhile replaces the void left by elimination of its hypnotic effect.

That very good things can fill the gap left by conventional means of amusement was indicated in two incidents I heard about recently. One had to do with a lengthy power failure caused by a severe storm in the Pacific Northwest. A mother interviewed on a radio evening news broadcast explained how happily her family adjusted to this event. She told how they had enjoyed sitting around the kitchen table, lighted by candlelight. They were talking, playing games, sharing popcorn and enjoying one another's companionship as they had not done for years. She said that the whole family became aware of how little time it had spent together as a unit and how much it valued a new empathy it had been unaware existed.

Psychologist and broadcaster Joy Brown recently spoke of a family that reduced the use of television to weekends in a serious effort to improve the school success of its children. An arrangement was made whereby the children could choose weekday programs to be taped for viewing on the weekends, but no television viewing would be allowed from Monday through Friday. The children's mother reported that her children's grades improved even more than she had expected, but that there were other benefits to the new arrangement that were even more surprising. Paramount among these was increased communication. The family found itself reading to one another, laughing and playing games, having family discussions that arose from assigned schoolwork or from casual conversation, which just hadn't occurred when TV dominated the evenings. A family decision to cancel cable television led to savings that were spent by regular family outings to a cinema, or other cultural or sporting events chosen by the family as a group. The mother commented on how they had suddenly discovered how much they enjoyed each other.

There are things about restraint that are true even if they are not obvious. Daniel Webster recognized that even "liberty exists in proportion to wholesome restraint." Consider the fact that while we have liberty, the liberty is to enjoy our own rights without destroying the rights of others. When a group of individuals walks down the street singing in boisterousness, the liberty can suddenly turn to license — to abuse of others — if the camaraderie and joyfulness should lead to hurling rocks at streetlights or some other form of property damage. As the English statesman Edmund Burke pointed out in the 18th century, it is necessary that there be voluntary self-restraint in order for society to function in a healthy manner. Serious consideration of his reflection indicates much of what is missing from society today and lies at the root of much social and economic error:

> Men are qualified for civil liberty in exact proportion to their disposition to put chains upon their own appetites; in proportion as their love of justice is above their rapacity; in proportion as their soundness and sobriety of understanding is above their vanity and presumption; in proportion as they are more disposed to listen to the counsels of the wise and good, in preference to the flattery of knaves. Society cannot exist unless a controlling power upon the will and appetite is placed somewhere; and the less of it there is within, the more there must be of it without. It is ordained in the eternal constitution of things, that men of intemperate habits cannot be free. Their passions forge their fetters.[7]

We live in some sort of frustrated acceptance of the idea that we must be busy, busy, busy. We run from one event to another and rarely allow ourselves time for reflection on what we are trying to accomplish. As Thoreau commented: "Pause! Avast! Why so seeming fast and deadly slow."

Dr. Albert Schweitzer recognized in 1923 that we are denying ourselves the opportunity to live with worthwhile goals in mind. In his words, "The revival of thought which is essential for our time can only come through a transformation of the opinions and ideals of the many brought about by individual and universal reflection about the meaning of life and of the world."[8]

CHAPTER 9

Tuning in to the Creation

In the relations of humans with the animals, with the flowers, with the objects of creation, there is a whole great ethic scarcely seen as yet, but which will eventually break through into the light and be the corollary and the complement to human ethics.

Victor Hugo

Let's recapitulate for a moment.

Since long before humanity arrived, life has poured forth inexhaustibly from the earth — for ends that are beyond our understanding. As a thinking species, we would like to be able to explain the essence of the cosmos. In spite of our best efforts it remains a mystery. Numerous creation stories have been proposed and we can choose to believe one or another of them, or we can tailor a combination of them to suit ourselves. But we have achieved no consensus that can be proudly hailed and confidently explained in textbooks. That there is deep meaning in a personal sense still remains a matter of hope and of intuitively sensed but unseen evidence. It is unfortunate that convictions obstinately held result in animosity toward others holding equally sincere convictions. It is not illogical that peace on earth and good will toward other beings must spring from the tilling and cultivation of our own essences. Given a spark of the infinite, it is necessary for us to nourish that spark into a sustaining glow that will light our way to a level of civilization characterized by the kindness and benevolence that define the word humane. It would perhaps help us to realize that heaven is indeed under our feet as well as over our heads. This is the field upon which our better natures must cope with the weakness of self-gratification achieved at whatever cost to anyone or anything other than our selves.

Though vectored by parents, we spring from the soil of the earth through some mysterious alchemy in which spirited life inhabits matter. We look around and behold a tree, a flower, or a shrub. It is obvious that these are rooted in the earth and thus not at all difficult to understand that they are nourished by it. But because we are mobile and seemingly independent actors in life, it is easy to ignore the fact that our lives are also rooted in the earth; each day our bodies ingest earth energy for bodily heat, for growth, maintenance, and repair.

Unfortunately, we who are ourselves earth have become so sophisticated, such self-elected superior beings, that we cannot bring ourselves to grip with the glaring truth that we have wilfully and carelessly become estranged from our matrix. Nature, which Carlyle called the time-vesture of God, the mother and father of all generations of parents, has been relegated to an enemy that must be conquered, mastered, or beaten into submission. The wingbeats of folly are now clearly audible. Our lack of respect for the earth is disgraceful — and ominous.

About six hundred BC the *Tao te Ching*, attributed to Lao Tzu, identified the universe as a sacred vessel that was not made to be altered by humans. The *Tao* advised that the world would be ruined by tinkering with its established order. Basic to the *Tao* was the idea that we are incapable of comprehending the totality of the universe.

The late David Bohm, professor of theoretical physics at Birkbeck College, London, would have entirely agreed with this ancient belief. As a theoretical physicist, he emphatically declared his conviction that the wholeness and integrity of the cosmos is a reality. He observed us trapped in our reductionist habits. The outcome of separating various aspects of nature in our technical endeavors, he noted, is that we bring about fragmentation, which induces further fragmentation of our own thought processes and leads to increasing forms of social disorder. Bohm contended that we cannot break apart the intricate order of the world without affecting our own integrity. Likewise, we cannot solve specific social problems without considering the whole of society, nor treat parts of the body without affecting the whole body. He referred to the cosmos as a seamless whole in which there is a dynamic interconnectedness of everything. Eternity is now, as well as in the past and present, and thus today's events are productive of eternal reverberations.[1]

Bohm foresaw that there would be great difficulty in correcting the fragmentation that characterizes modern activities and goals. A deeply ingrained condition of behavior and thought characterized by ruthless ambition, unending wants, and all too many shattered psyches marks the shaky apex of industrial success.

Recognizing that our integrity has dissolved rapidly amidst the processes that dissolve the integrity of our surroundings, Bohm concluded that necessary changes in ourselves must proceed simultaneously with changes in our actions. Rebuilding wholeness in ourselves would only be possible through deeds leading to restoration of wholeness in what we euphemistically call the environment. Pious *talk* about a more holistic way of acting is not a substitute for *deeds* that might help undo as much as possible of the chaos we have caused and labeled misleadingly by such comforting words as development and progress.

In effect Bohm argued that we must make some sort of integrated quantum leap in both our behavior and our worldview for the obviously important sake of our continued existence. He contended that what we are presently doing does not work, and may lead to our extinction.

What Dr. Bohm saw as the glaring error in the present worldview is the extremity of the extent to which we have permitted ourselves to be obsessed by self-centered goals. He identified this as an error in our concept of measurement. With our studied disdain for ideas that we consider to be antiquated or unsophisticated, we have written off long-held values that recognized a Golden Mean or *right measure* that determines appropriate goals. As a reference he pointed to the Greek tragedies which depicted that suffering results from unreasonable expectations. While we understand the unhealthful aspects of over-eating, extreme fatigue, and excesses in general, we do not seem capable at present of recognizing the looming disaster that results from "wanting it all and wanting it now." In describing the path that we need to follow to end fragmentary thought and action, Bohm referred to the idea of *moderation in all things*. He commented that virtue has long been "regarded as the outcome of right inner measure underlying man's social action and behavior." Bohm used the idea of ratio or proportion to explain how we can solve many of our problems and identify a road to recovery. We must use our judgment to establish a sense of proportion that we can perceive both intellectually and through our senses. There are already many people who are convinced that the common goal of endless acquisition is as unreasonable as the more easily comprehended fate of extreme poverty. While there may be some sort of superficial agreement with the idea that there is no such thing as enough profit or enough money, more sober thought will at least suggest that such an idea approaches a serious form of mania. We are already far past the point of reasonableness in our exploitation of all things.

To consume everything today and save nothing for the future makes no more sense nationally or internationally than it does in a household. And although it is suavely pleaded that those who would slow down the pace of "economic growth" are irrational, we have overlooked the presence of the important word "ratio" in the excesses we label as rational. We disdain any true balance between what is done and what is left undone, between the exploited and the unexploited, the altered and the pristine, between judgments made by the mind and others made by the insight of soul-force.

It is only because we are morally irresolute that the economy has first priority in our lives. We need a nobler ideal, such as creating a genuine civilization, developing integrity in humanity, or devising a theology of the earth. As it is, we have focused upon the lowest common denominator, and are following our economy down to ruin. Realizing that the earth is everyone's overparent, it is easy to agree with Plato's words: "No true lover of his country would bring himself to tear in pieces his own nurse and mother."[2]

All about us we can discern the desacralized landscapes that are left by the passage of progress. We can smell and hear the titanic, never-ending rumbling and roaring of our mechanized society. All seems to be taking place according to some feckless human plan, acted upon with such momentum that society now teeters on its tiptoes, threatening to crash in one stunning fashion or another. It has been, and is, a society of too much. Too much use of antibiotics leads to antibiotic resistance, to the development of tougher disease organisms, and the weakening of the body's natural defence system. Too much industrial pollution has led to the steady deterioration of the ozone layer and the appearance of the most lethal antibiotic of all — Ultraviolet B. Too much deforestation has led to shrinking water tables, avalanches, climatic instability with attendant woes of floods, and higher wind velocities. Massive soil loss accompanies mechanized agriculture; focusing on computer literacy interferes with a more important form of literacy. It may be, as poet Robert Service said, "that each fresh move is a fresh mistake."[3]

Facing the facts, it could be said that we have been "asleep at the switch." But there are strong signs that there is also an awakening occurring, and even if it is in the very nick of time, this awakening offers hope. What a pleasant change it is to note that the "Yearning for Balance" report, which followed a study initiated by the Merck Family Fund, reveals the impressive fact that the deepest aspirations of Americans are non-material. In fact, most of the people who participated in the study revealed a sincere commitment to simplify their lives. The strength of this desire is further evidenced by the action taken by 28 percent of the participants, who took pay cuts over the last five years in order to improve the quality of their lives.

It is truly hopeful that so many individuals have made the personal decision that there is a better way to live than to be shackled to the golden car of commerce. Their choices show that there resides deep within the instincts of humanity an intuition that comes forth to lead when idolatry proves itself insufficient — a true awakening of the soul.

We are seeing, in many places and among many people, a tuning in to creation. Note the words of Bruce Cameron, vice-president of the Angus Reid Group that, "It came as a surprise to officials when major studies were done on the four mountain parks, and four out of five people said the parks should be expanded rather than limited in size." There is growing evidence that people expect much more from governments and from corporations than a balanced budget and statistics declaring that the corporations are making higher profits. They are tired of make-work political projects, which are offered as consolation for the automation that makes higher corporate profits possible, and tired of the unemployed becoming the sacrificial victims of these excessive profits. For most of the last decade people have indicated strong concerns about toxic chemicals, air and water pollution, and their effect on health. We are becoming aware that our personal health and quality of life are but reflections of the health and attributes of the entire creation. The world is ripe for change and only the most obtuse still measure their quality of life in terms of ostentation and possessions.

We undoubtedly could benefit from some of the stubborn conviction that guided more individualistic thinkers a few generations past.

A couple of summers ago we had supper with some friends who had a guest visiting them from one of the New England states. Our host was quizzing him about the town-meeting form of government that has been a tradition there for years. It was the New Englander's contention that people remain astute to the difference between pseudo and real needs of the community under such a form of government, and told us this story.

In the community where he grew up, there had been a long-standing respect for the wisdom of the village elders. Each year at the annual town meeting there were several comfortable wooden-backed benches that were occupied by the hoary-headed patriarchs of the community. It was customary for people who wished to have money appropriated for a particular purpose to insert an article in the "warrant" for the annual meeting. The one he recollected was an article "to see if the town would raise the sum of $500 to build a fence around the local burying ground," (this would be a much greater sum today). The reason given for building the fence was that a neighboring community had done so, and the local community did not wish to seem less respectful toward its own deceased. The usual procedure was that the people responsible for the particular article would speak on behalf of it, and others, as they saw fit, would rise and give their opinions. Always, he said, before the people voted upon the article, there would be a pause, and heads would turn toward the back of the hall to see if any of the aged citizens wished to add a comment. After the usual discussion following the proposal to fence the cemetery, heads turned and it was noted that someone was indeed rising from the back bench to remain standing with his hands resting upon a cane. There was a respectful pause to await his opinion. He began with the observation that he figured he had as much respect for the dead as anyone else, and more perhaps because many of them had been lifelong friends. He also commented that he didn't believe in "monkey-see, monkey-do" and didn't feel they needed to build a fence just because somebody in the neighboring community had built one around their cemetery. He summed up his views in his inimitable New England twang: "I cain't rightly see what for we need to build a fence around that there burying ground. Us'uns on the outside sure aren't in a hurry to get in there, and them on the inside aren't about to come out. I cain't rightly see what we're fencing in or fencing out, and don't see what fur we need a fence." The teller of the tale chuckled, and told us that the article was voted down, and commented that frills and window-dressing didn't stand much chance but people did vote for things that were really needed.

The interesting thing about the old patriarch's observations was that his vision took him to the heart of the matter. He understood, as many did not, that a fence is a structure that has the function of setting something apart that has actual need of inclusion or of prevention from straying. Once he had pointed out that there was no such need in this instance, people who were voting for or against additional taxation saw little reason for a structure clearly delineated as unnecessary. To be sure, in the minds of some individuals, there might have been a cosmetic consideration that a fence would be attractive, but the old-timer had also indicated that respect for the dead was more an attitude of mind than of matter.

It is of course possible that people today might look upon the old man's words from diametrically opposite viewpoints. Some might think of his comments as "old fashioned" and of no value at all. It might be argued that his were counter-productive remarks since they denied someone the right to sell materials for the fence, and someone else employment in doing the building. Those of opposite persuasion would recognize an underlying wisdom that is currently in short supply. Significantly though, the patriarch functioned as an independent personality, considered the topic from the vantage of his long life and his own uniqueness, and exerted his influence upon his community by expressing ideas previously not considered.

What is important in the example above is the function of individual reflection in the formation of decisions. Dr. Albert Schweitzer repeatedly expressed his concern with the extent to which individuality of thought had been stifled by the over-organization of society. He was particularly distressed at the manipulation of society by economic forces of self-interest, which he reasoned would spoil peoples' ideals of civilization. It was his idea that only by free individuals can true civilization be realized.

It troubled Schweitzer that existing public opinion "is maintained by the press, by propaganda, by organization, and by financial and other influences which are at its disposal." It was his conclusion that such an engineered means of spreading ideas is unnatural, "and must be opposed by the natural one, which goes from man to man and relies solely on the truth of the thoughts and the hearer's receptiveness for new truth." He likened the forces of propaganda agencies to Goliath enrobed in "the mighty armor of the age" facing unarmed David, whose most effective weapon was the human spirit.

Dr. Schweitzer left no doubt of his conviction that the only solution lies in the deepest realm of individual being, in the soul-force, which, once activated, can become the swelling bud of a true humanity. Only in its flowering will there ever be that long-awaited goal of peace on earth and good will toward all. As Schweitzer wrote: "The history of our decadence preaches the truth that when hope is dead the spirit becomes the deciding court of appeal, and this truth must in the future find in us a sublime and noble fulfillment."[4] It is no mere play on words that soul-force is the sole force that will achieve this end.

In modern society we have neglected the idea of a balance between practicality and idealism. Practicality was espoused by one British Columbia politician who in banal fashion referred to the odor of pollution as the smell of money, and who scoffed at the idea of conservative forestry practices by asking what God made trees for if he didn't mean them to be cut down. Dr. Paul Ehrlich, a much-published Stanford University biologist, closed his 1970 book, *Population — Resources — Environment: Issues in Human Ecology,* by declaring that while there have always been visionaries who spoke of such things as love, peace, and beauty, they have been silenced by practical men who praised smog as a sign of progress and who argued in support of "just" wars. But his final thought on the matter was expressed in these words: "It must be one of the greatest ironies of the history of *Homo sapiens* that the only salvation for the practical men now lies in what they think of as the dreams of idealists. The question now is: can the realists be persuaded to face reality in time?"[5]

It is sobering to consider that even in 1970 Ehrlich felt there was evidence to suggest "that the capacity of the planet to support human life has been permanently impaired." Ehrlich also stressed that there is no technological panacea for our problems, although technological means can help, as in the reduction of pollution. The principal hope for solutions, he contended, lies in human attitudes toward such things as population, environment, economic growth, reduction of worldwide tensions, and technology itself.

The matter of attitude really lies at the heart of what I refer to as tuning in to creation. What is really involved is a bit of humble recognition of our absolute dependence on the earth for everything that pertains to our livelihood. This means dispensing with our illusions of omniscience in being able to solve the many dilemmas we have already produced. It is interesting to think in retrospect of a little article written by Norman Cousins, former editor of the *Saturday Review of Literature.* Cousins was an observer at atomic bomb tests conducted by the U.S. government shortly after the end of World War II. So impressed was he by the awesome spectacle that he wrote that humanity can only justify its existence as long as "it can control the conditions it creates."

The likelihood that we can control what we have already done is reminiscent of an old tale told about a relentless gossip who finally realized the error of her ways and sought forgiveness from her priest, and a suitable penance for her behavior. It was a windy day and he took her to the belfry of the church and tore several sheets of paper into tiny bits and cast them to the wind. He pointed out to her that it would be as difficult to repair the harm her gossip had done as it would be to retrieve all the pieces of paper that blew helter-skelter before the gusty breezes, but that her penance demanded that she make the attempt.

Dr. Hans Selye, a much-honored pioneer in the theory of stress disease, spoke enthusiastically of the *vis medicatrix naturae,* a "healing force of nature which works from within." He reminds us that 24 centuries ago, Hippocrates, the Father of Medicine, believed that "disease is not only suffering (pathos) but is also toil (ponos), the fight of the body to restore itself toward normal." Selye writes that this is an important idea, which is constantly being rediscovered. In Selye's book, *The Stress of Life,* he states that one of the principal reasons for writing the book "was the wish to share with others the serene and elevating satisfaction which comes from understanding the inherent, harmonious beauty of nature." Experiencing nature he felt was an aid to daily life, just as deep religious faith or a balanced philosophical outlook give roots to internal stability: "There is an equanimity and a peace of mind which can be achieved only through contact with the sublime." The visible joy a child exhibits at seeing a brightly colored insect, a rainbow, or an animal such as a moose or bear is an impressive response to the abundance of mystery. Unfortunately, the astonishment of youthful experiences becomes eroded by sophistication and by the onerous shackles forged in devotion to getting and spending. Dulled by the demands of practicality, people sacrifice their todays for the promises of wealth and leisure tomorrow. A cause for stress is apparent in the sacrifice of awe and wonder about life itself for the sake of daily routine. It becomes easy, Dr. Selye suggests, to substitute a little extra overtime (or alcohol), for more meaningful experiences.

Those inspired by their work, those who find great pleasure in seeking and knowing or in unraveling some intriguing mystery, retain a youthful outlook on life. They are motivated by enthusiasm (*en Theos,* or God within). Theirs is a spontaneity that is not ossified by the demands of utter practicality. By contrast, in Selye's words: "The most acquisitive person is so busy reinvesting that he never learns how to cash in." People who call themselves realistic and practical in the quest for fame and fortune, suggests Selye, rarely have as realistic and practical goals as do the dreamers who pursue their own ideals with devotion.[6]

There have been books written about people seeking their roots. Such books have usually focused principally on returning to one's place of birth, to familiar faces and scenes. But we hear little about returning to the deeper roots which bind us to the earth. Quite to the contrary, we have developed a whole industry that would even deny return of our dead bodies to the earth. In effect, we attempt to defeat the decomposition system by infusing our dead with chemicals. And more lately there has been the development of cryogenics. Our insensitivity to our source has enabled us to turn our backs upon our origin. We gaze upon the stars and think of other planetary systems that we can also mine and develop for profit. We spend billions playing the game of space cadet, while the foundations of our existence on earth crumble beneath our unheeding feet. Needless to say, we would be far better off spending those billions in trying to undo some of the damage already done or, better yet, not even attempting to accrue those billions simply by leaving more resources intact. Powerful as our technological skills and aspirations may be, they are as nothing compared to the incredible natural forces of the universe. As an example, consider how penicillin was once thought to be a "magic bullet" capable of curing any bacterial infection, and a mere half century later some bacteria have developed astonishing resistance to virtually all antibiotics.

The unspeakable catastrophe we invite, with adamant unwillingness to modify our actions, seems to re-echo the observation of evolutionary biologists that extreme specialization always greatly increases a species risk of extinction. In our case we have defined "rational" to suit ourselves and justified this by saying that 'truth is relative.' Yet, as Spanish philosopher Jose Ortega y Gasset pointed out: "Our own spirit is alien from both of these positions; when we attempt to assume either of them we feel we are being mutilated."

Realization of the holiness of nature has manifested itself over and over throughout history. Spinoza saw God apparent in nature, and understood both God and nature to be mutually interpenetrating rather than standing in juxtaposition to one another. Goethe found delight in the thoughts of Spinoza, and in his old age told Eckermann, his confidant, that, "Nature is always true, always serious, always severe, it is always right and mistakes and errors are always the work of men. It disdains the incapable, it gives itself up and reveals its secrets only to that person who is honest and pure and capable" (Feb. 13th, 1829).[7]

Musing upon the patterns formed by frost coming from the ground in spring, Thoreau too was moved to comment: "There is nothing inorganic. Those foliaceous heaps lie along the bank like the slag of a furnace, showing that Nature is 'in full blast' within. The earth is not a mere fragment of dead history, stratum upon stratum like the leaves of a book, to be studied by geologists and antiquaries chiefly, but living poetry like the leaves of a tree, — not a fossil earth, but a living earth, compared with whose great central life all animal and vegetable life is merely parasitic."

It is when we start to question our goals in life that we begin to retrieve our individuality. We have been a pleasure-bent society pursuing goals that are characteristically engendered by vanity, status and acquisitions. We are overdue for a change in our lives, one which entails serious reflection about the meaning of life itself and the innate order of the world in which we live. We continue in our ways by curtailing our thought in such fashion that it deals almost exclusively with our personal aspirations and the aims and intents of the highly favored industrial society in which we live. It does not require deep reflection to recognize that we are heavy feeders at the banquet of life. Consider, for example, how luxury food items grown for affluent tables constitute a denial of basic food supplies for the poor of other nations. Can we lightly assume the right to impose starvation on less fortunate individuals because of balance of payment problems brought about by an imposed economic system?

Reflection upon the foregoing can lead to the realization of endless social injustices that exist, and for which we allow only a murmur of criticism. It is precisely because we elect to live in haste and superficiality that we have no time for reflection, and this valuable tool gathers dust upon the remotest shelves in our minds.

If we consider the basic structure and integrity of the earth we encounter even deeper consequences of our actions. As zoologist Edward O. Wilson points out in his popular book *The Diversity of Life*, 27,000 species of organisms are rendered extinct each year in tropical rain forests alone. This number is made more graphic by his identification of the miraculous strategies organisms must employ "to survive and reproduce against nearly impossible odds."[8]

To tune into creation it must be brought into consciousness. Unfortunately the living world has been assigned a nebulous, rather bureaucratic term called "environment," and has been relegated to the same status as urban background noise, which people learn to ignore. In order to call attention to emergency vehicles and to dangerous situations we have devised various flashing lights and sirens to override ordinary sounds. If we could awaken from the trance in which progress is carried on we would install flashing lights and sirens on factory chimneys, on outlet pipes carrying dangerous chemicals into water bodies, and even on vehicle exhaust pipes that pour vast amounts of hostile chemicals into what was once called fresh air. In Canada a packet of cigarettes may have a label warning that smoking during pregnancy can harm your baby or that tobacco smoke can cause lung cancer. Consider what labels might be placed on automobiles or aircraft — that driving or flying can kill you; or consider what labels might be placed on bottles containing alcoholic beverages. If we are going to warn people of dangers inherent in various products or devices, we should embrace this technique without hesitation and without exception. Yet these far greater menaces to our health are ignored. "There has always been a price on human safety," said the chief representative of a power company. His organization was building a dam that overshadowed a community of thousands of people in the path of the enormous potential energy that would be unleashed if the dam failed.

The fact of the matter is that if we had the respect for creation that it deserves we would act upon that respect. We would thus curb the destructive energies within ourselves that cause us to abandon restraint and tear apart the intricate miracle of life that we can only partially understand at best, and that we can emulate only to the most rudimentary extent.

Considering that bigness has become so pronounced that governments are endlessly struggling to counter daily problems without having time or energy for long-term thinking, the ball has been cast into the court of individuals. If any serious improvement is to be effected it must start at grassroot level. This is a difficult individual initiative, and has been stifled by over-organization through which we have begun to rely on group protests or demonstrations rather than upon personal actions.

While we have orchestrated present events by our own lack of zeal, and by our willingness to let someone else do our thinking for us, we have unwisely ignored any personal responsibility toward our planet. American dramatist Robert Sherwood expressed his view of our strange come-uppance in *The Petrified Forest* (1935): "Nature is hitting back. Not with the old weapons — floods, plagues, holocausts. We can neutralize them. She's fighting back with strange instruments called neuroses. She's taking the world away from the intellectuals and giving it back to the apes."

More explicitly we can say that individuals of conscience are required in large numbers to assess their own ways and to remedy them through reflection, study, analysis, and adoption of changed behavior that is less destructive, more constructive and in some instances even reconstructive.

Let us not underestimate the effect that an individual can have upon mass society. There is much truth in Emerson's often quoted remark that, "An institution is the lengthened shadow of one man."

The recognition of the cumulative effect of personal effort was expressed by psychologist and philosopher William James:

> I am done with great things and big things; great institutions and big success, and I am for those tiny, invisible, molecular moral forces that work from individual to individual, creeping through the crannies of the world like so many soft rootlets, or like the capillary oozing of water, yet which, if you give them time, will rend the hardest monuments of man's pride.[9]

If we are to move toward harmony with the All, it will be through nurture of our inner selves, through awakening the soul and selflessly offering love, concern and care for the land and all of the life it sustains. At an even deeper level it will be through attaining reunion with the mystical quintessence that sponsors life force and the astounding beauty quietly portrayed in the starry nights, the sunrises and sunsets, and the countless sublime vistas that present themselves gratuitously to our senses and our intuitions.

Life is the school we all attend, and although we have been sadly failing the grade, we are still invited to change our ways and pass with flying colors. Indeed, we may have to spice our insights with, "Humility that low, sweet root / From which all heavenly virtues shoot," but we have evaded our innate understanding until the eleventh hour and cannot afford to tarry a moment longer.

In the next two chapters I would like to discuss tools we can use to heal the breach between us and the seamless whole in which we move, live, and have our being. The focus will be upon prayer, silence, and reflection.

CHAPTER 10

Re-Engagement: Prayer and Silence

Certain thoughts are prayers. There are moments when, whatever be the attitude of the body, the soul is on its knees.

Victor Hugo

Prayer is usually thought of in relation to formal religions but many people have come to view all religions, formal and private, as attempts to respect a deep meaning that is sensed to exist in the universe. God, Brahma, Allah, Buddha and the Great Spirit are just a few of the names for the creative power as visualized by people at different times and places in the world. The insistence of particular faiths that they have a monopoly on truth is aggressive and defensive. It is unfortunate that the obstinacy of sects has acted as a barrier to the development of peace and respect among various peoples of the world.

That a variety of religions have sprung up throughout the world speaks well of humanity. Wherever and whenever people have lived there has been an innate sense that the world is too great to be meaningless. Awe may lie at the root of the conclusion that there must be more meaning to existence than we realize. The world detectable to the senses has been deemed part of something far greater — a spiritual meaning that lies at the very heart of life.

Both in our private lives and in formal religions there has been a search to establish union with the great power deemed to be the quintessence of all that is. Prayer stems from human efforts to contact that which is greatest, to seek harmony with it, to understand, and in an admirable sense, to act in accordance with the will and laws of that which made and makes possible our consciousness of ourselves and of that which we comprehend as a beacon illuminating the path of life.

Prayers are inspirational, offer meaning to replace meaninglessness, commend sharing in place of grasping attitudes, kindliness instead of brutality, and suggest in a still inactivated awareness the concepts of peace on earth and good will toward everyone and everything.

In a world in which the tendrils of techno-fascism have steadily been spreading through the soft tissue of society, prayer remains as the ultimate form of democracy. All the petty despots and bureaucrats can be bypassed and a direct appeal can be made to the Supreme Ruler. As long as there is prayer we are unlikely to succumb totally to a mechanistic ideology. No e-mail, fax machine, telephone, telegraph or letter writing is needed. And although you can't expect a lightning bolt answer, did you ever get one from a politician?

Since prayer is an outreaching, it signifies that our self-assurance is more limited than we pretend, and that in our troubled moments we feel the need for guidance. It does not require much thought to realize that frail, mortal beings such as we really are, have little justification for the self-aggrandizement involved in egotism. Throughout history there has been much emphasis placed on the benefits of humility. Confucius saw it as the foundation of all virtues, as protection from self-love and avarice. St. Augustine observed that, "It was pride that changed angels into devils; it is humility that makes men as angels." More recently Albert Einstein, uncomfortable and embarrassed by notoriety, commented, "There are plenty of the well-endowed, thank God...It strikes me as unfair, and even in bad taste, to select a few of them for boundless admiration, attributing super-human powers of mind and character to them. This has been my fate, and the contrast between the popular estimate of my powers and achievement and the reality is simply grotesque."

I recall, years ago in school, becoming acquainted with the humorous anecdotes of *archy and mehitabel*, written by Donald

Marquis. The protagonists were archy, a cockroach, and an alley cat named mehitabel. The book was purportedly written by archy who, in a previous life, had been a writer. His companion, mehitabel, was the reincarnation of Cleopatra. They both lived together in a house, and referred to the master of the house as "the boss." Nostalgic for his role as a writer, archy espied a typewriter with paper in it, and each evening after dark would resume his efforts at creative writing. The book was written entirely without capital letters because archy could not depress the shift key of the typewriter as he was writing. Indeed, in order to type, it was necessary for him to hurl himself into the air and land on each individual key.

Marquis, being a serious individual, combined humor with philosophical musings. Hence, roughly remembered, archy wrote: "as i was crawling through the holes in the swiss cheese the other day, i got to wondering what a swiss cheese would think if a swiss cheese could think and i came to the conclusion that if a swiss cheese could think, it would think it's about the best thing there is, just as everything that can think, does think."

Reflecting upon archy's thoughts, I realized that it is very easy to become overimpressed with one's importance. As archy expressed it, a man may seem pretty important to himself, but to a mosquito, he's just food!

Humility is not the only root of prayer. Whether one has certainty that there is a greater meaning to life, or an equal certainty that there is no such meaning, we are all aware of our own mortality. Part of life is the desire for achievement, and respect from our peers. Many strive for importance and recognition and society, in response, has devised innumerable titles and marks of status to gratify this yen for recognition that seems to be a universal characteristic of human life. Nor is such desire a distinctly human trait, for a dog running from person to person in greeting both gives and seeks attention, and it might even be said that a squirrel pumping its tail, chattering and chirping from a tree limb, does not want to be overlooked.

It is as though we are all bonded to otherness, innately aware of separation, and often moved toward re-union with the multiplicity we lack in our individuality. Prayer often occupies our thoughts when we are overcome by loneliness or when we are weakly striving to escape the mire of doubt. This has been freely admitted by many highly admired persons who have unashamedly sought counsel or comfort from a higher power. Abraham Lincoln vouchsafed that, "I have been driven many times to my knees by the overwhelming conviction that I had nowhere else to go. My own wisdom, and that of all about me, seemed insufficient for the day."

An expanded idea of what prayer is can perhaps be gained if we think of the silent Benedictine monks who spent a great portion of their lives digging, clearing and building. Much farmland in Europe resulted from the toil of this monastic order as, by small degrees, the wooded swamps and thickets in which they worked became arable land that they tilled with the Benedictine tenet that "to labor is to pray" (laborare est orare). The work of these monks was an attempt to restore a world that St. Benedict found to be in physical and social ruin. The toil was undertaken by following nature's guidance, and by patiently and gradually bringing the land to ebullient health and productivity.[1]

The famous Benedictine monk St. Bernard (1091–1153), with his own insight into nature, told those he invited into his Order: "Believe me upon my own experience, you will find more in the woods than in books; the forests and rocks will teach you what you cannot learn of the greatest masters." In his study of Holy Scripture, St. Bernard commented that he had no other teacher than "the oaks and beeches of the forest."[2]

Prayer then, may be much more than we commonly recognize it to be. While it may be virtually uncategorizeable, this is appropriate because there are billions of individual people on the planet, each of whom is unique. The modern penchant for organization does have its limitations. We may well divide people into groups based on such measurable things as color, race, creed, or financial status; but the uniqueness of which I speak is of a higher (or highest) order.

Our limitation has been described by quantum physicists who point out that the objective study of nature really eludes us because we are inside nature, a part of nature, and view it from the restrictive force of not being able to detach ourselves from it physically. We likewise bring our opinions with us into whatever we do, and try as we may, we are unable to detach ourselves from these opinions. Obviously, those with a pre-formed opinion for or against the idea of prayer will find evidence to support their view, because things supporting our views are clearly visible while those supporting an opposite view will seem vague, troublesome, inconclusive or unconvincing.

One of the more cynical definitions of "pray" appeared in *The Devil's Dictionary*, which began as a column in a weekly paper in 1881 and later became a book. In fairness to Ambrose Bierce, its author, it should be pointed out that his barbs were democratically aimed at the various sacred pomposities and cherished absurdities of his time. His trade was "humor" and he has supplied writers and speakers over the years with some of the cleverest witticisms of the English language. The definition Bierce offered of "pray" was, "To ask that the laws of the universe be annulled in behalf of a single petitioner confessedly unworthy."[3] The definition reminds me that we have no operating manual for Spaceship Earth, nor do we have an official copy of the "Authorized Laws of the Universe." It does appear however that we have decided not to live by the ones we do know about in moderate detail. For all we know, prayer and the effects of prayer, may be very much a part of universal law. Certainly we are surrounded by evidence that we are in urgent need of assistance in unsnarling the knots with which we have trussed ourselves.

Prayer, in short, is a very natural quest for help and guidance. Such instinctive seeking may be rooted in the racial history of our species, and is perhaps entwined in the reality that every living organism comes from something greater and is compelled to seek its source.

It is easiest for us to pray for immediate concerns. Hence prayers for health of self or others, for help in solving present problems, for reduction of stressful concerns — all such things are common causes of prayer.

When the chips are down, we frequently turn to prayer. Famed war correspondent Ernie Pyle suggested that "there's no such thing as an atheist in a foxhole." But, even though God was frequently implored from the depths of battlefield despair, no such generality fits all individuals. The stimulus for prayer need not be life threatening. Consider, for example, a dyed-in-the-wool athlete confronted with a crucial moment in her or his career. Perhaps the stimulus is a potential game-winning field goal opportunity in the dying moments of a football game, or a chance at a series of potentially game winning, foul shots immediately after the buzzer signifies the end of a basketball game. The individual on the spot — the place-kicker or the foul-shooter — whether dedicatedly religious or not, may well ask for outside help, for equanimity and even for direct help in the moment ahead. Where does the request for assistance come from? Is it from our cultural heritage, or from some lurking vestige of faith derived from unrecognized interiority? We cannot identify the source with certainty, but know that in moments deemed as crises, prayer often results.

Moments of truth in sports events are just one sort of example. Students may pray before a difficult examination. Job applicants may do the same before an important interview by a potential employer. We may pray for the return of a lost pet, never knowing until that moment how important that animal has become to us.

In many instances life itself becomes a prayer. While this may seem to necessitate a looser definition of prayer than the making of a direct appeal to the Divine Power for assistance, it is still inadequacy searching for completion. It may stem from a particular life undertaking, or a particularly stressful event in our lives, or from both of these. We all know people whose dedication to a single cause has turned almost every action in their lives into a form of reverence or prayer. Motherhood is a prime example, or the life of Mother Teresa, or those seeking to help victims of AIDS.

It wasn't until I started mulling over the idea of prayer that I realized a lot of things I do myself are a form of prayer. I usually pick up a lot of cones from trees when I am walking. I then dry them and shake out the seeds, which I later broadcast when I take walks in various places that have been over-logged or particularly in places where clear-cut logging has been so extensive that natural seeding can hardly take place any more.

This autumn, squirrels cut down hemlock cones in vast numbers — the tips of branches, often with twenty or thirty cones attached lay scattered everywhere in the woods. Squirrels, like people, can be over-zealous and many of the branch tips were left uncollected. I picked up hundreds of the cones and put them in flats where they opened as they dried, then transferred them to paper sacks and shook the seeds from the cones. The result was thousands of seeds for later dissemination.

Because I was thinking about the nature of prayer, I realized that my own activity constituted a prayer of sorts — the more so perhaps because I feel that broadcasting the seeds is a thing that should be done out of respect for the earth. Now I realize that in the actual process of spreading seeds, I am offering them to the winds, the earth and the power of life that causes seeds to germinate and grow. I have no control over which ones, or how many, will come alive and thrive; and I also realize that this is a matter of choice by powers considerably greater than my own — perhaps I should say by power astronomically greater than my own. But my intent is only that I shall try to be a vector for such growth to take place. The rationale behind it is that I am absolutely convinced that we do not know what we are doing in obliterating forests. This is verified to me by the fact that I often walk in places logged several decades ago where there has been little natural restorative growth, and by the admitted fact that much land has been classified as NSR, or Not Sufficiently Restocked.

My conviction that there is deep underlying meaning to life also constitutes a reason for writing things that are not as popular or successful as tales of human "conquests" of nature, or intrigue relating to activities of spies, military ventures, violence or horror. I sometimes find myself thinking that about the time we decided we were wiser than nature and knew more than her, she decided to let us play out our fantasy to the very end. Today there is increasing evidence of the connectedness of all living organisms and of the ability of healing energies to be transmitted. This suggests that prayer may be very important in the healing of the earth and its inhabitants. Physician and author Larry Dossey suggests that prayer will be recognized as a potent force in medicine and that its use will become so pervasive "that not to recommend the use of prayer as an integral part of medicine will one day constitute medical malpractice."[4] We are certainly in a race today between our own destruction and our ability to awake from technosleep and change our attitudes and actions. Prayer, in a psychological sense, would assist us to develop the will to change. And to those who recognize prayer as communion with forces greater than our own, it might bring the type of help we can hope for from no other source. "Pray unceasingly," urged St. Benedict. "More things are wrought by prayer than this world dreams of," declared Alfred Lord Tennyson in *Morte d'Arthur.* It seems appropriate that the call to prayer is a personal decision and a personal activity. That its height, breadth, weight and length cannot be measured and made part of a formula, may be frustrating to those whose faith lies only in what is quantifiable. But it is a form of confidence in creation which recognizes that we are encompassed by a universal order. It is confidence in the awesome integrity of this earth, the immediate creation daily revealed to our senses, that calls upon us to lift ourselves above the view that materialism is the most important purpose in life. Prayer can lead to the awakening of personality. An awakened personality can deal with the best of past and present in human accomplishment, can assess what blend of action is suitable to address life's problems, and give vision to a future that will be more balanced, more nearly whole, and more predictive of harmonious life on a healthy planet. An individual reaching out for greater understanding is less apt to be victimized by self-pride. She or he will be unashamed to ask for Greater insight in order to be able to act in the fullness of an awakened consciousness.

Silence is a singular thing, a quality that stands on its own. Though it might be emphasized by birdsong, by soughing of breezes in the branches of trees, or even by the howl of a wolf, bugle of an elk, or hoot of an owl, it is merely enriched — intensified — by these natural sounds. There was a time, before the din of machines filled the air, when silence ruled the land. It had not yet been forced to retreat to lonely canyons, dense forests or alpine meadows. It was a part of life, a characteristic of landscapes, an aspect of life which taught "the trick of quiet."

Have we created a noisy, superficial world and banished silence to such distant hinterlands that, without its balm, we are rarely able to find enough peace to think for ourselves?

I enjoy this story of a burly logger, Big Swede they called him, who came to the city years ago from the land of caulked boots, crosscut saws, and baked beans three times a day. He was tattered and grimy and first bought himself a hot bath wherein he luxuriated for an hour. Then with his ragged duds about him, and his wages in his pocket, he set off to buy some new clothes. The merchant he encountered was happy to adorn him in a complete new outfit, then walked around Big Swede admiringly to congratulate him on his handsome and dignified appearance. "I have just what you need to complete your outfit," he said, bringing forth a stylish felt hat.

"Five dollar?" enquired Big Swede.

"Oh no, not for this hat. This is a twenty-five dollar hat!"

"Seven dollar," growled the Swede.

"No, no. Twenty-five dollars. It's worth every cent, and you must have it — for then you will be in style."

The Swede took the hat from him, turned it round and round in his hands, set it on his head for a minute, took it off again and looked at the top and sides. "Vere are the holes in the hat?" he asked a bit suspiciously.

"Holes? What holes? This is a fashionable hat, what do you mean by asking about holes?"

Big Swede laughed handsomely, and replied: "I mean the two holes for the ears of the yackass who vud pay tventy five dollar for this hat!" The sales pitch ended. Big Swede paid for the goods he had bought and sallied forth. The merchant put away the hat. Big Swede turned out to be unimpressed with the vanity of style. Unlettered perhaps and more suited to the "land of big silences" than to towns, he knew what he wanted and needed, and above all he knew what he didn't want or need.

And do we not all need silence in order that we may have time to come to grips with who we really are? Rooted in silence by our ties to nature, we ignore our heritage and forego the pensive times in which thought can be fashioned. Individuality is grist ground from contemplation of the living world about us. No longer do we awaken subtle sensitivities attuned to sights, sounds, scents and other information now masked by urban clamor. Unlettered buck-skin-clad backwoodsmen, crude as these ancestors are considered to have been, lived life close to the land and summarily rejected the over-organization that typifies society today. Their exploits, admirable or not, did less lasting damage to our planet than modern boardroom barbarians togged in three piece suits have done in the 50 years since the end of World War II.

Amiel describes the intense peace of soul found in privacy and silence (Jan. 2nd, 1880):

> Here there is a sense of rest and quietness. Silence in the house and outside. A tranquil fire gives a feeling of comfort. The portrait of my mother seems to smile upon me. This peaceful morning makes me happy. Whatever pleasure we may get from our emotions I do not think it can equal those moments of silent peace which are glimpses of the joys of Paradise. Desire and fear, grief and anxiety are no more. We live a moment of life in the supreme region of our own being: pure consciousness. One feels an inner harmony free from the slightest agitation or tension. In those moments the state of the soul is solemn, perhaps akin to its condition beyond the grave. It is happiness as the Orientals understand it, the happiness of the hermit who is free from desire and struggle, and who simply adores in fullness of joy. We cannot find words to express this experience, because our languages can only describe particular and definite conditions of life; they have no words to express this silent contemplation, this heavenly quietness, this ocean of peace which both reflects the heaven above and is master of its own vast depth. Things return to their first principle, while memories become dreams of memories. The soul is then pure being and no longer feels its separation from the whole. It is conscious of the universal life, and at that moment is a centre of communion with God. It has nothing and it lacks nothing.

Few days go by when I do not at some time appreciate the silence that can be enjoyed amidst the woods and mountains where we live. During the day there is traffic, particularly logging trucks, along what was for many years a gravel road and is now a paved highway used mainly for the extraction of resources. In summer the road serves an increasing number of tourists. There are lulls in traffic though because much of it is regulated by the schedule of the Arrow Lake ferry that arrives at Galena Bay from Shelter Bay on the opposite side of the lake at about twenty minutes past the hour. Some years ago the ferry ran only during the daylight hours. But with the use of radar it now runs until midnight and takes a break until early morning.

Except during holidays, traffic is still quite light in evenings, and there is a noticeable settling down of silence upon the earth. During spring mornings and evenings, varied thrushes sing the world awake and asleep. By early summer the Swainson's thrushes help them at this task; and at irregular intervals, cascading comments from a few veeries help twilight descend upon the land. At such times of day we are often walking in the woods where even-song of birds seems part of silence itself, making stillness more noticeable by harmonious contrast. This is even more evident when darkness and silence hold the world gently in their grasp. The *hoo-hoo* of an owl, now here and now there, reminds all that it can move through the night on silent wings.

Though the ritual advent and departure of each day are cosmic events respected by most living things, they have been dispelled by unremitting production efforts of the human species. Just as we keep the world of darkness ablaze with light, so it seems the continuous noise of "progress" eliminates silence from all but the remoter places on earth. The feeling of anomie, the sense of hollowness that is spoken of as characteristic of modern states of anxiety, may be alleviated by the restorative power of nature more readily than by any other means. Silence, one of these forces, I venture is more of a balm to the harassment of busy-ness than the pharmacist's pill or the psychiatrist's couch.

Today's increased stress levels, partially due to unremitting noise and confusion, have led to an increasing exodus of people from cities to rural areas. While an extra home or even a modest cabin, particularly if the site be on a lake or pond, is a matter of affluence, more and more people seek rural experiences. Not all of these people have the same motives for seeking less-frequented places, but a good number of them are in search of quiet.

Although we live in the country, one of our greatest enjoyments is to go farther back into the mountains. There are old mining and logging roads that provide access to sub-alpine or alpine country of great beauty and immense majesty. Of late years we have taken people from the cities into such places, and have heard interesting comments. One man who had been quietly drinking in the beauty for some hours, came out with the remark, "If there's any place you wouldn't be surprised to meet an angel, it's up here!"

People, we have found, come to love the quietness and peace of out-of-the-way places. Normally garrulous individuals become subdued. Sometimes they stand for a long while looking from a mountainside at the sprawling landscape below. They also find that simple activities such as berry picking are gratifying. This is an activity at which silence prevails as individuals move on separate paths from one beckoning bush to another. Often, toward late afternoon or evening as shadows are lengthening, someone will speak of the wonderful surrounding silence, of having forgotten or perhaps of never having realized that such places exist. Invariably, it seems, people express the desire to do the same sort of thing again soon. Feeling a bit estranged from these activities, some prefer to go to such places in company, but others start exploring on their own and speak enthusiastically of new places they have discovered.

Silence, it seems, does beckon to many people. It is, after all, an element in which individuality is fashioned. In silence we strike up acquaintance anew with an inner self that has often not been encountered for a long while. Taking time to know oneself is of great importance in a society that has emphasized participation in group activities to such an extent that a person can wind up with very little opportunity for self-development. People tend to ignore their obligations to society. but really should function as thoughtful, constructive citizens who have reflected and formed their own convictions, and are willing to act on them. While it may be easy to sit back and let other people do most of the thinking, this really denies society the benefit of other valuable insights. An admirable society will not come about if capable individuals rely upon some anonymous "them" to solve the problems of the times in which we live. Social improvement will be a result of individual improvement and of active participation in the issues that need everyone's input. The worth of a state cannot be greater than the worth of the individuals composing it.

Confucius expressed this truth well when he said:

> Things have their roots and their completion. Affairs have their
> end and their beginning. To know what is first and what is last is
> the beginning of wisdom.

Those who desire to create harmony in the world must first establish order in their own communities. Wishing to establish order in
their communities, they must first regulate their own family life.
Wishing to regulate their own family life, they must first cultivate
their own personal lives. Wishing to cultivate their personal lives,
they must first set their own feelings right. Wishing to set their
feelings right, they must first seek to make their own wills sincere. Wishing to make their wills sincere, they must first increase
to the utmost their own understanding. Such increase in the
understanding comes from the extension of their knowledge of all
things.

Things being investigated, their own knowledge will become
extended. Their knowledge being extended, their own understanding will increase. Their understanding being increased, their
own wills will become sincere. Their wills being set right, their
own personal lives will become cultivated. Their personal lives
being cultivated, their own family life will be properly regulated.
Their family life being properly regulated, their communities will
become well-ordered. Their own communities being well-
ordered, the whole world will become happy and peaceful.

From the greatest of men down to the masses of people, all must
consider the cultivation of the personal life the foundation of every
other thing.

Silence is a prerequisite in the cultivation of our personal life,
and perhaps has always been a need of our species. A quiet room in
our homes away from the jangle of telephones and the intrusion of
all forms of media can be an island for the long, long thoughts of
youth or maturity. For those uncomfortable away from the urban
world, a den can be a haven for reveries or simply for basking in the
luxury of introspection. One should never be surprised if thoughts
cast into the void come back well-muscled at a later date.

The more venturesome will find endless opportunities for
adventure of all sorts in the world of soil, rocks, forests and sea in
which our racial and personal history is entwined. There are group
activities that offer opportunity for strenuous exertion in the outdoors, but still allow time to be alone, to look at the silent stars and

permit the vastness of the universe to infiltrate mind, heart and soul. I recall a man who sat atop a mossy boulder for half a day "just looking and thinking," he said, and told me later it was "a glorious experience."

I have noted on several occasions the richness and independence of personalities developed by long years spent in pursuit of an individual dream. Lack of formal education is no impediment, in such instances, to an innate scholarly nature. I am reminded particularly of Paddy Carroll, a prospector unspoiled by his own success, who became poet and philosopher and a man of deep peace as the years unrolled before him. I asked him one time if he had any idea how much of his life he had spent by himself, in his search for minerals. He told me that he had wondered that himself and had calculated that more than a decade had been spent "on the trail." "I'd be way out in the back country, maybe up the Turnagain River somewhere, and when I heard the loons giving their storm warning calls in autumn, I'd head out for home." It interested me that he always carried a book or two with him, and would lie propped on his elbow reading by the light of his campfire. Poets were a favorite of his and he could quote astoundingly from them.

"No, I was never lonely," he said. "I was surrounded by life. It's a living world and I was always aware of some Great Presence, something that loves us all...I have no fear of death whatsoever. When you die you return to the elemental wealth of the world. You float in the clouds, dance in the leaves and gurgle in the streams...I lived out where I belonged. I'd rather be a packsaddle and frying pan prospector than be shackled to the golden car of commerce."

His own life had given him an awareness of the power of nature to heal the ills of humankind. "I've lived all my life with the woods, the birds and bees. If we got young people out in nature where they belong they wouldn't sop up all the worthless values of society... It will take great people to get us back on the track, and a great person, I believe, is one who raises his voice against the social injustices of the times in which he lives."

A rare prospector in the sense that he did make a big find that left him unspoiled, his values transcended metallic wealth and are expressed in a poem he labored on beside his campfire. He named it *The Prospector*:

There's a swish of brush on his old canoe
As he tramps the portage trail,
Where the Pegwa flows to the Albany
As the lights of evening fail.
There are rapids and riffles and sweepers bad
In the path of his old canoe —
There is gold on the rim of that ancient shield
There is gold, and he'll find it too.
From the rugged hills of Couer d'Alene
And the far off Kootenay
To the golden sands of the Cariboo,
He has hunted the hills for pay.
His head is bowed to the tumpline's toil,
On his face the weather's scar,
On his feet the dust of the desert grey
And mud from the glacier's bar.
His tent shows white on the timberline
And the ash of his campfire cold
Is stirred by the breeze of the Yellowknife
On his endless search for gold.
He has wandered far on his lonely quest
He has sought and found the prize —
It is felt in the grasp of his eager hand
And seen in his smiling eyes; —
The gold of the golden autumn hills
As they rise o'er the shimmering lake,
The Gold of the dawn on snowcapped peaks
When myriad birds awake,
The gold of a gorgeous sunset grand
At the close of a desert day —
The gold in the hearts of his fellowman
— There never was better pay.

For the most part, nature is silent and unassuming. Yet it contains mighty forces. The incoming energy of the sun arrives silently but sets in motion the photosynthetic engine that provides for life on earth. The earth rotates without advertising to tell us what it is doing and why; the constant motion of solar bodies proceeds in response to gravity and we hear little of it, although, in mountain country, spring avalanches produced by melting snow on steep slopes sometimes rumble and crackle as mud and rock masses are set in motion. When the frost demon wrenches the land, its iron grip is so silent that the cracking and complaining of distant trees sound like an irregular volley of pistol shots. So audible was the effect in the icy hush that the month of January was known to native tribes as the Moon of the Cracking Trees. It is easy to understand why a pagan could feel the Mighty Presence in nature. It is still there!

There is another reason, a very serious one, why we need to pursue silence. Think back to the easy way in which Cyrus the King manipulated the Lydians. He controlled these people by giving them the sensational and spectacular forms of amusement to which people easily succumb, and which keep them in a trance-like state, obliterating all concern they might have about more meaningful issues.

In the middle years of this century, behavior modification and operant conditioning were of interest to psychologists such as B.F. Skinner. While these ideas were discussed in many university classes and employed to some extent in education, they were of vast interest to those who control society — to military and political leaders, big businesses, advertisers, and managers of the mass media. Unfortunately the employers of behavior modification techniques often tended to be people more concerned with keeping or expanding power, than with influencing human behavior to make a better world.

The keynote of operant conditioning is to reward desirable behavior. For example, how might consumerism be rewarded or encouraged? With credit cards of course! If people respond by buying more impulsively, by putting off payment and thus incurring increased debt through interest charges, or by travelling farther or more frequently than they can really afford to, the success of credit cards is assured. Moral responsibility for people enticed into hopeless debt is simply denied.

The management of behavior by opportunists, and that is what they are, has led to the world of bread and circuses we live in today. Many comparisons have been made between the last days of the decline of the Roman Empire and the steady decay of our industrial society.

So we have another reason for escaping from round-the-clock bedlam into an inner world of thought. It is said that silence is consent, and that by not objecting to the malicious intent of manipulators, we agree to being manipulated. Unless we break the pace at which the manipulators would have us run, we will never escape the unthinking behavior that simply has us ask "Where?" and "How fast?" From silence, and the introspection which results, will come the power to forge our own goals and take control of our lives.

History names various sages and prophets who have experienced their forty days in the wilderness. Why this number of days has become a sign of retreat into silence in order to obtain insight is difficult to explain. Many contemplatives have lived lives in remote situations where tranquility was the norm rather than the exception. I find it so vastly satisfying a medium that a few hours in town is enough to suffice for a considerable time, and always return to the quietness of home place with vast relief that it will not be necessary to leave it within the near foreseeable future. Quiet thought, lengthy walks in the woods, fields and mountains; days spent toiling in garden, or working on the winter's wood supply; evenings spent reading; time spent looking and appreciating the stunning beauty of nature; for me, these really suffice to form a life that has ample meaning.

Our uniqueness is both a limitation and an opportunity afforded by life. It enables each of us to view the world from an individual perspective and it is from conscious harmonizing and blending of these perspectives that a true civilization might be achieved. Unfortunately the loudest, most dominant and persistent voices reject the quieter thoughts that might establish peace, both on earth and toward the earth. Bellicose attitudes can only be curbed by deliberate cultivation of finer instincts. The rough sod of our selves will yield only to the ministration of the yeomanry of ideals. Life or education for life, if focused only on short term goals, assures that our own species will be ephemeral.

Some modification of the vision quest assigned to maturing youth by native tribes would be a refreshing change to the consumer oriented education now supplied by society through its schools. An individual who is not encouraged to meet himself or herself face to face in silence and solitude may well blend into mass society, but only through sacrifice of realized selfhood.

In this sense, some number of days in the wilderness, or in a suitable meditative setting, may be a *sine qua non* of maturation. Forty days in what eventually leads to serenity, is not the heroic ordeal that many would consider it. Having lived in relatively remote places for far longer than forty times forty days, and having spent lengthy periods alone here or in other places, it seems true that one learns to confront the meaning of life. As Lord Byron wrote of time spent in solitude in natural settings:

> There is pleasure in the pathless woods,
> There is a rapture on the lonely shore,
> There is society, where none intrudes,
> By the deep sea, and music in its roar;
> I love not man the less, but Nature more,
> From these our interviews.[5]

A total infusion in urban society ultimately produces people of dependency, forever imploring governments for assistance in pulling their own chestnuts out of the fire where they have been thrown. Even the dominant powers of industry cannot function without interest-free loans, government grants, and must, as now, implore their workers to tighten their belts and take wage cuts so the affluent can continue banqueting their way through life.

It is ludicrous that wild, natural places, the safest places in the world, are often considered hostile, while in cities, doors and windows must be barricaded at night and streets become centres of violence when shadows fall, with people afraid to leave the security of their homes.

Walking in the serenity of woods, or ascending above the forest into the scattered trees of sub-alpine country and thence into alpine meadows is an experience steeped in awe and majesty. Silence in these places is vibrant with meaning and serenity. One learns that the universe is home, and will at least sense that some immortal companion walks by her side, and helps in the solving of problems

and the reconciliation of doubt. When for a time I lapse into looking and listening, and am aware of no conscious effort on my part to
follow any particular line of thought, I am suddenly the possessor of
new and enticing ideas never before entertained. It is as though the
invisible companion says, "Here, try this idea for a bit."

CHAPTER II

Re-Engagement: Reflection

Men can live without air for a few minutes, without water for about two weeks, without food for about two months — and without a new thought for years on end.

Kent Ruth

It is an over-simplification to comment that reflectiveness involves looking before you leap. But, if you imagine what may result from actually leaping without looking, you can infer substantially the value that may accrue from thinking over an issue carefully before committing yourself to it.

In order to be reflective, an individual must be willing to take time to think. Most people have had the experience of making an instantaneous decision, a snap judgment, and later finding that it was wrong. One of the things consumers are warned about is the folly of impulse buying. We read of high profit items being placed at the eye level of shoppers, where they will be quickly noticed. People often respond to such a readily visible product by reaching out for it and stowing it in their shopping cart. Time and effort has been spent determining the colors and shapes of packages that consumers find attractive, and a handsome product strategically placed is readily sold. Saleability is further enhanced by a well-known product name drilled into the human mind by advertising. Mental acuity for shopping can be sharpened by reading labels, by studying consumer reports, by demanding quality, by waiting for sales, and by thinking carefully before buying any product.

"I buy only what I need," observes an acquaintance of mine

who has had a trapline for many years, "but every time I go into the supermarket to get my groceries I see tactics of marketing that make me realize how carefully I have to set traps for kinds of animals that are trap shy...and by golly I can't help saying that if wild animals were as foolish as people, there wouldn't be any left at all."

A habit of reflectiveness is one that is useful in many circumstances. Conduct brought about by impulse is notoriously apt to be unsound. Since reflectiveness refers to an ingrained habit of considering events and beliefs in respect to their appropriateness and consequences, it serves to determine whether or not a given action is warranted. To a certain extent we have all learned that experience can be a costly lesson and it is likely that we all have to derive some wisdom from the school of hard knocks. It is preferable that we learn some things by vicarious experience. We know that a stove is hot when it is being used, and most individuals do not have to touch it and burn themselves in order to be aware of this hazard. In youth we learn from others that knives are sharp, that care must be exercised in steep places, and that we should look both ways before crossing streets. We thus develop some habitual behavior that safeguards us from harm. We also learn, through lapses of attention, that it is wise to act with attentiveness.

But there are more subtle things that require serious thought rather than mere attention. Early in life we are subjected to temptation and to the beliefs of others. As we gain in experience an individual choice must be made whether or not a specific belief or pattern of attention is warranted. When presented with evidence or influence that favors holding a certain belief, we endanger ourselves if we act primarily by impulse. It is far better to be thoughtful and consider the evidence a belief should rest upon, and also to think about where it would lead. This involves reflectiveness or serious thought in which we must determine whether a thing is right or wrong and whether it will lead to good or evil. To gain the necessary perspective on any topic of importance, time is needed for consideration and the topic must be evaluated from as many vantage points as possible. The wisdom of the old Latin motto *Festina lente*, which means "make haste slowly," is apparent. The idea of looking before one leaps therefore can be applied to many things.

There are many customs and proverbs that make up the vast

fund of thought called common sense; and reflectiveness, when matured, does entail a background of knowledge that will give an individual a broader view of life and insight into how causes produce effects. Studiousness is an obvious asset, since through study the factual basis for reflection is increased. The idea of thinking a bit like a trap-shy animal is pertinent, because such an animal will walk around and around a suspicious site in order to consider it from all possible angles, and will depart from the possible trap if it remains suspicious. Not long ago in this area there was a destructive accident involving drunken driving and serious injuries. We learned there was a person who was asked to accompany the group in the vehicle but who refused because she felt insecure at the thought of going with the others. Needless to say, the individual was very happy she did not go along, and it is apparent that serious reflection can often be a life-saving force. Today's close commitment to action and change has made it easy for us to forge ahead without weighing issues beforehand, or allowing any time for reflection.

It seems natural that an individual might ask what all this material is that requires reflection. But almost any sort of enterprise needs fairly regular accounting. If this is neglected for too long, any endeavor might find itself upon the rocks, stranded somehow while the rest of the world goes along its way.

It is not too ridiculous to imagine that each of us sails our own good ship *Enterprise*. We are lubbers when it comes to sailing our craft, and we meet unusual tides proceeding in random directions, encounter storms that might be considered emotional, intellectual, spiritual, or physical. To borrow from an old poem, "we are the cook, the crew and the captain too," of the craft in which we voyage through life, and it would pay dividends for us to learn about ourselves, about the calm seas and vicissitudes of the ocean of life upon which we are embarked.

It certainly wouldn't hurt to quite regularly ask ourselves the questions: "How am I doing?" "Where am I at anyway?" "Am I on the right course?" "How come I felt good about this particular thing, and bad about something else?" "What can I do to improve the way I am doing things.?" "Can I really respect myself?"

And then there are the bigger questions: "What is the meaning of life anyway?" "Is there a God?" "Is there anything at all out there?" "Is there anything worth working for?"

I remember hearing about the idea of an "experiential continuum." This simply referred to the fact that we live through a continuous chain of experiences, good, bad, and indifferent. The idea of the continuum is that each night we can say to ourselves, "I am what I was yesterday, plus what I learned today. Each day I become a day older, a day more experienced, and hopefully a day wiser." The thrust of the experiential continuum idea is that each day we should reflect upon the happenings of that day, and help them to merge into a bigger and hopefully better understanding of life. Not a bad way of looking at things it seems.

One of the problems involved in assigning undue merit to the great volume of information that abounds in the world today is that such information may impinge upon our senses but never become useful knowledge. All knowledge, as English philosopher John Locke explained in the 17th century, is derived from experience that is specifically the combination of sensation and reflection. From the simple ideas provided by sensation, we compare, compound, and abstract the foundation of our complex ideas. Basically then, it is reflection that must filter and digest the useful stimuli and provide nourishment for the human spirit. It could be that, without intending to do so, we have developed a new version of the famous Roman orgies in which people ate and ate until forced to vomit, and then commenced eating again. Today we quantify information, and assume that sheer volume of ideas is meaningful. But ideas also need digestion, hence reflection, in order to be of any value. And it is obvious that production of goods from unripened ideas, before their actual value and likely harm has been ascertained, can, and has, led to serious malign effects.

When life was simpler and people more scattered, there was time and space to think and develop a sense of individuality. The existence of strong opinions made it less likely we could be numbed into acceptance of the goals of present mass society. Economy had another meaning — it was a way of living in which expenditures were kept a degree or two below one's means. Many people understood well that to want less was to have more, and one of the precious things one had more of was independence through freedom from debt.

There was also a greater sense of community before the attitude of impersonality was presented as an advantage in the quest for material success. It would be a great benefit to present society if we could again realize that civilization is a dream to which we all should contribute. If we took more time to ponder the meaning of life we would succumb less readily to the muzzling of personality required to be part of the economic machine of today.

Reflectiveness then must address itself to the question of the meaning of life itself. The number of people who act with a sense of hopelessness, who would like to have an effect upon civilization but feel that they cannot make a difference in the world through their own beliefs and ideals, is ample evidence that we have succumbed to the suppression of the spiritual heart of our being. We travel through life cluttered with possessions, craving this and that thing we do not have, all the while failing to realize that the reduction of our superfluous wants is the fastest way to empower the spiritual nature that lies dormant within us.

Pity the person who must have everything, who must flaunt his affluence; he is a slave to one of the shoddiest reasons for being that exists. When we walk by a showroom window and must have the glittering object displayed within, we are forging new chains with which to shackle ourselves. When we buy an object because it gives opportunity to display our affluence to others, we act from sorry motive. The greatest possession in life is life itself — life which affords time to think, to discover our own individuality, and to contribute from our uniqueness, whatever will be of benefit to a true civilization.

We have a serious need for reflection and there is enormous evidence to support the necessity of change in our patterns of thought and behavior. Just from scanning the known facts, we do live on a quite ancient planet. This is well supported by scientific knowledge, and not objected to strenuously by most of the major religions. We, as fairly recent arrivals on the planet, have chosen to make monumental changes that are proving to be quite unsupportable. It is not at all uncommon to hear of serious concern as to whether or not we will largely destroy ourselves.

Our religious constructs may assure many people that we have a special position in the universe and are immune from limitations affecting other beings. We have accepted a self-serving dichotomy that establishes us as the highest species surrounded by millions of lower species placed here for our convenience. In recent years, however, more people are beginning to question this belief. And, as has been noted, there are scriptures that call our illusion of central position in the universe into question.

Somehow I don't believe, at all, that the assignment of lesser importance to ourselves, does serious damage to religious feelings. In my own wanderings and musings I am continually impressed by the sense of sacredness that emanates from the earth. The more natural and unaffected a setting is, the more palpable is the sense of serenity proceeding from the surroundings.

Now, of course, I realize that the quickest way to disparage such an impression is to refer to it as something imagined, as something that "T'aint so," and is capable of affecting only those individuals who are stubbornly "counter productive" or otherwise unimpressed with the arbitrary hodgepodge that is superficially deemed to be progress.

In spite of whatever disparagement there may be, I feel most comfortable in my certainty that I am one with the earth, and am happy to have had that conclusion for many years. When I stand or sit in quiet, lovely places, and there are many such places, I know that the sense of religiousness is a product of all that surrounds me and all that is registered by my senses. As a matter of fact, it seems that the most profound religiousness pours forth from the earth, and from its lofty mountains, sparkling lakes, majestic forests, its sunny glades and shady nooks. It is detectable from every viewing place, from landscapes rolling away to the horizon, from the breath of the breezes, the plopping rain and from the silent snowfall turning autumn browns to wintry whites. I know that I am not the only one to consider the earth as a cathedral.

Although I am less comfortable in cities due to my own sense of being most at home in a more remote setting, it is important that urban people do not lose sight of their own basic dependency on nature. It is easier in cities to accept the imposed value systems without considering their effect upon the intricate, interwoven reality of the natural world, which has provided so many options for different life styles. There are so many people and so many demands placed upon the sustaining world that we are far past the point at which we must reduce our demands before we throw away the future of our species.

From experience it seems that reflection is a natural process that awaits those moments when the busy, day-to-day affairs of life no longer need to be kept in the foreground of our minds. Given a bit of peace, and being able to saunter along in a pleasant place, it is possible to placidly ruminate, letting thoughts come and go as they choose. In this process our minds seem to organize themselves in a most effective manner. As our eyes drift over the scenes we view, our ears also register sounds as varied as the crackling noises of band-winged grasshoppers or the pleasing "quick, three beers" call of the olive-sided flycatcher. Sometimes there is a more startling noise, as when a grouse rockets away from beneath a bush a few feet away, or when a large mammal crashes through the brush and suddenly falls silent as it continues on its way more stealthily.

Two realizations come to mind. One is that such experiences are foreign to urban life. The second is that some individuals have little desire to be in rural places and have little interest in wild creatures. Urban settings probably make reflection more difficult. They are more noisy, more full of busy-ness, more loaded with stimuli of all sorts — flashing signs, endless visual displays in shop windows, moving traffic, variously dressed people — what could be summarized as countless distractions. Still, there are places for thought such as quiet churches where serenity can be found, or libraries where one may sit in silence even if the book before one is merely a prop. Other settings can be devised which enable reflection, and there are many people who have established a room to serve as an in-home retreat. I recall one such inner sanctum where the taped sound of ocean waves produced an aura of peace that served as a pleasant background for thought. There are also people who take great pleasures from heated greenhouses that enable them to putter and feel a closeness with living things. Local parks or arboretums can offer other areas of retreat in cities. And of course, no matter where you are, there is great joy that many people experience by feeding birds. From the enthusiastic comments made by those who feed and watch birds, it would seem that nature pays an uncommonly high interest rate for the investment made by those who feel close to her wild offspring.

I have occasionally been afield with people who look upon outdoor pursuits as some form of strenuous exercise or as a matter of getting into condition. Perhaps because of natural laziness, or because I feel much at home in the outdoors, I prefer an unhurried pace, and know from experience that such a pace affords enough opportunity to cover an adequate amount of ground.

Above all though, I have concluded that moving along at a natural pace affords an excellent opportunity for communion with self and others, and with some grand and serene presence that cannot be readily described since it exceeds our descriptive powers — a presence so vast and all-pervading that it is truly beyond words. At such times I have suddenly found myself wondering if the essence of the tenor of nature is anything less than the awesomeness to be expected in the enduring cathedral of the creation. Just as we ourselves have emerged into individuality from the wholeness of the universe, so we may re-enter it just by stepping into a world less trammelled by human aspirations. Even though an area may have been logged in an appalling fashion not long ago, once abandoned by human exploitation, the flickering force of healing and restoration soon becomes visible and will work at its own pace, though the pace will be much slower than economic optimists would have us believe.

We do fail to give credit to the fact that the religious impulse that has generated vast organized religions originated within nature itself, and I would suggest that the original impulse is still found in nature and is truly the greatest impetus we have to a feeling of reverence and wonder. Its ritual is seasons and sunlight, clouds and shadows, thundering waterfalls and chattering streams. The choir, vastly reduced by humanity's near sightedness, is birdsong, coyote and wolf howl, elk bugle, squirrel scolding and owl hoot. No stained glass windows block the view and services are not at prescribed hours, but day, night, year, and century long — a never ending promise that a divine presence is here always.

There is increasing evidence that our view of progress is illusory. Our narrow focus on economic goals has led us into one of the blind alleys that invites each species to its own immolation. The model exhibited by our planet demonstrates that change is constant, but proceeds at a measured pace. Even the vast Laramide Revolution that formed the Rocky Mountains through folding and thrusting action upon a geosyncline beneath Cretaceous seas, did not occur overnight, but over a period of millions of years. Catastrophic events such as axial tilts, polar shifts, and cometary collisions are part of cosmic history, but the planet does not generally exhibit the sort of frantic haste illustrated by our own species. It is not surprising that there have been calls for a moratorium on progress, even from Nobel laureates, over the last half dozen decades.

It is obvious that we need to slow down and thereby subject the present insatiable demand for authoritarian power to a cooling off period that will allow the enzymatic effect of reflection to act upon it. In the delicate balance between the individual and society there must be enough individuals who reject the lethal lure of excessive power to curb the runaway effect of proponents of ridiculously narrow views, the current one being that the World Trade Organization should rule the world for the sake of business. The masses have been rendered docile through the instrument of sustained propaganda. Reflection is the key to the awakening of individuality and to recognition of the reality that human irresponsibility has unleashed a high-speed catastrophe approaching a conclusion of its own making.

It is natural that the puzzling matter of immortality creeps into the reflective mind from time to time. Such ideas are enticing and stimulating, open doors to thoughts of permanence that are tantalizing because they speak of the mystery of life. We know that we forget many events that took place only a short while ago; therefore, it is not inconceivable that if we have lived past lives they have faded from memory. This would make sense if, as the ancient thinkers suggested, we drink the waters of the river Lethe (forgetfulness) before setting forth upon a new life. There seems to abide more strongly in some than in others, a sort of intuition that speaks of continued existence(s) that form the pathway of an immortal soul that will always have a part to play in the unfolding of the universe. David Hume spoke of palingenesis, the doctrine of rebirth, as "the only system to which philosophy can hearken." Admittedly we know very little and, admittedly, we have many foolish pretensions.

Our love affair with technology and economy shows more and more signs of being an extreme and unworthy fantasy. Our estrangement from the real world and the accompanying decisive attitude that we have created the "true reality" should suggest that we are incompetent authors of a workable scenario of life.

Even in the late 20th century there is a flat-earth mentality that defends business-as-usual, and denies that we live in anything other than the best of all possible worlds. Entrenched interests have dug in so deeply that they are blinded by their own sense of infallibility. But they have suffered a great loss of public faith. This in turn is triggering an increased awareness of the need for self-reliance, and an increasing disbelief in the good intentions of politicians and industrialists who have long masqueraded under the assumption they know what they are doing. There is already a new democracy of soul initiated by skepticism, and there is reflection from the need to assume responsibility for one's own future. If we can weather the storms of our times, it is unlikely that we will make the mistake of believing that there is an elite group that can be trusted to run the world. And, as we learn to think about things and to accept the universe as it is, we may recognize the possibility that our intuitions ascribing deep meaning to life may be the pole star that beckons us to a more constructive way of being than we might otherwise know.

Give consideration to this poem entitled *The Law,* written by Ella Wheeler Wilcox (1850–1919). The poem is a single example of many art forms stimulating more profound thought.

The sun may be clouded, yet ever the sun
Will sweep on its course till the cycle is run.
And when into chaos the systems are hurled,
Again shall the Builder reshape a new world.

Your path may be clouded, uncertain your goal;
Move on, for the orbit is fixed for your soul.
And though it may lead into darkness of night,
The torch of the Builder shall give it new light.

You were, and you will be; know this while you are.

Your spirit has traveled both long and afar.
It came from the Source, to the Source it returns;
The spark that was lighted, eternally burns.

It slept in the jewel, it leaped in the wave;
It roamed in the forest, it rose from the grave;
It took on strange garbs for long eons of years,
And now in the soul of yourself it appears.

From body to body your spirit speeds on;
It seeks a new form when the old one is gone;
And the form that it finds is the fabric you wrought,
On the loom of the mind, with the fiber of thought.

As dew is drawn upward, in rain to descend,
Your thoughts drift away and in destiny blend.
You cannot escape them; or petty, or great,
Or evil, or noble, they fashion your fate.

Somewhere on some planet, sometime and somehow,
Your life will reflect all the thoughts of your now.
The law is unerring; no blood can atone;
The structure you rear you must live in alone.

From cycle to cycle, through time, and through space,
Your lives with your longings will ever keep pace.
And all that you ask for, and all you desire,
Must come at your biding, as flames out of fire.

You are your own devil, you are your own God.
You fashioned the paths that your footsteps have trod:
And no one can save you from error or sin,
Until you shall hark to the spirit within.

Once list to that voice and all tumult is done,
Your life is the life of the Infinite One;
In the hurrying race you are conscious of pause,
With love for the purpose and love for the cause.

It is impressive to realize that in the 20th century, we have moved from Model T Fords to space travel. Astronauts have walked in space and on the moon. But there is glaring disparity in that we have not yet attained sufficient wisdom to live in harmony with the earth. We have made a drastic choice and have elected to pursue the luxuries of life rather than the necessities. Consider, for example, the internationalization of sport and recreation and how popular it has become to flee halfway around the world to escape the meaninglessness of our lives at home. Experts assemble to solve major problems caused by impact of our industrial society and all too often rationalize, postpone, or mask their inability beneath still another call for more studies to be made. Though they may assemble from afar, each person brings the self-same spirit with him that attended in his home. If our contemporary philosophy will not permit us to stop or radically alter behavior inimical to life and health at home, then an international delegation saddled with the same philosophy will do no better when it meets in Katmandu or Milan. Professional vagabondage enables us to display knowledge of the symptoms of societal disarray, while the real world crumples beneath our feet because we are too effete to accept our dependent relationship to an enormous ball or rock, dirt, water and air that we disdainfully smother beneath the excreta of an industrialized world.

It is not sufficient to state that we are in dire need of reflection and study. It is a necessity for our continuance that we take time to ponder without delay upon our relationship with the world and its author. This must be done while there is still time to readjust our thoughts and actions, and at least moderate our immoderate expectations.

Since I truly believe that deferring such crises as global warming and its causes is tantamount to suicide, I offer a few of my own thoughts for consideration. After all, our fragile physical bodies, which draw their stamina and health from the earth, are in absolute need of this terra firma for the development and survival of sound bodies that can host sound minds and spirits.

In the short-term sense we are imbued with exuberance for our own species. This is not surprising, although on a warier and longer term we should recognize our relationship to and reliance on other species and qualities of our environment. Our species interest is demonstrated with great frequency by the Emmies; Oscars; gold, silver and bronze medals; blue, pink, and other colored ribbons; titles of Miss This or Mr. That; titles of nobility or honor; and memberships that we bestow upon one another. In my outdoor ramblings I have idly wondered a time or two whether or not I was seeing a Corporal or Private Golden Mantled Ground Squirrel, or whether I was watching a first-, second-, or third-class Saw Whet Owl. I recall reading after one of our many wars that there was a sign at a driveway along a highway which read, "General Smith — Private Way." An unimpressed veteran, a mile farther, put up a sign that read, "Private Smith — General Way." *Sic transit gloria mundi!* (Thus fades the glory of the world.)

I have also wondered whether our grandiose assumptions about human beings have blinded us to recognition of ourselves as one of many kinds of related beings, as simply a part of life. Could it be that we so desperately seek reassurance of our significance that our psychological myopia becalms us in a human lagoon of self-interest? What this boils down to today is that we are so obsessed with humanity, and only a small segment of it, that we cannot accept the obvious reality that we are destructive tenants on this planet and are harassing the landlord into issuance of a summary eviction.

Our own literature abounds with analogies we might reflect upon in assessing our true relationship to our planet. Considering the earth as a living entity we might think about words written by satirist Jonathan Swift in *On Poetry, A Rhapsody* (1733):

So, naturalists observe, a flea
Hath smaller fleas that on him prey;
And these have smaller still to bite 'em;
And so proceed, ad infinitum...

As an observation of human importance in the face of time, Percy Bysshe Shelley in his poem *Ozymandias* (1817) spoke of a huge, crumbled statue in a desert waste which bore the legend:

My name is Ozymandias, king of kings:
Look on my works ye mighty and despair.

Shelley went on to say:

> Nothing beside remains. Round the decay
> Of that colossal wreck, boundless and bare
> The lone and level sands stretch far away.

In *The Republic*, Plato observed that, "No human thing is of serious importance." Yet he steadfastly maintained in the same work that, "The Soul of men is immortal and imperishable." And, at least in the sense that we are obviously carried along in a river of life that comes into the present from our genetic past, and continues into an even more indecipherable future, he is understandable. The sensible organism that is our being today may be no more than a way-station that extends through the lives of millions of ancestors, and is a transit point for the arrival of unknown numbers of descendants. Just as our river of life had its origin on this planet, so our life systems depend on the continued health of earth.

Compared to the life span of earth, our own life expectancies are minuscule. To be sure, we may appear in the river of life in many forms — this being one of many possibilities that have entered human thought. But the brevity of human life was long ago recognized in Ecclesiastes (1:4), "One generation passeth away, and another generation cometh: but the earth abideth forever."

It seems simply realistic and respectful on our parts to cherish the earth and to live in such a manner as to cease heaping abuse upon it. Very few people are so unthinking and unethical as to accept the hospitality of a friend and trash his home while there. Despicable indeed would be the individual who fouls the home of his host, tears apart the walls and wainscoting and otherwise despoils the hospitality of the owner. People would be all the more reluctant to take such steps if the owner was a burly, powerful individual. One would be foolish to rely on his host being forever patient. Can we expect patience from the earth forever?

There is much evidence that this world is rooted in an intelligent creative force. Nature's integration is of a higher order than hit-and-miss human endeavors. My intuition tells me that our economic obsession is infantile. We have lost sight of the role we are meant to play as parts of an unfolding Whole. Nowhere can I see such obligation as we have to the earth. If we have loyalty to family there is no closer relative than the earth. There is no greater friend. It provides all of us with our daily bread, with the water and air we imbibe to keep us alive. It is not merely an ancient relative but the sponsoring force of life.

Looking a bit farther we can see the earth as aesthetic stimulation for virtually all the art forms we know. Did the idea of melody not appear vividly in the songs of birds, and has great music not emerged from the sounds otherwise prevalent in nature? Think for example of Rimsky-Korsakov's *Flight of the Bumblebee*, or Hayden's *Toy Flute*. Is there not percussion in the sound of thunder and is there not marvelous and recurrent blending of color in the sunrises and sunsets, in the flowered meadows, the shimmering lakes and grasses? Are we not inclined to ponder when shadows grow long in the hush of evening, or to gaze in awe when the pulsating light of stars leads us to speculation upon the meaning of the universe and of life itself? Nothing seems so peaceful in my memory as a night spent under the stars in an alpine meadow high above the hubbub of daily life. I remember gazing at the stars, noting an occasional meteorite streak across the sky, and feeling at home with the universe. I don't remember falling asleep, but do remember awakening in the morning to see a yellowish-white mountain goat billy, grazing a bit, but mainly staring at me from a dozen steps away. "What was that all about?" I asked myself that day as I roamed in the alpine country. Was it just a happenstance or one of those close encounters of another kind? After considering whether our meeting was simply a form of universal gravitational attraction of one object for another, or mere curiosity, or intent, the best I could come up with was that we know little of the cause of anything that happens.

I am convinced that the earth and its sponsor is a far safer depository for the human soul than the economic system we venerate. Earth has been paying dividends called life for ages.

When majestic visions of oceans, prairies, sky, forests and mountains unfold before our eyes, does there not seem to be magnificent order that is a more trustworthy guide to life than the chaos we create through the narrow vision of technology that dominates current human values?

If we stop to think about it, a true respect for the earth would be the most sensible of reasons for bringing peace upon the planet and the necessary goodwill toward fellow beings, which would be an expression of that respect. The real tragedy of war is not that we annihilate each other. War is a long standing result of persistent barbarism, a criticism of nationalistic pretensions, and even at times of our religious zeal. Sadly, it is an imposed condition in which the blood of the young, innocent, and gullible is shed for the sins of the guilty who profit from war and whose incompetent leadership make it possible.

Of course in the business sense, war is the ideal stimulus for mass production. We build machines to blow them up so that we can build more for the sake of even bigger explosions and of course greater profit. But think of the impact upon the earth; the thermodynamic effect of 10,000 sorties and burning oil wells in Iraq; 2,4-D, 2,4,5-T and other biocides sprayed haphazardly in Vietnam, not to mention Rome plows and Johnson and Nixon bomb craters; the nuclear blasts in Japan and hundreds of other test blasts; the sinking of oil tankers and other ships in World War II; the lethal to all life implantation of millions of land mines; and on and on. Think also of the choice biological items that modern barbarians would use in the name of sophisticated warfare. Warfare is such madness and such injustice to the planet that supports us all, that the termination of military mania would probably be the first significant step toward civilization. But of course we do not take time to seriously consider that this contemporary belligerence is like the behavior of overcrowded laboratory animals, or is an increasing sign of pre-extinction behavior from a species incapable of positive changes. A serious attention to war-making might result if the initial battles, by public decree, were fought by the legislatures of the opposing nations and by leaders of the business interests that would profit from military endeavors.

Concern for the earth ultimately enters the domain of religion. Historian Lynn White attained unusual prominence for his observation that the ecological crisis stems from a Judeo-Christian lack of concern for nature. Since people in general have a utilitarian attitude toward nature, I am more impressed with White's suggestion that the efforts of St. Francis of Assisi to establish a brotherhood and sisterhood of all things on earth is an indication of the direction our own thoughts should follow. It is amazing that so few people have developed the insight to feel a genuine empathy with the natural world; and our lack of such insight is truly ominous. White further notes that St. Francis was "the greatest radical in Christian history since Christ," and one of the great miracles about his life "is the fact that he did not end at the stake, as many of his left wing followers did." White proposed St. Francis as a patron saint for all ecologists.[1]

According to Father Murray Bodo, O.F.M., who has written extensively on St. Francis, Francis believed that every living creature was a creature of God and anything that "demeans and devalues the creature demeans the Creator."[2] Loving all the creatures of the earth is a natural outcome of the love for God. While my own attendance at churches has been spotty, I am sure that if I had often heard the message of reverence for all living creatures including the earth, I would have found religious services more convincing. The love of earth itself is simply an extension of the First Commandment because the love of God automatically calls for love and respect of all that we call creation. Since the definition of faith as found in Hebrews (2:1)012 includes the "substance of things hoped for" and "the evidence of things not seen," my own faith rests upon the principle of necessity — that we will ultimately find it necessary to live and respect the totality of creation. With such a change we will find civilization possible, and without it we will not have learned enough to continue in the school of life. Even religions must grow from the self-serving to the higher plane of service toward all life.

CHAPTER 12

Life as Challenge and Privilege

*Is civilization progress? The challenge, I think, is clear; and,
as clearly, the final answer will be given not by our amassing
of knowledge, or by the discoveries of our science, or by the
speed of our aircraft, but by the effect our civilized activities
as a whole have upon the quality of our planet's life — the life
of plants and animals as well as that of men.*

Charles A. Lindbergh, Jr.

A friend of mine served as a U.S. Marine in the Pacific during
the island hopping days of the Second World War. But his
military career was ended by a severe facial wound that led to extensive medical work needed to reconstruct a shattered jaw.

His return to civilian life seemed meaningless. His immediate
need, he felt, was to search for his own self. Coming from a devout
Catholic family and having relatives who had embarked on voca-
tions with the church, it was not surprising therefore that he found
his way to post-war France and entered a monastery as a novitiate.

His tiny room, called a cell, had a small window near the ceil-
ing through which he could only see the sky, and a few treetops. It
had a single bed, a small bureau, a wash basin and pitcher for water.
A communal bathroom was down the hall. It seemed to suit him,
and was obviously designed for contemplation.

He found the simple work at the monastery enjoyable. Always

having been an active man, the use of his muscles for uncomplicated manual labor was pleasant. He also appreciated the plain diet and the absence of unnecessary conversation. From that standpoint, he said, he could always have remained a monk.

But he found it hard to concentrate on prayer. He kept reliving four years of military experience. Some memories sobered him, and brought tears to his eyes. Other robust, lusty reminiscences made him laugh, once loudly enough so that he found others staring at him in astonishment. The frequent calls to prayer were uncomfortable. At times he could respond with empathy, but often he could not.

Concentration failed when he tried to say the rosary at night and he would have to begin the prayers over and over again. But there was one prayer he said he learned that made sense, and he repeated it frequently to himself during his last months in the monastery. He told me that he still said it every day, and sometimes more than once:

Dear God:
Life is a challenge. A challenge is a privilege.
Make me a worthy vessel.

And then he said, with the old grin that he had lost for a long while: "Try it. It works. And it's true!"

When the day came for him to tell the abbot that he wanted to leave the monastery, the abbot blessed him and said: "I knew that you did not have a vocation to be here."

However, monastic life had been worthwhile because my friend had found a workable analysis of the meaning of life that served him faithfully through the years that followed.

Indeed, much has been said about life in attempts to analyze it. It has been called a moment in the sun; a path from cradle to grave; an affair that is nasty, short, and brutish; an experience that is filled with sobs, sighs and sniffles; an experiment; a bubble, a dream; a wraith; and many other things.

The apparent hopelessness of arriving at the core of meaning regarding our existence is demonstrated in Edward Fitzgerald's free-ranging translation of *The Rubaiyat of Omar Khayyam*. His translation of the 12th century quatrains created by the Persian poet is notable for having captured the spirit rather than the letter of the original work. The following stanza offers a synopsis of sincere effort to really comprehend the riddle of life:

> Myself when young did eagerly frequent
> Doctor and Saint, and heard great argument
> About it and about: but evermore
> Came out by the same door where in I went.

The few lines speak of experiences that are common to many people, perhaps even to most people. Here we travel along on the pathway of life, quite often aware that we know very little about whatever meaning may be attached to our existence. We pay attention to the words of learned individuals, experts of this or that discipline; or we sit at the feet of those reputed to be exemplars of spiritual knowledge. We fill ourselves as much as we can with the knowledge and awareness of others, hear things that are convincing and reject other things as nonsense. We are nourished to a varying extent by the ideas of others, and of how well those ideas merge into our innate credulity and uniqueness. All too often, we learn that what seemed like a true and complete formula for living life, upon digestion, makes us conscious that we must continue our search.

All of the foregoing is an indication of the fact that life offers continuous challenge. Upon consideration it can also be seen that challenge exists at many levels that vary from simple to complex. Our way of life makes the extent of challenges even more mind-boggling because entrenched values demand conformity and label those who seek a less destructive way of life as counter-productive.

When I walk along broadcasting seeds onto the earth, I am reminded that even before conception there is a challenge that is faced by would-be living things, whether they are plant or animal. The seed must come in contact with that which will sustain life. This is true of a spermatozoon seeking union with an ovum, or a seed that must make contact with fertile moist soil that will initiate and sustain growth. Once this challenge has been successfully met, it is obvious that chance also plays a lifelong role in the growth and maturation of the individual life that has been initiated. Having pointed out these fundamental conditions, it seems excessive to trace the harrowing circumstances that ensue before 30,000 tree seedlings have yielded to "survival of the fittest" and resulted in some 300 mature trees on an acre of ground. Similarly, although we have tipped the odds so that higher percentages of people survive into maturity, we do not really know how much we have affected the qualitative by favoring the quantitative aspects of life. The well known concept that animals are healthiest in an under-stocked habitat, must also apply to people, and therefore suggests that our problems can only multiply as our numbers increase.

Whatever our lives are, they are active rather than passive. They involve doing and experiencing. I recall one day when I ate my lunch sitting on a granite boulder alongside a foaming mountain stream called Glacier Creek, only a short distance above where it merged its water with the Fish River. All about me there were other granite boulders very light in color but sprinkled with black inclusions. Aware that some quantum physicists suggest awareness at all levels of existence, I wondered about what sort of consciousness might exist in an inert boulder. Certainly it would be a more passive form than ours since independent motion is not an attribute, and without an outside force imparting motion, the boulder would remain in its present location. Over centuries or millennia it would gradually disintegrate and crumble into soil. Perhaps, I mused, the boulder's present existence is a resting period between more adventurous forms of existence, a time to assimilate, to brood, and contemplate. I don't find it as difficult as some people do, to consider that intelligence and awareness might be present in each boulder or in every object we see. Animism holds no terror in my mind, nor do I feel it opposes otherworldly religions to reflect that we may live in an extremely conscious world — after all, we do talk freely of spirit being omnipresent.

Thinking of the boulder and of its apparent impassivity, I compared its stolid composure with the endless decision making involved in our own active lives, and especially with the great mobility afforded by current affairs. Whereas a boulder, as a condition of its physical attributes must remain where it is, we are guaranteed a restlessness and indecisiveness by virtue of the ever-changing perspectives of life that we are granted. An intelligent boulder would have the leisure to spend a few centuries looking forward and backward, seeking the first principles of existence on the one hand, and the purpose of this particular life on another. This may seem unimportant until we look at a particular aspect of our own lives. Our orientation is primarily what we consider "forward" in a direction arbitrarily labeled progress. Our sciences, also "forward oriented," seek mainly for necessary facts to enable the attainment of momentum toward innovations that cascade from industry as the new and latest things that everyone must work to possess. The search for first principles or basic meaning in the universe are relegated to the out-of-reach grapes that the fox disdained because of the difficulty involved in harvesting them. This has resulted in a shockingly over-balanced society with its head in the clouds and its feet braced by nothing really meaningful. The best we have been able to come up with as a spiritual guide is the idea of personal salvation without any responsibility for whatever we trample underfoot enroute to that goal. Unlike the boulder, we have no time to realize that all our aspirations rest upon the enduring earth that supports us at every moment of existence. We understand that our buildings must have solid foundations before they can tower into the sky, but we build our own lives upon the shifting sands of circumstance without the sills of granite that would provide them enduring support. Much work and thought indeed is needed to correct the problem we have created for ourselves. I am reminded of an acquaintance who bought a log home built atop flat rocks laid upon the ground. The rocks shifted and the house began to settle in one corner. It was necessary for him to jack up the house, excavate beneath the logs (an extremely laborious job), and pour a foundation that would support the log home before it began to rot. His situation was not different from the one we are in today, and we must indeed do much extra work and develop considerable self-restraint, to rectify hasty oversight.

Unlike the boulders that lay about where I ate my lunch, we are not fully-formed, nor must we remain as we are and reside in the place where we first became conscious of ourselves. We do not live our lives in rough-hewn fashion and can elect to retain amorphous, chaotic thoughts or else can create the facets of whatever mixture of nobility, flexibility or crystallinity we establish as our goals. It has been easiest for us to enthusiastically jump on the modern bandwagon of materialism. By letting rather unproved leaders do our thinking for us, it has been simple to entirely ignore or even scoff at the possibility that there is a divine or philosophical foundation to life. Spiritual laziness makes it easiest to enjoy the temptation of a steady parade of new things, and to carelessly forgo those out-of-reach grapes, luscious though their promise may be. This is probably a most serious and irrational failure on our part, one of those easy-way-out options made when it is uncomfortable and restrictive to face facts that demand fundamental change.

Humans once considered the spiritual foundation of life to be the source of primary knowledge and arrived at the conclusion that failure to recognize this underlying structure would permit only a less adequate form of secondary knowledge. Action taken in accord with primary knowledge was labeled sacred, whereas actions derived from secondary knowledge could only be profane. We may not be very comfortable coming to grips with such an idea. It's easier to lump all actions as relative without making serious effort to consider the foundation of their existence.

Looking around though, it isn't difficult to spot many of our ideas and their manifestations as more profane than sacred. That we even consider such alternatives as nuclear war and its space age evolution of "star wars" is utterly profane. The military use of biological warfare to any extent, from defoliants to induced diseases, indicates an unquestionably profane level of barbarism as the quagmire in which "realistic" thought has its roots. In an even larger sense the word profane aptly describes the industrial behemoth that would sacrifice oceans, lakes, rivers, forests, soil, air, and widespread life forms to the equally profane belief that profit is the *summum bonum* (greatest good) to which human life (to the exclusion of all other life) should be devoted.

It is interesting to note that we employ challenge in many ways for the sake of personal improvement. A golfer's handicap is a constant reminder of the need for improvement. Basketball players attempt to improve their shooting percentage, and records are kept of the percentage of shots made from the floor and from the free throw line. Pass completion percentages and average yardage gained in attempts carrying the ball serve for measuring the success of football players and keep players striving for improvement.

Keeping score is basically a method of recording an individual's or a team's success at meeting challenge. Salary raises, promotions, and honors of various sorts are likewise score-keeping tactics along the pathway that defines what we call upward mobility. The rewards that may be attained are also a stimulus toward conformity, toward thinking like the company thinks or in a manner that mass society approves.

It is easy to see that an over-organized society can provide sufficient challenges to keep individuals moving largely in the direction that is deemed appropriate. Add to the easily recognizable challenges pertaining to work and to the nebulous thing called success, other pursuits such as "fitness" derived from exercise machines, and relaxation and enjoyment employing electronic machines such as television, and there remains little time for an individual to allow serious consideration of the nagging inner reminder that things are not exactly what they should be. This is also an example of how allowing the mundane to control our lives, does in fact allow the mundane to become the profane.

Fortunately however, individuals do pursue some challenges on an entirely personal basis. Here, to a certain extent, the golf handicap, handicraft facility, horseshoe pitching skills, fly-casting ability, or crossword puzzle performance all demand some inner persistence and innovative ability. An individual may step outside purely self-serving attainments and try to raise beautiful flowers for the sake of beauty itself, or try in some manner to help others, or to assist in efforts toward a noble goal such as peace on the planet. The privilege of thinking for ourselves does enable us to cast aside such habit forming soporifics as electronic entertainment and to develop our own individuality as an alternative to mass entertainment.

Centuries ago, thinkers advised that democracy could only survive when citizens remained continually active and took part with a high level of consciousness and vigilant concern in the daily affairs of government. But, they pointed out, when people primarily seek self-gain and leave government to political forces alone, there results a decline in social behavior that leads to anarchy, which ultimately becomes so bad it is replaced by tyranny. There is strong evidence of the progression toward tyranny in anarchic behavior today.

The pathway to the human soul is kept alive more through the things that are unique about us, than through the endless conformities that require obedience rather than heartfelt empathy. A century and a half ago, Thoreau noted that education often makes a straight-cut ditch out of the meandering thoughts of children. So the peremptory goals of mass society would channelize our own thoughts, focusing them on a narrow, arbitrary goal that is the antithesis of the success it claims to be. A society living beyond its means, exploiting everything it can find to exploit, is out of step with the lessons we can learn from nature simply by observation. In spite of the impressive manipulative skills of technology, it is rooted in futility as long as we continue in ignorance of the endless subtlety and complexity that is the reality of nature. We are foundering because of a hasty assumption that we know "enough" about nature to impose our will upon it. The proof of our own adaptability to survive does not yet exist, and our diminishing chances depend upon a rapid drawing back from continued meddling with planetary order, coupled with significant amelioration of human engendered toxicity. Before any success at all can be attained, there will have to be a spiritual awakening that lets us function with far less ego and far more humility. Not surprisingly, everything does hinge upon the transformation of ourselves that must precede the transformation of social structure.

If we let ourselves look at the increasingly severe storms that are flattening towns, sliding houses off muddy slopes and causing thousands to evacuate their homes due to unprecedented flooding or hurricanes, we might think of the ancient doctrine of Karma. Whether or not we believe in esoteric doctrines, it does seem that we are receiving increasing violence resulting from the violence we have imposed upon the planet. It is about time for us to walk upon another path and learn that if we act upon Earth with understanding and compassion, we will be recipients of comparable qualities. To the scoffer who comments that it is a little late to change when swirling in the sink before departing down the drain, I would say that it is still more admirable to die trying to get out of the current than to pretend we are simply on a pleasant river ride. Going with the current is being caught in what Carlyle called the "center of indifference." The task, as he expressed it, is to pass through indifference on one's travels from the negative to the positive pole.[1]

The challenge that impatiently awaits our response has to do with our continued existence. It involves a far more holistic perception in which we recognize ourselves as part of the vast community of life. We must call upon tremendous willpower and unformed character, not yet really displayed. It is within our intellectual capacity to subordinate our desires to the reasonable possibilities that would provide us with enough without doing further destruction to the vital fabric of our ecosphere. No doubt there was a time in the history of our species when we were ignorant because of our own naivety. We simply were not experienced as a species and did not have a vast cultural heritage to pass on to our offspring. Nature wisely imbued us with a sense of awe and with the innate conviction that there was power greater than our own. Fortunately we did not at that time have the tools to enable us to become such earth wreckers as we have become. Too hastily though, we devised religions and philosophies that imagined us to be the focal point of the entire universe. As we became more competent at fabricating tools offering us an increasing degree of mastery, we cast aside the sense of wonder and awe. We succumbed to the idea of sophistication, which enabled us to worship our own accomplishments without recognizing that in the process we were taking apart a world that was beyond our capacity to restore. We made the fundamental mistake of assuming that this vast life-giving and life-nourishing planet upon which we are privileged to live, is an actual possession that we can deed, lease and exploit to our heart's content. The condition in which we now live was referred to by philosophers as double ignorance, a condition of being ignorant of our own ignorance: "He who knows no life save the physical is merely ignorant; but he who declares physical life to be all-important and elevates it to the position of supreme reality — such a one is ignorant of his own ignorance."[2]

The easiest path to follow is that of succumbing to the surrogate world that we have devised. The constant titillation it affords is an effective block to recognition of the challenge of our existence. Does it not offer enough variety to satisfy anyone's appetite for activity? It is only by taking a stand within oneself and withdrawing from the superficial world we have called reality, that we can enter the real world. It may not be at all far-fetched to say that in deep thought our own essences are in harmony with the essence of life itself. In seeking there is finding, but thought and reflection must replace the shallow materialism we have elected as the purpose of life.

There is enough dissatisfaction with the apparent meaninglessness of the often referred to "rat race" that more and more people are having to resort to tranquillizing drugs to prevent psychic collapse in one form or another. The beauty of response to the challenge of trying to find something more meaningful is that we will realize the absoluteness of a prior attachment to God and the universe, which makes the surrogate world's claim on us seem irrelevant. We can gain a perspective that allows us to see the essential silliness of devoting ourselves to endless change and acquisition. The awakening of humility (humus, earthiness) will rapidly dissolve the unjustified egocentricism that has been such a stumbling block to spiritual growth. In humility we can realize that life is a privilege that has been conferred upon us. If we become more free, more capable of loving and understanding life and yet do not have the conviction of an absolutist religion or a pure philosophy, is that so bad? Should we really expect that the absolute law of the universe was written out for our sole benefit? Was Tennyson wrong when he expressed the thought that there is more faith in honest doubt than in half the creeds? Or was Cervantes lacking insight in claiming that the road is better than the inn? Have we overlooked the law of conservation of energy and matter and the fact that we ultimately return to the elemental wealth of the world? Could it be that we continue on our way to float in the clouds, dance in the leaves, and gurgle in the streams? Are we perhaps creatures of forever? There are people who assert with confidence that the concept of immortality is a myth. For all we really know, *mortality* may be the actual myth.

Some certainties in life are indisputable. One is that we are earth-born and will be healthiest if we eat food produced upon an earth that is not saturated with chemical compounds that are foreign to the physical makeup of our bodies. No matter how many laws are passed permitting an arbitrary number of parts per million or billion of industry's poisonous creations to be found in our food or water, such laws are simply fatuous. Human law may have adopted the maxim that "the law concerneth itself not with trifles" *(de minimus not curat lex)*. But it is an entirely different matter in the laws of nature where little and great are only terms of comparison, for nature knows no trifles and, "Her laws are as inflexible in dealing with an atom as with a continent or a planet." We have no justification for assuming traces of poisonous elements or compounds to be insignificant because we cannot immediately determine their effect. There is increasing incontrovertible evidence that humanity is *of* nature, not above her.

As it is with food, so it is with every bit of the ecosphere in which we are privileged to enjoy our present moment in the sun. The most fundamental challenge of our existence resides in our relationship to the ecosphere. At present we suffer from a ludicrously magnified sense of our own importance. With the unfounded assumption that we have dominion over the ecosphere we have hacked away with might and main and have made a shambles of the world about us.

The basic challenge of our existence is to renege our illusions and dedicate ourselves, within the truly limited scope of our competence, to restore the imbalances we have created, and to work toward a harmony with earth that we have shattered in our unrecognized impetuousness and immaturity.

An idyllic tale of meeting challenge and privilege, of sacrificing one's wealth for the purpose of giving life to others was told by Lafcadio Hearn in *Gleanings in Buddha-Fields.*

Hearn begins his volume, which was originally published in 1898, by relating a story which he calls "A Living God," a tale of quite ordinary Japanese people, their customs, qualities, and their religion of many gods who were distinguished ancestors, and of a person in particular, who had so distinguished himself that he was venerated as a living god.

Throughout Japan, Hearn tells us, there are Shinto shrines made of unpainted wood that turns "under the action of rain and sun, to a natural grey, varying according to the surface exposure from the silvery tone of birch bark to the somber grey of basalt."

So appropriately designed, and then weathered are these isolated *yashiro* that they blend into the landscape like nature's own rocks and trees, seeming like boulders and vegetation to have derived their own existence as a "manifestation of Ohotsuchi-no-Kami, the Earth god, the primeval divinity of the land." Although ancient Shinto myths speak of a very large number of *kami*, which are manifested as mountains, trees, birds, beasts, plants of all sorts and human beings, Shinto is more than a collection of multiple deities, and is identified as a single, cosmic religion, with all things sharing the *kami*, superior or divine nature.

Although the Shinto religion was overshadowed by Mahayana Buddhism in the 8th century, reconciliation was offered by Buddhist leaders in the 9th century, and the Shinto *kami* were identified as manifestations of Buddha, thus leading to a long-lasting pattern of Buddhist and Shinto coexistence. State Shinto was disestablished after World War II, but Shinto still exists as a religion in various forms. There are about 80,000 shrines in Japan today, and domestic Shinto focuses in many homes around the household *kami* shelf *(kami-dana)*, which is dedicated to the tutelary *kami* of the family.

Hearn speaks of the untranslatable nature of many of the Shinto terms that we loosely render as "temple" or "shrine." The "august houses" of the *kami* have their historical roots in ideas and beliefs that are thousands of years old. Their antique origins give them their special nature. The impressive realization is that millions of people for thousands of years have worshipped their memorable dead before the yashiros, and millions still believe these memorials are occupied by invisible but conscious personalities of sages, teachers, warriors, rulers, and other heroes of the past. Realizing what the yashiro have represented over the centuries makes one "apt to reflect how difficult it would be to prove the faith absurd," as Hearn says.

Hamaguchi Gohei, a farmer in the district of Atila, located in the province of Kishu, was one of those rare individuals who was honored by having a yashiro built for his spirit, and by being revered as a god while he was still alive. And it is easy to see that he performed an act having great merit.

When nature presented an unusual challenge to Hamaguchi, he was already a successful, respected individual — the headman of his village. His farm was on a plateau above the community which stretched along the ocean shore, with some houses and small farms scattered at intervals on the terraced slopes above. Of significance was Hamaguchi's good view of the sea, for the day of his challenge was a day on which a tsunami occurred. It was an earlier event than the overpowering wave of 1896 that swept the north-eastern provinces for nearly two hundred miles, demolishing scores of towns and villages and killing thirty thousand people. Nonetheless it was a wave that none of the people who saw it would ever forget.

It was a late autumn afternoon and Hamaguchi could see preparations being made for a harvest celebration at the *ujigami,* the Shinto parish temple in the village below. Most of his family had already gone down the hill to help decorate the village in preparations for the festivity. He was alone except for his ten-year-old grandson. The day was unpleasantly hot, earthquake weather as it was commonly called, and a mild earthquake had suddenly shaken the land, very likely an aftershock of an immense seismic event that took place farther away. The mild shock did not alarm the villagers who were used to the many tremors that affect earthquake-prone Japan. When Hamaguchi looked up and out to sea he saw that the water was "running away from the land." People below had noted the ebbing water but failed to recognize the monstrous significance of sea water retreating from the land. But Hamaguchi was old and experienced, and knew the meaning of this forerunner of a tidal wave.

His response to the challenge was immediate, and was instinctively based on the tradition that entire communities — children and all — were expected to respond at once to the threat of fire.

"Tada! — quick, very quick! Light me a torch," Hamaguchi shouted. His grandchild responded at once, and the old man hurried to the adjacent field where hundreds of rice stacks, most of his invested capital, awaited transporting. Hastening as rapidly as his aged legs would carry him, he began lighting one stack after another. The dry stalks flared up immediately and the freshening seabreeze lighted rank behind rank of the stacks. Columns of smoke arose and formed an enormous cloud.

The bewildered child ran behind his grandfather, asking: "Ojiisan! why? Ojiisan! why? — why?"

But Hamaguchi had no time to respond. All his flagging energy was needed to produce the cloud of smoke and flame that might rescue the villagers. A single thought occupied his mind and governed his actions: "Save the four hundred neighbors who would respond to the fire."

Even as he was firing the last of the crop, the big bell in the temple on the hillside began ringing; and because of the smoke, the flame, and the ringing, people came swarming up the hill, eager to help in whatever way they could.

Water in the sea was still retreating from the land when the first villagers arrived, and the child babbled with fear that his grandfather was mad. The people too were beginning to wonder about his sanity when Hamaguchi called out to them: "Let it burn, lads! — let it be! I want the whole *mura* here. There is great danger — *taihen da!*"

People kept arriving. Hamaguchi was well loved and deeply respected. Men, women, babes in arms, girls and boys — they all had come to help. When all but a few stragglers had arrived and people wondered why Hamaguchi seemed uninterested in the serious matter of his burning rice crop, they voiced their concern. They could not understand this thing — letting the crop burn!

Then the old man shouted: *"Kita,"* and pointed to the sea. "Say now if I be mad."

And the people stared into the twilight eastward "and saw at the edge of the dusky horizon a long, lean, dim line like the shadowing of a coast where no coast ever was — a line that thickened as they gazed, that broadened as a coast-line broadens to the eyes of one approaching it, yet incomparably more quickly. For that long darkness was the returning sea, towering like a cliff, and coursing more swiftly than the kite flies."

"Tsunami," shrieked the people and then all other sounds were obliterated by a sound greater than a thunderclap, as the colossal wave crashed upon the shore with enough force to cause a shudder to be felt through the ground beneath people's feet. Spray from the impact surrounded them in a cloud and people automatically retreated from its menacing aspect. And when they could see the village site, it had disappeared beneath a thrashing sea that raged over where their homes had been. "It drew back roaring, and tearing out the bowels of the land as it went. Twice, thrice, five times the sea struck and ebbed, but each time with lesser surges; then it returned to its ancient bed and stayed — still raging as after a typhoon." Of the village nothing remained but two straw roofs tossing in the water, and the temple like a sentinel on the hill.

Then Hamaguchi was heard to say quietly: "That was why I set fire to the rice." He was now almost as poor as the poorest among them, but by his quick foresight, and willing sacrifice he had saved four hundred lives.

The people of the village had no money and could not replace the wealth he had lost, but when they rebuilt their village, they built a shrine to honor Hamaguchi as a living god.

He lived out his life in his thatched home upon the plateau he farmed. His children and his grandchildren lived with him as simply as before the great wave, while his soul was worshipped in the shrine below. People still visit and pray to the soul of the good old farmer who saved others in the time of their distress.[3]

The challenge is still present today, the challenge to reduce energy use, to curb the tidal wave of pollution, the challenge to place the well-being of the community and the world above personal self-interest, the challenge to look upon one's work as something more than "just a way to make a living." And the privilege of sacrifice is also existent, but is contingent upon recognition of the importance of all life and the Great Mystery in which we live.

In 1958, British ecologist Charles Elton, suggested specific attitudes we should keep in mind as we carry on activities on earth. This conscious self-questioning he recommends as we go about our daily business is realistic, and poses great possibilities in a world that places strong self interest ahead of responsibility. Elton basically challenges those who intend to drain, plant, spray or substantially change any portion of the land to consider what damage is being done to pre-existent conditions. What resident plants and animals will be extirpated? What natural beauty and uniqueness will be shattered? What further damage will be done to the increasingly precarious health of ecosystems? Basically he asks us to act with sensitive conscientiousness and to preserve as much of the natural order as we can.[4]

It would be another worthwhile challenge to revise our priorities so that the major economic target would be the restoration of the earth. Because economics is a humanly devised discipline, it would be entirely possible to identify increasing real wealth with increasing health of the earth and its inhabitants. Bettering the conditions of life and the health of the ecosphere is a sane and admirable goal. There was a time when we recognized the value of a truly loyal opposition to the heedlessness of the worshipers of unrelenting acquisition and the exploitation that has been cynically called development. Today we value only conformity and have no patience for those whose sobriety has led to centuries old warnings that we are proceeding on a path of self destruction.

With moderation as a respected factor in life, humans could have enough in a quantitative sense and much more in a qualitative sense. We need to recognize at the level of our souls that we have been privileged to receive the gift of life and that the challenge is for us to respond to the gift by developing the best qualities within our being.

CHAPTER 13

Walking on the New Path

Two roads diverged in a wood, and I —
I took the one less traveled by,
And that has made all the difference.

Robert Frost

Human history has recorded many creation myths. One of the more distinguished of these was presented in Chapter Five. The idea of living things constituting a ladder of experience enroute to an exalted state appealed to many thinkers and served to remind people that human beings were something short of perfect in their present form. Unfortunately the more popular creation stories contradict this belief and suggest that of all the things in the universe only people are important.

Coupled with conviction of our paramount importance is the irrational belief, started by optimistic settlers in North America, that the resources of this continent are inexhaustible. In his book, *The Quiet Crisis*, then U.S. Secretary of the Interior Stewart T. Udall challenged the assumption that the continent would forever drip milk and honey into avid mouths, as still another myth which he called "The Myth of Superabundance."[1]

Though warnings have been issued for years by responsible groups and individuals there seems to be little willingness on the part of politicians or industry to come to grips with the fact that we live on a finite planet. Their concerns, except for election oratory and self-congratulations for cosmetic, token, conservation efforts that will not inconvenience the industrial giant, are obviously superficial.

The farthest we have come after years of strident denial is to finally admit that global warming and severe climate change is a reality. In spite of hundreds of millions of dollars spent by fossil fuel industries to deny the fact that global warming is taking place, the truth surfaced because the evidence of severe storms and unusual climatic excesses has become too common to deny. It is noteworthy that the insurance industry is advising governments of the necessity of reducing carbon emissions, or in so many words, the use of fossil fuels. Basing its efforts for change on the increasing costs of claims resulting from weather-related damage, it offers the financial community outstanding evidence that we can no longer afford to neglect serious action. Weather-related insurance claims increased from $17 billion in the decade of the 1980s to $48 billion for the first five years of the 90s. Economic losses from floods, storms, droughts, and other weather related disasters reached a new record of $60 billion in 1996. According to Munich Re, one of the largest reinsurance companies: "Loss of life and property from natural disasters has been climbing for two decades. Economic losses from natural catastrophes during the last 10 years (1996–2006) have totalled $566.8 billion, exceeding the combined losses from 1950 through 1989."[2] This statistic mocks political and industrial foresight, and raises a question about our current view that nothing is more important than business. Prior to the year 2000, 60 of the world's leading insurance companies were urging governments to reduce carbon emissions, but they are still increasing.

There is widespread awareness that human activities have become a threat to our survival. Industrial pollutants are ubiquitous and there are virtually no ecosystems, including the broad oceans, that have not been rendered toxic and imperiled by our recklessness. For instance, there are "dead zones" in the ocean, such as the 17,000-square-kilometre (6,560 sq. mi.) area where the Mississippi River ejects over-fertilized agricultural waste into the Gulf of Mexico. The huge resulting algal blooms deplete the water of oxygen, thus causing all other life in the area to die.[3] In ways such as this, human activities show that the idea of super abundance is indeed a myth.

Although such events had not been foreseen, we have been given many warnings. As a single example, U. Thant in his position as Secretary-General of the United Nations, warned the world that there was perhaps a decade left in which we would have to settle our ancient problems, curb the population explosion, and end the arms race. As he foresaw the unfolding of events, if a global partnership did not forge new co-operative efforts among nations, it was very much feared that problems resulting from human impact on earth would be uncontrollable.[4]

On November 18, 1992, "The World Scientists' Warning to Humanity," co-ordinated by the Union of Concerned Scientists, was released. It bore signatures of 1575 scientists from 69 countries, including those of more than half the living Nobel laureates. The warning said that we have a few decades at most, and perhaps only one, in which to remedy threats that immeasurably diminish human prospects. The warning called for population stabilization, reduction of greenhouse gas emissions, curtailing of air and water pollution, a cessation of deforestation, plus formulation of a new ethic of caring for the earth, and recognition of the earth's limited capacity to care for us. It was suggested that caring for the planet was "enlightened self interest" and not a matter of mere altruism.

Another way of looking at the current impasse with which we are faced is to think of it in terms of motion. When our industrial momentum was taking its toddling infant steps, it had to overcome the inertia of an older civilization, of a pre-industrial mode of thought and its accompanying way of life. People then were at least as reluctant to change their ways as people today will be to give up their dependence on motorized transport and the nearly endless list of other devices that advertising has made us think of as necessities. Present attitudes concur with the second law of motion effect, which states that an object in motion in a given direction will continue in the same direction unless a force is applied to cause it to change. Although our fascination with an ever expanding economy and increasing Gross National Product depends on the unheeding blind-ness that is the fashion of our times, nature is clearly stating that the third law of motion is coming into effect: For every action there is an equal and opposite reaction. Brush fires in Mexico and Florida, record-making ice storms in the eastern provinces of Canada and the northeastern United States, tornadoes where they do not usually occur, droughts, intense heat and cold, these are but a prelude to what we can expect if we do not wake up to the absurdity of our own pretensions.

Rationalization is a means used to push present problems into the future. But how long can we rationalize mounting ecological problems stemming from continual degradation of the earth? Doleful predictions as to our fate are already numerous. George Santayana in *Soliloquies in England* (1922), expressed this well in his observation that humanity is "a perpetual caricature of itself; at every moment it is the mockery and the contradiction of what it is pretending to be."

It is quite interesting now to look back upon the projections offered by Princeton University professor of international law Richard Falk in his 1971 book, *The Endangered Planet*. Falk recognized that the 1970s were typified by a growing politics of despair in which it was becoming increasingly more obvious that the problems of society were too big for governments to handle. If society continued on the same path, the 1980s would be a decade in which the world's leaders, a confident elite, would exert more and more repressive control in order to safeguard their own privileges. Although token concessions might be offered to appease the poor, the aid would not be great enough to prevent burgeoning animosity stemming from real deprivation and suffering. With nuclear capability extending throughout the world, the grim possibility of ultimate terrorism could become an imminent reality. He suggested that the 1990s would be a decade in which the politics of catastrophe would be unable to avert an enormous disaster of ecological or thermonuclear nature. He felt that the existing order of nation-states and corporate domination would necessarily yield to a world-oriented reorganization of political structure to replace nation-state systems. The 21st century he foresaw as little other than an "era of annihilation." To be sure, Professor Falk did offer an alternative scenario, which did not occur, one in which the 1980s might have been a decade of mobilization toward changed goals and the 1990s a decade of transformation in which population and economic activity was stabilized into a format that might respect and adhere to the recognizable limits of the life support systems of the planet.[5]

We in the western world have enjoyed our economic ascendancy and the life of "wine, women, and song," not to mention increased materialism, and have assumed it would last forever. Well-established studies of boom and bust cycles were inadmissible to the new world order of science, technology and subservient politics. Air, water, and soil could forever be used to dilute pollution. Folklore that the piper must eventually be paid was considered as simple to postpone as corporately and politically deferred debt. The books can always be juggled.

Consider, though, the disturbing set of figures which suggest that environmental stress is directly affecting the well-being of the living organisms with whom we are most closely related. There are five classes of vertebrate animals: fish, amphibians, reptiles, birds, and mammals. We are members of the class called mammals.

Since the 1960s the World Conservation Union (still abbreviated IUCN from its former name, The International Union for the Conservation of Nature) has published the *Red Data Book* listing all known animal species in the world that are threatened with extinction. Representative numbers of fish, amphibia, and reptiles were among those surveyed, and in 1996 the status of all birds and mammals was included. This involved nearly ten thousand species of birds and some 4,400 mammal species.[6]

The 1996 publication showed 4 percent of birds were in immediate danger of extinction and 7 percent vulnerable; 11 percent of mammals were in immediate danger, another 14 percent vulnerable, and 14 percent approaching vulnerability; 10 percent of amphibians surveyed were immediately threatened and 15 percent vulnerable; and 8 percent of reptiles were in immediate danger with 12 percent vulnerable.

The 2004 IUCN Red List shows 15,589 species threatened with extinction, including 12 percent of birds, 23 percent of mammals, and 32 percent of amphibians, and among reptiles, 42 percent of turtles and tortoises. While assessments have not been completed for all threatened species, study reveals that among birds, the albatrosses, cranes, parrots, pheasants and pigeons are more threatened than other groups. Among mammals, the ungulates, carnivores, primates, dugongs and manatees are particularly at risk. The Red List notes that the "non-ramdom distribution of threats across the tree of life means that entire evolutionary lineages are liable to go extinct very quickly." Seeing that we ourselves are primates, this should warn us that we are playing with fire.

It is hardly acceptable today for an individual to question the prevailing definition of progress. However, I do not feel it is an exaggeration to say that if we really acted upon our intelligence we would change our ways and begin a full-scale emergency program to restore the health of our planet. We are already victimizing one another (and future generations) by causing problems that we may never be able to solve, e.g. ozone depletion, and reduction of biodiversity. An ounce of prevention may not only be worth a pound of cure, but may prevent incurable circumstances from arising.

We should ask ourselves the question popularized by Bill Cosby, modifying it only slightly to enquire: "How long can we tread water?"

Thoreau made a thought-provoking comment that, "Superfluous wealth can buy superfluities only. Money cannot buy one necessity of the soul." His statement is particularly relevant because it acknowledges the necessity of having a certain amount of money but also conveys the idea that a point is reached at which one has enough. As for the things of the soul that money cannot purchase, there are spiritual, emotional and aesthetic qualities that are not measurable with a monetary yardstick. The good, the true, the beautiful — love, honor and justice — are too often sacrificed on the alter of materialism.

Thoreau carried his idea a bit farther, claiming stoutly that a person "is rich in proportion to the number of things he can get along without." Most of us eventually realize that the incessant accumulation of possessions can become excessive and frustrating. We hear much advertising designed to make us want new, improved gadgets. While there is no end to the number of things that businesses offer for sale, there is a distinct limit to the number of things that people need to survive. Discriminating between things needed, and things not needed does require some thought. But Thoreau was right in pointing out that the ability to recognize that you do not need a thing is in itself a measure of wealth. A friend tells me that he always looks at an item he wants in reference to the number of hours he will have to work in order to buy it. He says that he simplifies the matter of purchasing, because life is measured in time, and time is grace. There's no "overtime" to life itself. He claims that the highest priority in his life is free time: "I look at something I don't need and say to myself that as far as buying it, I might just as well be fishing when the fish aren't biting. Some people go downtown to see if there's something they want to buy, but I know without going that there's nothing I need. I don't feel it's my social duty to keep the economy afloat."

Many people understand that we are overdue for a genuine assessment of what we have called progress, and it is likely that a serious study of the matter would determine simply that we have constructed improved means for arriving at unimproved ends. We will not be on the trail to progress until we realize that it is not to be found in the accumulation of wealth but in the improvement of character.

It has seemed obvious to me, for most of my adult years, that the earth, which nurtures life, is more important than the people who inhabit it. Through self-serving religions, insatiable wants, and quite incompetent leadership, we are arriving at the only end that can be expected from unreasonable expectations — the end of our selves. The world is a proving ground for all species, not a playground for an especially privileged one. The cards aren't dealt that way.

We have arrived at a very difficult dilemma. Perhaps for a species such as ours, with its modicum of intelligence, it was inevitable that we must stumble our way toward a moment of truth. It seems likely that the world's Armageddon must be the battle between our physical cravings and the quintessence that resides within us — the phenomenon referred to as the still, small voice, the spark of being, or the virtually indefinable quality we call soul. And in the final analysis, soul is not a quality that belongs to a church, a state, or an obsession such as materialism. It is instead a form of potential energy lying deep inside everyone and perhaps within everything, a seed that belongs to the creative reason of the universe. We sense it as a larger phenomenon than ourselves, and have respectfully considered it the omniscient, omnipotent, and omnipresent God. If we need mayor or city manager for our conurbations, a president or premier for our states, and a paterfamilias for our religions, why should we be surprised that the universe needs a pilot at its helm? If, through introspection, we should arrive at innate truth, it will tell us that, "yes, we do indeed owe responsibility to the original gift of creation, which is the historical parent of the ceaseless tide of created beings that stems from its fertility." Whatever our religions and philosophies may be, their point of origin was here on earth. Whatever metaphysical assumptions we may have, we can only live in one world at a time. We can hardly qualify for a higher orbit unless we can establish peace and harmony in our own communities and our own world. In our present condition we would probably litter heaven and write graffiti on the walls of the celestial city. Businessmen would no doubt be anxious to develop it!

Almost everything we need involves sacrifice. But sacrifice can also be gratifying. We can understand the feeling of satisfaction that comes from quitting smoking or drinking, from losing weight by exercising and cutting down on fattening foods. As Pico della Mirandola pointed out, we have the choice between stoking the fires of the beast within ourselves or satisfying the more spiritual impulses we feel. We can hedge, snuffle, polish our sophisticated veneer and pretend to a man or woman of the world image but, as the old philosophers used to point out, we are continually forced to make choices between actions and desires that smack of the profane or approach the sacred.

As I sit here writing this on a Monday morning, there are some 600 forest fires burning in British Columbia. The evacuation of Salmon Arm (a community of 15,000 people on the Trans-Canada Highway) has been partly accomplished and the remaining citizens are on a ten-minute evacuation notice. A forest fire covering more than 5,000 hectares is threatening the city, and high winds are expected in the afternoon as a front moves in from the north. The fires throughout the country are very likely the result of global warming, which has caused an exceptionally hot and dry summer with temperature records being set across the nation. As I am writing, a loaded logging truck occasionally rumbles down the highway in front of our home. Deforestation is one of the causes of climate change, and this is an often-published fact, but the forest sector is impatient for more dollars. The general attitude of the forest industry was well expressed by the chairman of timber giant Louisiana Pacific: "We don't log to a ten-inch top, or an eight-inch top. We log to infinity. Because we need it all. It's ours, it's out there, and we want it all. Now."[7] This is a classic example of the unbridled greed exhibited by a corporate world devoid of ethics and of any sense of moderation.

The foregoing attitude also represents the final unravelling of the climate systems that have kept the world liveable. While those whom it suits may claim that this is not so, knowledge of the relationship between forests and climate has been around for a long while. For example, *The Canada Farmer, A Fortnightly Journal of Agriculture, Horticulture and Rural Affairs,* Vol.1, No.1, dated January 15, 1864 (Toronto) published this: "The wholesale destruction of the forests of Canada is an evil that begins, at least in many localities, to demand a check...the shelter needed by many crops in exposed situations is removed, and unfavourable climatic changes are taking place which can be clearly traced to the wholesale and indiscriminate destruction of timber. A little exercise of judgment, forethought and taste would mend matters very much. For example, why cannot some of the young wood be preserved when land is cleared, to form groups which shall at once ornament the landscape, furnish shade for stock, and act as a wind-break when cold and biting blasts sweep over the fields?"[8]

The forethought offered in *The Canada Farmer* was not unique. In the same year, 1864, George Perkins Marsh, early in his 22-year career as American ambassador to Italy, published his enduring classic *Man and Nature, or Physical Geography as Modified by Human Action.* Summing up the essential nature of forests in protection of farming, in retention of water by tree roots to keep streams running year-round, and displaying an ecological awareness still unapplied today, Marsh wrote of the effects of over-logging in Europe and of vast sums that had to be spent to partially correct danger from avalanches and recurrent floods. In offering his conclusions in what amounts to an early plea for a land ethic, Marsh wrote:

We have now felled forest enough everywhere, in many districts far too much. Let us restore this one element of material life to its normal proportions, and devise means for maintaining the permanence of its relations to the fields, the meadows, and the pastures, to the rain and the dews of heaven, to the springs and rivulets with which it waters the earth.[9]

Extensive damages still follow forest removal. In the Pacific Northwest of the United States hundreds of landslides occur annually. Ninety four percent of these slides originate from logging roads and clear-cuts. Debris torrents from deforested watersheds caused billions of dollars worth of damage in a single year (1996).[10]

Much as we prefer not to disturb our dream of life, every logging truck carrying logs to market, and every vehicle flatulating its way along the highway is helping to finish off the stability of our climate and of ourselves.

Noting the tolerance the earth has long given to our habits of flooding the air with noxious gases and the living waters with sewage and industrial effluent, she might also have reminded us that she is now presenting us with the ultimatum we can see if we use our eyes and minds. We have a limited time to respond with changed behavior. We live in a vast ecosphere that we understand fragmentally and should remember that while ecological systems have resilience, they also have limitations, and when these are exceeded ecosystems can collapse with rapidity.

The strange thing about our situation is that we have been led into a trap because of our own complacency. Years ago when the concept of division of labor emerged, it may have been derived from as simple a thing as a family diverting a small creek to provide water for its garden, and then allowing its neighbors to use some of the diverted water in exchange for the plowing of a field. And so division of labor has continued, and provided many benefits to people, but it has now proceeded so far that we have allowed others (politicians, industrialists, advertisers) to even do our *thinking* for us. This has produced a power structure of aggressive exploiters whose concern is limited to short-term values and profits. Blinded by their sense of immediacy, their newest moves turn out to be their newest mistakes. If we could learn from nature we would correct our major blunders and then become as deliberate as she is. Our haste to change would be vastly modified. Over confident leaders would not be compelled, as often as they are now, to invent new smoke screens to mask the fact that the ecosphere is rapidly disintegrating as the result of the megablunder of heedless exploitation.

Some idea of the way progress might have altered if we acted upon our knowledge may be found in the fact that global warming was anticipated as long ago as 1896 by Nobel-winning Swedish chemist Svante Arrhenius. He recognized that people were burning fuels such as oil, coal, and wood at an increasing rate each year. His scientific background enabled him to understand that huge amounts of carbon dioxide were emitted into the atmosphere from the combustion of these fuels. In April 1896, an article written by him was published in the London, Edinburgh, and Dublin *Philosophical Journal*. In it he explained that, "We are evaporating our coal mines into the air," and that the addition of so much carbon dioxide must be altering the transparency of the air and causing the less transparent air to act as a blanket, which in time might cause the earth to become heated to an extent that people have never before known. His article was extremely thorough and predicted that a doubling of carbon dioxide in the air would cause mean earth temperature to rise between five and six degrees Celsius.[11] The accuracy of his predictions was verified by computer modelling in the 1960s, and the amount of carbon dioxide in the atmosphere does increase each year. In spite of a tremendous mass of data that verifies the steady accumulation of greenhouse gases, newspapers representing corporate interests have for years denied that we need change our ways to accommodate reality.

Another example of ignoring scientific findings that might have led to a less damaged atmosphere is that we are only now becoming serious about developing reliable propulsion engines for vehicles, from fuel cells. Yet the fuel cell was first designed by Sir William Gove in 1839. The fuel cell combines hydrogen and oxygen in an electrolytic reaction and generates low voltage electricity. In Gove's design the electrolyte was sulfuric acid. It has not been in the interest of the fossil fuel industry to develop fuel cells. But fuel cells have been used in space vehicles and experimental electric vehicles. Their reliability and longevity have made them useful in remote relay stations and their high power and low weight recommend their widespread use in propulsion systems. The byproduct from the fuel cell reaction is water.

Our behavior needs to be altered in ways that call for sacrifice of many conveniences we have allowed ourselves to think of as necessities. Many items that make life more pleasant are far from essential. They may indeed be embellishments to an automated lifestyle, but our resource and energy hunger is leading to shattered ecosystems that are collapsing under planet-wide toxicity. It will be a difficult thing for many people to moderate affluent lifestyles. Though it is quite easy to get along without luxury that has never been possessed, it is otherwise when people are already accustomed to wasteful substitutes for the expenditure of their own energy. We must face the difficult days required by sober realization of the problems we have produced.

Shopping disease, vigorously promoted, makes it very difficult to maintain personal autonomy. While shopping has become a sort of holy pursuit in the Western world wherein people do not have many pressing tasks to accomplish, it resembles a school of fish trying to swim past a multitude of baited hooks. We don't like to think of ourselves as gullible victims of systematic selling but, like pack rats, we are attracted by glitter and color, as well as by a collectomania that has led to far more possessions than are needed. Since it is exceptionally easy to succumb to the temptation for a low down payment (or none, as the economic climate becomes riskier), and for so-called easy terms, people become soundly hooked by their own impulsiveness. If they repeat their follies, they are kept in a state of servitude, striving with might and main to pay off their debts and the interest upon them. There is much wealth to be acquired by reducing wants, and serious wisdom in not buying a thing until you can afford to pay for it — or in not buying it at all. How often do we buy an object only to discover later that we rarely use it? It is not only fish that must learn to pass by the baited hook.

We need significant change quite desperately. Society is over-organized and is being run with only enough cosmetic input from advisory committees to keep people minimally happy — to offer them the condolence of an occasional fleeting thought that their input may matter. The trouble with being run from the pinnacle, is that the sated individuals at the peak are a very long way from the foundation. Stratified by the wrong sort of success, blind and deaf in the illusion of importance, the attitude of today's economic leaders resembles Gratiano's description of human behavior to the Venetian merchant Antonio in the *Merchant of Venice*:

> There are a sort of men whose visages
> Do cream and mantle like a standing pond
> And do a wilful stillness entertain,
> With purpose to be dress'd in an opinion
> Of wisdom, gravity, profound conceit,
> As who should say, 'I am Sir Oracle,
> And when I ope my lips let no dog bark!'[12]

If we did not have a vast moral problem at the root of society, in the very soil of its existence, we would not have produced leaders so mesmerized by monetary profit that they have succeeded in piloting the world's ships of state, which after all are more like rowboats of recklessness, upon the jagged rocks of retribution. We apparently prefer to continue as we are doing but, however many excuses we make, we are unravelling the fabric of planetary life. We have a flippant unconcern and a "let them eat cake" attitude toward exploited nations whose bread-making abilities have often been sacrificed to the demands of techne. As a single consideration, think of the thousands of people moved from food-producing lands for the sake of hydroelectric "development," and of tens of thousands who live directly downstream from the monstrous potential energy temporarily held back by high dams. Consideration of basic human rights is nil when a new mega-project promises new opportunities for power, fame or profit. These shallow aims suffice for the dismantling of ecosystems that have supported abundant life for millennia.

We do indeed need a massive renewal of human ideals, from the ground up. Those at the peak of success, who have expected the lion's share of life and admiration as well, may buoy themselves up for a moment or two longer, but the reality of earth is a great leveller. Mountains may rear snowy peaks, but the geological force of peneplanation eventually renders mountains into molehills, proving that gravity exerts its inexorable force upon objects both large and small.

We really do not have time for scapegoats. There are no doubt endless worthy candidates for the "Illustrious Order of Scapegoats," but they are best left to the mills of the gods, which are rumored to grind exceedingly fine. We have a planet to make liveable again. This is an enormous chore, a very worthy one, perhaps the first worthy chore humanity has ever had, and if we could bury our hostilities toward one another and work devotedly for an aim bigger than ourselves, we might walk again on the path toward civilization. We may have art galleries, symphony halls, universities, and manners that tell us how to behave when we are having a fashionable tea; but a world that can count 26 million dead in World War I and 53 million dead in World War II,[13] and has a vast stockpile of nuclear and biological weaponry on hand, can hardly expect its application for citizenship to be approved by a judge of the Universal Court.

Let's say that we became serious about the matter of restoring the foundation of our life, the earth. We would need, first of all a change in attitude that would awaken us individually and also awaken our ossified institutions.

We might remind our churches, for example, that they have seldom emphasized the fact that we need to respect the creation. After all, if they are in the business of teaching respect for the Divine, one way of showing that respect is to pay scrupulous attention to the health of the pristine gift of a beautiful and bounteous earth, a place that any thoughtful person should appreciate with every iota of being.

Certainly the task before us is monumental, and the odds are not encouraging. But it is true that the first step in any enterprise often seems the most difficult, and it is already long past the time when human ingenuity must be applied to clean up the mess that human ingenuity has created. Now is the time to address ourselves to the problems of pollution, over-population, deforestation, over-production, over-consumption, global warming, the diminished ozone layer, and our dwindling resources.

All things could change upon recognition of the great need that exists for people to think for themselves and to become aware that the foundation of our lives, the earth, is slipping out from under our feet. I suspect that the greatest civilizing influence on our souls is the earth itself. Life in harmony with the earth may be a forsaken ideal but it still contains more promise than life in the crowded hives of sin which the cities have become. Wheeling and dealing, jockeying for status, vying for importance, and departure from the sights and sounds of nature, are all steps by which we further distance ourselves from the true values of life.

It may well be that many of the problems with violence among young people, with crime, drugs, alcohol, suicide, and our vulnerability to stress is simply a derivative of the idea that as we sow, so shall we reap. Because we have sowed meaninglessness, we reap it in our daily lives.

Our continued existence now depends upon our ability to confront the greatest challenge our species may ever encounter. Looking at it from a Christian perspective, we must recognize the responsibility assigned in the Book of Genesis that we were put upon the earth to dress and keep it, and to make it like a garden.

There is something to be said in favor of looking upon an enterprise constructively. Let's say that we have many disillusioned people around, including many frustrated young people with no apparent future before them.

Instead of giving up on the whole matter of our future because it seems unsolvable, let's kick out that defeatist attitude, and summon up the courage to tackle the problem and solve it. This can be done with the help of our educational institutions. Let's help our young people become aware that they are the first generation ever to have the chance to save a planet, to take real steps that might make the future become a little brighter every day, to make the planet more habitable, the air more breathable, the water cleaner, and the soil healthier. The time is ripe for a turn-around generation to reverse the foibles of its predecessors. The power of an idea whose time has come is real.

To be sure, there is nothing easy about the whole task, but there is everlasting truth in the old axiom that, "In the Beginning was the Word." The phrase is an inspiration in itself because, as Plato suggested, ideas rest at the heart of life, and the *idea* of restoring the planet and ourselves to health must exist before the task itself can begin.

There are at least two obvious and opposite areas in which our efforts to change should be made. There are things that would need to be done, and other things that would need to be undone. There are things we have omitted to do, and other things that we have done excessively. In general, we have omitted to clean up after ourselves in many shocking ways. We pour all kinds of effluents into water and air all over the world. On a major riverway, settlements take water for human consumption on the upstream side of the community and pump sewage into the river on the downstream side. It is not unusual to see mocking signs saying, "Flush the toilet, the water is needed in...," the sign completed by the name of a downstream community. As scientists have pointed out, diseases that afflict the family home may be vectored by the faucets that deliver our water. It is difficult to accept the truth that the water we drink may have already passed through eight or ten other people.

Instead of stopping the pollution of waterways, we filter and chlorinate water before it is consumed. But the chlorination of water may result in chlorine compounds that cause mutations. This was called to people's attention in a Washington Post column by Nobel laureate Joshua Lederberg in 1969.[14] Thus, with all our grandiose technological aspirations we have turned our backs on proper sewage disposal and protection of water from excessive contamination. Many rivers, in fact, have become little more than sewage canals. Obviously the quality of fish and other life able to survive in such streams, the suitability of water for swimming and other recreational purposes, the aesthetic effects, even the wisdom of rinsing hands in such flowage, are impaired tremendously by omission of even the slightest concern for what we do. This seems a matter to be seriously questioned from the pulpits, since earthkeeping is an assigned responsibility of people. It is also a matter of such importance that the extent of our omissions should immediately displace the lurid sensationalism that keeps newspaper readers unaware of the bald fact that we are jeopardizing our very lives by ignoring the news to which we should be giving our primary attention.

There are also things we overdo. Having already mentioned ceaseless purchasing of unnecessary objects, it is unavoidably necessary to consider slavish relationship with mechanical devices — the most obvious being personal vehicles. Inasmuch as transportation is the largest single source of air pollution in Canada and the U.S., any voluntary curbing of private motor vehicle use is a step in the right direction. Reduction in the use of motorized machines of all sorts would help reduce the constant barrage of gases that enter the air. Motor vehicles are the culprits in production of nearly two-thirds of atmospheric carbon monoxide, one-third of the nitrogen oxides (which react to form particles and ozone), and a quarter of hydrocarbons, which also form ozone. Automobiles, trucks, gas-fueling hoses and refineries steadily produce benzene, a known carcinogen, and several other compounds that are considered probable carcinogens. These include acetaldehyde, 1,3-butadiene, formaldehyde, and diesel particulates when diesel engines are the power source. The United States EPA estimates that the air toxins produced from trucks and cars are responsible for half of all cancers caused by toxic air pollution. Travel by car and truck continues to increase and, like many other contemporary problems, a major change in attitudes and values must precede any significant change toward more hopeful behavior.

A long look at today's society will detect that many people are relying on counselling, psychological intervention at deeper levels, and are dependent on stress-relieving and mood-enhancing drugs. Unfortunately the value system, or lack of value system, in our society has accentuated material success and has paid very little attention to inner strength that ensues from a life of greater serenity. And serenity comes from self-examination, from the ability to soberly consider the meaning of life and to achieve a modicum of detachment from a society that admires undue speed, and spends much of its time racing from one nowhere to another. What is the need for the frenzied race for undefined progress? Would it not be wiser to clean up the mess we have made on earth than to throw away our energies and wealth in space travel? We have enough problems with inner space, and avoid confronting inner space problems. Instead we blithely look off into the fantasy world of a future that will not arrive because we are irresponsible in our behavior toward earth. Havelock Ellis saw human nature quite clearly in his observation that: "The sun and the moon and the stars would have disappeared long ago — had they happened to be within the reach of predatory human hands."

With a different attitude at the core of our being, we could turn things around. Perhaps through the employment of actual goodwill within ourselves, and certainly with a different attitude toward wealth (that it is to be shared for succor of all life) we could take a solid first step toward civilization. Suppose we used our media to educate people to the realities of life, rather than to entertain them at a rather low level of being. With reasonable possibilities for a fifty-year-long truce on earth, we could immediately free the trillion or more dollars a year used in the insane race for military power with which to destroy one another. Realizing that free enterprise should never have subsidized corporate welfare, we could free another 650 billion dollars a year that passes from one hand to another in an unholy alliance between politicians and big business. If informed voters were asked to choose between a space race and mobilization to restore the health of the planet, I am sure that the planet would receive top priority.

Certainly the world faces the loss of jobs, whether it is from stagnation of the present unrealistic economy or from more modest lifestyles necessitated by the insupportable burden we have placed on the planet. One benefit of a more ethical view upon life is that the gap between the very rich and the very poor would be narrowed. As Gandhi suggested, "There is enough for everyone's need, but not for everyone's greed."

Obviously a new concept of economy would be needed. We know, as never before, that there are no free externalities. The poisoning of air or water may start off as a nuisance, but soon moves to the stage where calcium and magnesium are leached from soil, lakes acidified, limestone and marble eroded by acid rain, and as we know, ultimately reaches the stage where organisms pay with their health and their lives. Our Gross National Product only increases because the profit side of the ledger has no counterpart to show the steady diminishment of resources, the increased fouling of the entire earth from pollution fallout, waste disposal, and from the fact that we have produced all sorts of synthetic materials for which there is no enzyme that will lead to biodegradation. The economy we have devised, is clearly formulated to suit a money-bedazzled business world that believes in free lunch forever and in never paying its debts.

And of course it should no longer be treated as counterproductive to even utter the thought that the party is over and it is time to pay the piper.

James Lovelock, an eminent scientist has catalyzed pioneer studies in planetary biochemistry, physiology, and climate regulation. His book *Healing Gaia, Practical Medicine for the Planet* suggests that "humans on earth behave in some ways like a pathogenic microorganism"[15] or a malignant growth. He contends that while our middle-aged planet is sturdy, it is nonetheless plagued by abnormal chemicals that are not made by normal planetary processes. The earth's ecosystems thus display severe signs of stress. He suggests also that a planetary dermatologist might well be concerned with extensive skin damage suffered by the planet due to removal of normal ground cover. Resulting desertification, and scrub land deteriorating toward the desert stage, may have lethal consequences.

Lovelock reminds us that vegetation on earth forms a living skin upon which we live. Denuding earth of its forests and other natural ecosystems is comparable to burning the skin of a human. The process we call transpiration by forests and other natural ecosystems is comparable, in his words, to "sweating." This release of moisture by trees forms cloud cover that produces rain. This in turn keeps forests alive and contributes to global weather systems, and to the existence of springs and streams that run continually. Trees and rain go together. Cut down the trees and, in effect, the clouds are cut down and the country begins to dry up and can support much less life. Lovelock reminds us that 21 million hectares of land are "degraded to scrub or desert each year." The yearly erosion of soil, as a consequence, amounts to 24 billion tons. The cumulative damage to the planet makes our economic pursuits seem like nothing more than the swan song of a species sliding toward oblivion.

A point to ponder upon is Lovelock's mention of the fact that when a human body has lost 70% of its skin, death usually results. According to his calculations we have now reached 65% destruction of the earth's skin, and there seems to be no sign of awakening on the part of our industrial colossus.

In continuing his comparison of our ways to a disease of the earth, Lovelock visualizes four possible outcomes of this affliction:

First, the earth, our host, will destroy us in the same manner that our bodies often win the battle against invading organisms. Earth's resistance is already launching violent storms, droughts, and temperature changes as a sign of its fevered state. Serious crop failures could well be in the offing. Wars, famines, and diseases, as Malthus suggested, will result from over-population, stress, and reduced ability to cope with events even beyond our imagination.

A second outcome is that we may be victorious in our war against our own earth, and will continue the degradation of its life support systems until they collapse. This is simply a lose-lose situation — a sort of unthinking species suicide in which we triumphantly destroy our planet. Our conquest of nature and eradication of ourselves will be the ultimate consequence of a parasite so weakening its host, that host and parasite both succumb. This would also indicate the ultimate insanity of an intelligent species that might control its own behavior and have more realistic values.

The third possible outcome would amount to an ailing species continuing to exist on a sickened planet. As the productivity of the earth declined, so would the health and numbers of organisms it could support. Both host and dependent species would suffer attrition and a seesaw state of jeopardy would exist with an unpredictable conclusion.

The fourth, or win-win, situation that we might work toward would involve a shift on our part from parasitism to another form of symbiosis called mutualism. As the name implies, mutualism involves an arrangement through which two dissimilar species can benefit from each other. We should not find a mutualistic relationship difficult to understand. The digestive tract of a healthy human, for example, contains more than 400 species of bacteria, with a total weight of about 1.5 kg. (ca 3.3 lbs.). Although a minority of the bacteria may cause disease, most live in a mutually beneficial relationship with us.[16] The dependence of insects on flowers is a form of mutualism that is well known. An insect such as a bee may derive food from nectar produced by a flower and at the same time carry pollen from the anther of one plant to the stigma of another, thus ensuring cross-pollination. Another example of mutualism is the transport and burying of acorns and walnuts by squirrels. These animals have been called uphill planters of oak trees because they bury and forget many of the seeds they harvest from trees. Other examples include the relationship between crocodile birds and crocodiles in which the birds pick leeches from around the teeth of the reptiles and the crocodiles in turn open their mouths so the birds can feed. Ostriches and zebras also have a mutualistic arrangement in which they associate in mixed groups. The ostrich is keen-sighted, and the zebra has sensitive scenting ability. Both species thus gain added protection from surprise attack by predators.

It's easy to see that change of enormous magnitude must be made if we are to avoid the three less palatable outcomes suggested by Lovelock. To reach an arrangement of mutualism between ourselves and the earth will require a generosity of spirit that is not typical of modern society. We have intelligence enough but are weak in that much-advocated compromise usually reduces our intelligent decisions to a lowest common denominator.

What we really need, right now, is a mysticism to control our mechanisms. Our final defense, and the only one powerful enough to work, is great strength of soul. People may wish to quibble about the existence of soul, but it is time to put aside such differences and call upon our greatest inner reserve of strength. One of the ways I have thought of soul is as the personal link we have with the universe and its greatest meaning. As I see it, we did not come into life as a mere product of chaos. We have borrowed our bodies from the earth, but we brought the seed of more sublime thought with us as an innate gift. Preoccupied as we are with sophisticated pleasures and possessions, most people still experience moments of puzzlement when it seems that we are missing some elusive meaning in our lives. That meaning may be the need to devote ourselves to that which supports our existence and provides for the growth of mind, body and spirit. These things to which we give lip service — such as peace on earth and good will toward all things — are real possibilities, but only if we think about such things as Pico della Mirandola's observation that we must always face the choice between trying to be beast or angel, of choosing the sacred over the profane. Our lives may be short, but need be neither nasty nor brutish.

CHAPTER 14

Needed:
A Theology of the Earth

Love all God's creation, the whole and every grain of sand in it. Love every leaf, every ray of God's light. Love the animals, love the plants, love everything. If you love everything, you will perceive the divine mystery in things. Once you perceive it, you will begin to comprehend it better every day. And you will come at last to love the whole world with an all-embracing love.

The Brothers Karamazov
Part II, Book VI, Chap. 3

We have long been aware that a small error may bring about a large misfortune. Think of the childhood adage, "For want of a nail a shoe was lost..." In the quotation above, from *The Brothers Karamazov*, Fyodor Dostoyevsky identified the essential quality we lack that puts all life on earth in danger. We do not love the earth! We consider it a non-living cornucopia of resources; simply there for our pleasure, use or abuse, whatever we wish. Religions have not helped. They have led us to believe that our future is in heaven, and that earth is an unimportant way-station. As I have indicated, the Bible states otherwise, but earth-care has been de-emphasized or even ignored.

And yet, the creative redeeming good-will that is at the heart of love may be the divine essence itself. I recall books written under the name of David Grayson that recounted tales of his rambling in nature in the first half of this century, days when highways were more like byways, and rural life was common. Grayson told of a walking tour of several weeks in which he continually passed rocks that had been painted with the words: "God is Love." He hoped he might eventually catch up with the person who was doing the painting, and finally encountered a man with a brush in the act of painting his single message to the world. And David Grayson, after talking with the man for a while, did ask, "Why do you paint 'God is Love' all along these roads?" And the man replied: "Because it is true." Reason enough!

With love as a guide we might recognize that our own integrity is dependent on the integrity of the earth and the maintenance (or restoration) of the natural systems that provide for healthy life. It is ridiculous to equate progress with a steadily growing GNP that does not recognize ever increasing GED — Gross Ecological Destruction.

Is it wisdom or foolishness to seek ever increasing funds for health care but to make only feeble efforts to remove the causes of poor health? Fine particulate matter from vehicles aggravates respiratory problems, notably asthma, which afflicts nearly twenty million Canadians and Americans. Is the ideal solution the installation of air conditioning in cars and homes everywhere? Where does this leave those who work or play outdoors? Should pedestrians wear oxygen masks? Should we continue to eject known and suspected carcinogens into the air and treat unfortunate victims with Draconian chemicals that do little more than prolong life through a lingering period often characterized by intense suffering? Is it not obvious that we are poisoning everything between the seas and the skies, as well as the seas and the skies themselves? Does the fascination of humans with weapons of mass destruction indicate the reality of the death wish commented upon by Sigmund Freud?

Although historians tell us that civilization declines mainly through the failure of political leaders to respond to challenges for change, it is abetted in its decline when citizenry amuses itself to death with endless trivia and focuses only on "how much we can get." Governments likewise fail even to govern themselves, for they also are guided by the prevailing mentality of these years.

Civilization is a goal toward which our society makes only feeble, pawing attempts, especially when there is a conflict between self interest and what is good for society. But civilization can only come about when we have refined our ideals and realized that the integrity of the earth and of all life is more important than self-aggrandizement.

The bedrock of our being lies deep within our interiority, the mystic region to which we assign the word soul. We may be cynical of any deeper meaning in life, but there is an inscrutable force within us that energizes at least some people to rise to their feet and oppose the social injustices of the times in which they live. Philosophers long ago pointed out that true justice is older than any state or governing body, while the type of justice that meets the aims and goals of the power structure of a given time is often crude and self-serving. Watered down justice, as Socrates pointed out long ago, is destructive even to those who administer it for, as he explained, the person who is wronged and suffers injustice may be injured in body or mind, but the one who does wrong to others injures his own soul by destroying what Socrates considered its greatest good: "the equable temper from which all fitting actions flow." As the actions of a period in history become more and more random, a loyal and audible opposition may serve as the only bulwark against oppression. Today's injustices can only be corrected by a quantum leap from the essence of the human soul. And the main injustice is to the earth.

The soul may be unknowable in the sense that it does not fit into the observable world of science. Yet people have recognized for years that there are inner qualities, more evident in some individuals than others, that urge them to strive toward perfection of self. This inscrutable force has often been identified as soul or what might be called the "prime mover" of individuality.

Circumspect science knows that it emerged from the human intellect and is at its best in working with things that are external and mechanical. Within its own limitations, science can only draw its skirts away from that which enters the domain of the philosophical or mystical.

The soul has been tagged as an essence that inhabits the deepest reality within ourselves. It precedes the intellect because from the soul stems the will, which, in its turn, directs the intellect toward tasks that include the sciences. Science therefore cannot stand aloof from the soul force that motivates society, or fail to take moral responsibility for the results of its research.

It might be supposed that science and religion are mutually exclusive of one another. However, Werner Heisenberg, a physicist who became a Nobel laureate in 1932, commented that there is a religious language and a scientific language, and we need BOTH of them.[1] Furthermore, he instructed, we should avoid weakening the content of either language by blending them. Science focuses primarily upon objective issues, but religion focuses upon objective *and* subjective issues. Heisenberg saw the world as a place of material plenty but one in which the trust (or faith) that gives life its meaning is missing. The role of theology becomes apparent in a single sentence in which he identified the plight of many people today: "We must try to overcome the isolation which threatens the individual in a world dominated by technical expediency."

While we may marvel at the attainments of science, we must realize that it has often been directed by many attitudes of the human psyche that are still barbaric. The human arsenal of nuclear weapons, agents of biological warfare, and biocides in general, indicates that we have not yet developed enough intellectual restraint to stand anywhere but on a powder keg. If there is one lesson we may derive from our sciences it is that it is unwise to create substances or conditions that cannot be controlled. Today's certainty can easily become uncertainty tomorrow. Nature's precaution that there should be an enzyme capable of breaking down each organic substance, displays a wisdom that should be applied to scientific tinkering. We have tons of nuclear waste that has been "thrown away" (into the oceans for example), although we now know that we have no "away" that is safe for disposal of such substances, and we lack the fortitude to spend the sums that are required to find a safe way to take apart the mess we have created. Likewise, we have invented chlorofluorocarbons that are so stable they will continue destroying the ozone layer for at least another century, and these were released into the atmosphere by millions of tons before their menace was realized. Haste makes waste indeed, and also creates new menaces. We have lacked respect or even a basic realization of the fact that we are but one kind of living organism in a complex, interwoven system of life. It is hardly an accolade for our self-importance to reflect that we may be nothing more than a monkey wrench in the mechanism of a living universe — an anomaly to be erased as we awaken the checks and balances that are a part of the legal code of the cosmos.

Wild and unadmirable as society has become, and in spite of perennial exploitation, hypocrisy, and the vicissitudes of daily life, there is a counterforce we have been given, an ace in the hole that we can play if we have the wisdom to use it. I am referring to the moral force that lies at the root of individuality. This is the deepest reality within an individual and is the still, small voice of soul that willingly counsels us when we let ourselves listen. When we run at reckless haste, chasing a will-o-the-wisp such as fame for the sake of fame, glory for the sake of glory, power for the sake of power, or wealth for the sake of wealth, we are seeking counterfeit goals. And the soul, which is aware of the folly of seeking vanity or mere temporal rewards, only occasionally nudges us to remind us it is there. But when we observe, inquire, and ponder for the sake of truth, and reach for understanding of what is eternal we are energized from the depth of our souls.

To attain infinity, unity and complete understanding, said the Brahman philosopher Shankara (788–820 AD), we must burn with desire for liberation from ignorance. Today the counterforce of soul is causing many people to despair of our present shabby goals of acquisition and display. They already smolder with zeal for things more meaningful. Deeply rooted morality is surfacing. It is groggy perhaps with reawakening, but attracted by the idea of sifting the essential things of life from the irrelevant, the eternal from the temporal, and the whole from the part.

It is not logic that we need said Shankara, it is insight; and he echoed the thoughts of his predecessor, Jaimini, an Indian religious leader of the 4th century BC, who noted that reason is like a lawyer and will prove anything we choose, for it seeks equal arguments for both sides of any issue, and weakens character while it undermines values. To train our reasoning powers in the lifelong education we experience will be nothing without the cleansing, enriching, and deepening discipline of the soul. And within each individual, in that discernible inner quietness, lies the answers with which we were born, those that show us the "right" path. Perhaps Socrates was accurate in saying, "We do not learn, we remember."[2]

What makes soul such a winner compared to the flotsam and jetsam of a super-manipulated society is that it is the bane of existence to those who would like to make people into full-fledged automata. That would be extremely convenient to the would-be arrangers of society who were referred to as the "Terrible Simplifiers"[3] by philosopher Lewis Mumford. While constant manipulation of peoples' minds is part of the inferences, half-truths, or no truths at all, that are lumped under the name of propaganda, the deep interiority of humans still tugs them toward truth in whatever reflective moments they have. In casual talk with individuals today there is adequate evidence to believe that the flame of life, the core of being, is becoming reactivated by the sheer inanity of synthetic wants that glittered for a time and gradually lost their luster. Much has been weighted in the balances and found wanting. More and more people are realizing that they must stand upon the rock of their own moral sense, and like Archimedes they want to move the world. Where? Quite likely toward sanity.

Some religions defend their own turf by scoffing at paganism and pantheism, but the spiritual codes of people who lived close to the earth offered far better protection to the planet. While churches present their own miracles as proof of divinity; those who lived close to the earth saw the endless miracles of growth, flowering, and seed production; witnessed the annual runs of fish by the millions into rivers and streams; saw the reappearance of herds of migratory wild animals; slept under the star-studded skies; and felt the impact of nature's constant awesomeness. And, they understood without definition that some Great Spirit constantly provided them with evidence of its presence. Theirs was a natural theology.

They were in awe of the earth, and quite properly felt a sense of reverence toward the bounty with which they were surrounded. They best knew the Deity by its works. We refer to the primitive people as uncivilized. But we have only substituted organized barbarism for the uncomplicated beliefs of an earlier time. For today barbarism dominates society in an efficient and systematic manner.

Boardroom Attilas lead their mechanized Huns to plunder and rape of the earth that would leave Genghis Khan green with envy. A basic truth evident to the primitive human has vanished beneath the suavity of skin-deep manners, the clink of cocktail glasses, and the engineering of profitable deals. The primitive knew, but the sophisticated does not, that the earth, which we do not own at all and inhabit for a very limited time, is the root of our being and the overparent of everyone. Looking at our behavior, we do not flatter God by suggesting that we are in His image.

It is tragic that we have never unified our many religious faiths by a "theology of the earth" common to them all. A given faith is often inculcated from youth. People are brought up to be strongly defensive of their faith, just as a nationalism learned from birth makes one prepare for militant postures against those from a different nation. Likewise a religious devotion to the earth, learned in childhood, would serve to instill beliefs that would prevent the continuation of such needless degradation of the planet as we see today. We can only survive our present crisis of earth mismanagement if our spiritual attitudes are substantially revised and lead to altered behavior.

I am speaking of a theology of the earth as if this had never been heard of before. But the fundamentals of it have been strongly advocated in ancient and medieval times. Unfortunately, present creeds have focused on homocentricity and eternal life while ignoring admonitions to dress and keep the earth, or to appreciate it as a divine provision for health and sanity. Who now pays any attention to the biblical instruction that the land is entitled to a Sabbath every seventh year, in which the fields are not to be sown but instead allowed rest? With the obvious disdain we have had for soil protection we cannot even entertain the idea of a jubilee occurring every fiftieth year. The fiftieth year was ordained to be a year in which neither sowing nor reaping of even voluntary growth took place, and was to be a year of forgiveness as well. But history tells us that these biblical instructions were obeyed only between the 5th century BC and the 2nd century AD.

For believers of creeds based upon the Bible, the thoughts presented above are obvious rudiments of divine instructions for nurture of the soil. For those lacking firm belief or any belief at all, they are indications that thoughtful minds since antiquity have realized the need for care and concern for the earth, and the need to moderate demands upon its fruitful soil. Though history offers many examples of abusive behavior toward the planet, salting the land after conquest, or destroying irrigation works as part of warfare, it also establishes wiser precedents for guardianship of the land. Words of caution regarding excess faith in science and humanism also appear in Isaiah (47:10): "Thy wisdom and thy knowledge, it hath perverted thee, and thou hast said in thine heart, I *am*, and none else beside me." And certainly we act today as though nothing but human beings have the slightest importance on earth.

I suggest a theology of the earth because it might provide a profound change of human attitude, which is desperately needed. It would enable us to face the truth that there are limitations on the capability of people and on human reason that we have been blithely exceeding. It is not the Psalms alone (33:5) that tell us the earth is full of the goodness of the Lord. The earth speaks plainly of that from every sun-kissed hillside and verdant meadow. It is something that is wrong with us that makes the earth a place of raging greed and of armored conflict rather than of caring co-operation. We have made a sufficient heaven into an obsessed hell. Our continued disdain for the planet indicates a colossal inability to give things their proper priority. Everything, we think, centers around human wishes, but before us was the planet. We scoff at any idea that it might have awareness, because we think of it as nothing more than a ball of earth and rock with a motley assortment of minerals useful to us. We forget that our own bodies dissolve into clay yet do not find it surprising that we have awareness. Our histories of royal families and of financial and political dealings, may be nothing more than the amazing illusions of a species of ectoparasites on earth's skin.

The question might be raised as to how theology relates to earth. This is clarified in checking a dictionary and finding that one of the definitions of theology is "the study of God and of God's relation to the earth." And religions suggest that we can know God through his works. So the study of God is something that is before us regularly, and is perhaps more fully visible to a person working or living in a natural setting than it is to one who resides in the altered landscapes and developed enterprises where the natural has been subdued by the synthetic.

It has been easy for us to lose awareness of the reality that the earth is our home. Liberty Hyde Bailey, a man who grew up among pioneers and Indians in Michigan during the 1850s and 1860s, studied agriculture and eventually held the deanship of New York State College of Agriculture at Cornell University. In 1915 he wrote a book entitled *The Holy Earth*, in which he spoke strongly of the need to focus on morality rather than in our dominion of the earth. In his words:

> We are parts in a living sensitive creation…The living creation is not exclusively man-centered. It is biocentric. We perceive the essential continuum in nature, arising from within rather than from without, the forms of life proceeding upwardly and outwardly in something very like a mighty plan of sequence, man being one part of the process. We have genetic relation with all living things and our aristocracy is the aristocracy of nature. We can claim no gross superiority and no isolated self-importance. The creation, and not man, is the norm.[4]

One of the milestones of thought on the existence of a divine power is the *Critique of Pure Reason* by the German philosopher Immanuel Kant.[5] Kant's writing reaches the conclusion that we can neither prove nor disprove free will, immortality or God by the use of reason alone. And indeed, many people believe that these questions can only be answered through the gift of faith. But Kant also suggests things that are useful to those who think about the possibility of a Supreme Power, even though they are not recipients of faith by bestowal. His thoughts indicate that reason is a very important step on the road to insight.

Kant's idea is that the moral force within us is an innate drive toward a measure of self-respect. That puts mildly what Kant states more strongly, that, "The *Ens summum* (Supreme Being) is an *ens rationis* (a creation of reason)...not a substance outside me." This allows latitude by which one can conceive that we are given a spark of the divine, an awareness of what is right and wrong. Kant does not look as much upon God as a force outside oneself but as a guiding inner commandment that exerts pressure upon an individual's reasoning power.

The acceptance of Kant's idea that we are governed by an inner moral force or moral sense appeals to the intellect as a practical means of reminding individuals of the likelihood of a greater reasoning power than their own, and of driving them toward the highest degree of perfection they can attain. The innate moral sense also may detect from the natural order of the world what Kant calls "manifest signs of an arrangement full of purpose, executed with great wisdom, and existing in a whole of a content indescribably various, and of an extent without limits."

Kant carefully makes an analogy to human art and suggests "the existence of an *architect of the world* whose efforts are limited by the capabilities of the material with which he works, but not of a *creator of the world* to whom all things are subject." He goes on to say that the existence of an all-sufficient being is not proved by the argument about arrangement or design. This would require a transcendental argument from experience and the intuition of one's mind.

We are able to understand the strife between our moral strength and our weakness. The moral sense urges us toward perfection, but our physical existence makes us vulnerable to sensual impulses. It is a paradox indeed, but may indicate the challenge of life, and the lesson it may teach through repeated failures. It is the conflict we experience that also suggests the immortality of the soul. If we have ideals within but cannot keep them functioning fully or constantly, we are able to know that superior behavior is *possible*. If we cannot attain the good, the true, and the beautiful in this short physical existence, we yet sense that our striving might lead to a continuation of being in which our ideals will be fulfilled.

Stepping away from Kant's thoughts just a bit, I would suggest that reason can lead one to a theology of the earth. Having watched the seasons throughout my own life, I am moved to think that earth's rhythms, from tides in the oceans, or spring greening of grass, to migration of birds, flowering times of plant species, all these and other things suggest transcendence in themselves. There is the intimation of a mystical, overarching presence so powerful and meaningful as to be truly indescribable. In fact this presence invites harmony with itself without an insistence of self-importance or any expectation other than the rightness of the natural order. Human interpretations of afterlife and of heaven, do not seem any more majestic than might be derived from respect and compatibility with whatever is part of nature's own way. We ourselves are a vast integration of cells, and there are such complex arrangements within and between organs and organ systems that our medical knowledge is limited at best. And it seems certain that we know the Deity even less, though we may be impressed by the thoughts of the patriarchs or sacred scripture. To live in this world with patience and appreciation, to marvel at things we can understand and yet continue to seek more understanding, these things are part of life. Life for many people is a prayer in itself as they try to live worthily in what is magnificent and understandable in part, but also is elusive as to its deeper meanings. To live in this one world as well as possible is certainly to fit oneself for whatever else may come later. But to ignore and abuse our home is something that somehow should be beneath our personal dignity.

History tells us that there came a time (circa 300 BC) when the old religion of Greece, with its pantheon of gods, no longer served to inspire society to the self-control and self-sacrifice necessary for social stability and collective survival. Educated Greeks called upon philosophers for a new worldview that would give meaning and value to life and lessen the terror of inevitable death. In answer to the discontent and need of people of that period, the philosophy of Stoicism came into being. Stoics understood that the problem of their age was the collapse of the theological foundation of morality.[6]

Before Christianity emerged from the mental and moral confusion of the Greek and Roman decline, the philosophy engendered by the Stoics helped pave the way with a dogma that stressed the necessity of faith, called for ascetic lives of simplicity and morality and emphasized the realization that all things are in God. It is not a wonder that Stoicism has been referred to as a root of Christianity, and much of its terminology is still a part of modern religion. Stoics who embraced retreat were called anchorites, and those who practiced self discipline were ascetics. Those who retreated from society into contemplative life were called "monachi" and their retreat was into a "monasterium." Maxwell Staniforth, a translator of the *Meditations* of Marcus Aurelius pointed out the derivation of the Trinity from different Stoic names for the Divine Unity.[7] He also comments on the treatise that was the foundation for moral philosophy in medieval times, the *Duties* of St. Ambrose of Milan. In this treatise the narrator is a Christian bishop but the ideas presented are those of Zeno the Stoic. Happiness is given as the ideal of life, and the happiest life is one lived in co-operation with nature. Virtue is indicated as "the highest good" and this is achieved by adhering to the pagan tenets of justice, temperance, prudence, and fortitude. Interestingly, Pope Gregory the Great (Gregory I), and theologians who followed, spoke of seven deadly sins: pride, avarice, envy, lust, anger, gluttony, and sloth.[8] To counter these, they offered four cardinal virtues, named wisdom, courage, justice, and temperance, plus three theological virtues: faith, hope and charity. Pride was ranked as the deadliest of sins, but it was felt that individual types of "sin" did not occur singly, but were intermeshed with others. Reason suggests that adherence to the original four cardinal virtues, embraced by philosophers including Plato and Pythagoras, would eliminate the need for falling into sin of any kind.

With some foundation blocks of Christianity having been tailored from the ideas of Stoicism, there is a major tenet of the Stoics that is more and more obviously a central consideration for survival. It is also a belief that would help subdue rampant humanism, and turn us away from the illusion that our "wants" are a good in themselves.

This major idea from Stoicism that we need to adopt as an ethic of being is that people are a *part* of God and of nature and that goodness may be found in co-operation with God and nature by observing and honoring the law of the world. The well-being of humanity is dependent upon, or subsequent to, the well being of the world. Preoccupation with the study of science should serve to determine the law of nature and then enable us to act according to that law. It is wisest to live in accordance to the wisdom of nature, not to destroy it.

From this belief naturally flowed the idea of asceticism. To live without luxury was considered more noble than a life of self-indulgence. The Stoics would have seen our battle to subdue the biosphere and replace it with a humanly designed noosphere as a form of madness. And certainly we are receiving enough shots across the bows of our ships of state — taking the form of vicious storms, dangerous ultraviolet rays from the sun, increasing average temperatures planet-wide, increasing desertification, environmental refugees, etc. — to know that we must change our behavior.

I sense that the Stoics were on the main track in a figurative and perhaps literal sense when they spoke of the universe as a living organism of which God is the soul, the source of universal law, and the infusing spirit that sustains all. Morality is willing surrender to the law of this world of which we are a part. Live according to the benevolence and orderliness of the universe, said the Stoics. This will bring *euthymia*, which signifies spiritual peace and well-being. Another name for life in keeping with the divine will was *eudaimonia*: a happy soul because in its effort it comes to resemble the Deity. And to extend that thought a bit further, as pointed out in the lengthy Vatican II documents, the environment is the rearing ground for souls and it therefore behooves us all to be respectful of it.

I have mentioned the Stoic idea at some length because it is a wise concept that could help to reverse the psychopathic frenzy with which our earth is being maimed, and through which our self-indulgent society is losing its foothold on life. We are apparently so confused by the ponderous verbosities of the laws created by self-serving legislatures that we feel superior to the earth that makes it possible to live. We cannot make laws that will prevent ice-storms, hurricanes, droughts or earthquakes. But we can make and enforce laws that will end the manic dumping of poisons into the air and water; and we can do positive things such as planting millions upon millions of trees to restore the carbon balance in our atmosphere.

What we need is exactly the broad concept that arose from the thoughts of the Cynics, Epicureans, and particularly the Stoics who endeavored to find a philosophy of life that would sustain humans in a theologically barren world. The point is often made that we have Christianity, but very few people act in a Christ-like manner. The question to consider is whether or not a theology can be other than barren if it is far removed from creation. In promoting the idea of human beings as the most important creatures in the universe, or as the purpose of the universe itself, the all-sustaining framework in which corporeal existence and spiritual seeking takes place is ignored.

Many people realize the need for change. They are sated with possessions, and would like a more meaningful life. It makes sense to them that we can only find enduring happiness by thoughtfully adjusting our aspirations and behavior to the purposes of the universal laws, which we sense must be more meaningful than our own. Human beings are not autonomous, but are dependent. The number of people of all ages who need psychological help today, suggests massive dissatisfaction at the deepest level of being.

There is no question that the restoration of our estranged species to the ecological niche it occupies in the natural world, especially in its basic thinking, will be difficult to accomplish. It is as though a massive Bacchanalian festival has been going on in the Western world for years. Now the decorations are down, damage to the site of the feasting is very noticeable, things are a bit tacky, and the costs, it is being learned, far exceed what promoters of the feast predicted.

A theology of the earth would be a step in the right direction. The earth, after all, is unique, and a theology of the earth would be a recognition of its divine origin and of the gift of life it vectors to all beings. Our attitude of conquering nature is an absurdity, unless our true aim is suicide.

In establishing such a theology, two purposes would be served. The earth would finally be recognized again, after years of neglect. We might look at our long fashionable idea of subduing the earth and realize that we have over-reached our abilities. What follies we have indulged in, an example being the illusion of importance that enables us to say that the earth and its myriad beings have no "standing" in our courts! It's rather obvious that Terra is helping itself to a bit more standing, in spite of courts, with every ice storm that engulfs a city, or every hurricane that makes matchwood of a community's buildings.

The second thing that would be accomplished is the setting of the stage for continued advocacy, which would awaken human thought and work to relieve some of the unreasonable demands and expectations made upon the earth.

A needed new perspective in reference to the earth would be

gained. Our present outlook would be recognized as outmoded, and seen as the reversal of reality that it is. Thus far we have had a sort of amateurish overconfidence that has enabled us to promote our modest technological accomplishments simply by labeling them "high technology." Given a few centuries in which we could learn to clean up after ourselves and to research the hazards of our new ideas before mass-producing more mistakes, we might reach the technological foothills, but Alps upon Alps will still rise behind the foothills. Before we can reach even modest heights, we will have to practice survival techniques such as an earth theology might afford.

A half millennium before the birth of Christ, the Chinese philosopher Confucius suggested that an important step toward the improvement of society would involve "rectification of names."[9] To Confucius this meant that there should be an exact correspondence between the titles given people and the fulfillment of their responsibility. People and things should be called what they are, he advised. A prince should not be called a prince unless he acted in such a manner as to be worthy of that name. High sounding titles mean nothing if given indiscriminately. Only when names are rectified can harmony exist between individuals and society. Note for instance, that we call an elected person "Honorable" although winning an election is often a matter of personal salesmanship, and support by organizations that have their own interests at heart. Elected individuals unfortunately, often behave in such fashion as to make a mockery of honor.

If names were rectified, many technological developments would more properly be called experiments. Consider, for example, the uncertainty of scientists at Alamagordo, New Mexico prior to the explosion of the first atom bomb. Before the test blast, physicists responsible established a betting pool. The low bet was that the blast would equal 300 tons of TNT, and bets ranged up to 45,000 tons. One physicist, Enrico Fermi, offered to take bets that the entire atmosphere might be ignited! Even with this range of uncertainty, the experiment was carried out. The blast equalled the force of 18,000 tons of TNT.

Given sufficient political blather and optimistic statements by promoters, a risky scheme can be made to sound like a sure thing. The conclusion of the 1988 World Conference on the Changing Atmosphere that, "Humanity is conducting an unintended, uncontrolled, globally pervasive experiment whose ultimate consequences could be second only to a global nuclear war," was a remarkably honest statement. This might be applied to development schemes ranging from the Columbia River Dams and the more than 45,000 dams over 15 meters high worldwide, to the unhindered combustion of fossil fuels, to mining endeavors that pollute and kill waterways, and other similar damaging projects.

Thus, we are surrounded by the sad problem that results when ethical concerns are abandoned and virtually anything that might make a profit or increase the power of the few over the many is condoned. In reality, it is a stunning lack of ethics shared by governments and industries that has brought about the stockpiling of more than 60,000 nuclear bombs throughout the world. It is nearly unbelievable that we have let ourselves become so intoxicated by technology that all caution is thrown to the winds as we jump from one fantasy to another. Can we really believe that we are moving toward control of the universe before we even learn to control ourselves? In Pope John Paul's (II) encyclical *Fides et Ratio* (Faith and Reason, Sept. 14th, 1998) he speaks of the need for upgrading the values of technology, saying: "If this technology is not ordered to something greater than a merely utilitarian end, then it could soon prove inhuman and even become potential destroyer of the human race."

The paranoia displayed over possible failure of computer systems in the year 2,000, and the resulting social panic that might have ensued, is a good example of social disarray caused by addiction to technology. In this instance shortsighted designers have lacked even the mild forethought required to remember that new centuries do manage to occur once each hundred years. It is a sad, just commentary to note that nuclear wars have nearly erupted because of computer malfunction, banks and other institutions collapse with computeritis on frequent occasions, and internet addiction is already looked upon as a disease. Perhaps the psalmist who advised that, "It is better to trust in the LORD than to put confidence in man," (Psalm 118:8) made more sense than those who would have us rely heavily upon machines. I certainly do not want to present myself as one who knows a lot about the Bible, but I feel that there is a lot more enduring wisdom in traditional literature than in the chimera of progress, politics, and power that paralyzes us today. The original monster of Greek mythology had a lion's head, a goat's body, and a serpent's tail. Today's Leviathan strives to be a seamless whole and studies hard to maintain a good press for itself. But it is characterized by nihilism throughout.

An earth theology could not reach prominence through religions alone. Things have slid too far toward dissolution. But religious groups could be magnificent catalysts, and could awaken many people to the absolute sacredness of the earth.

As a matter of possibility, an earth theology would form a true basis for ecumenism because all human life, and all souls of all beings, are nurtured on earth. True interdependence and inter-reliance of religions is indicated because any damage to earth is a menace to everyone's religion and everyone's existence.

An earth theology should teach new tolerance for the religion of others, and for the nations of all individuals, because the fragile existence of every living thing is bound to the earth and its health. Respecting the health of the earth could be a common bond between all peoples, and the terrible sin of separation could begin to knit beneath the ministrations of new attitudes. The words of the Bible support this idea of tolerance for we are told not to judge others (religions, for example), lest we (and our religions) also be judged. We are also reminded that, "In my Father's house are many mansions," (John 14:2), and it would seem that this admonition would be sufficient in itself to ensure peace and goodwill among sects. I'll have to admit that when I read about the many mansions, I hoped that there might be a few cabins in the woods for those who prefer living a less ornate life.

It would be timely for creeds to take a strong stance in support of protecting and restoring the earth. There is ample concern for the earth expressed in the Bible to merit strong, active support from religions, and the need for that help is immediate. More than a few people feel that the Sabbath as a day of rest and thought, has been wrongly sacrificed to the aspirations of commerce. A renewal of belief in the holiness of the Sabbath might be a great boon to the awakening and enlightenment of meditative souls. Some creeds indeed have been active ecologically and morally in many ways in recent years, but their voices have not yet reached the masses.

Reason does deduce the all-supporting role of Terra in providing for the growth of individuals — from uncaring creatures to ethical, spiritual and responsible beings. Neither churches nor states, businesses or individuals can recklessly abuse the foundation of their existence. The solution to our behavioral lapse can be found only in the reawakening of our souls, and the inclusion of the earth at the center of our morality.

When I sit in high places where the vista settles one's mind on sober thought, I think that the awesome beauty of earth invites the love and respect of everyone. Our home place is real and tangible. I comprehend a deep love and respect for the earth to be at the core of sensibility. Traditional religions attract some people, but not all. There are probably as many reasons for having faith or non-faith as there are people, and of course a person's exposure to religion in childhood has a strong influence. The wonders of the earth itself seem to me to be the beginning of religious impulse, and I have no hesitation in referring to it as the creation. Some people will object to calling it creation, but the same people may not find it strange to call a person who wins an election by the significant word "honorable." Overleaf I mentioned "rectification of names" proposed by Confucius. That probably still stands as one of the great ideas in the history of thought, and if names are rectified by their importance, the name earth would be dignified by an unimaginably flattering title, simply because it is vital to everyone of us. "Creation" is a respectful name for it, without even thinking of its exact origin, because it is endlessly creating new living things, day after day, or in the case of micro-organisms, second after second. St. Francis of Assisi referred to it as "Sister Earth, our mother," and that is appropriate too because it indicates the utter respect it deserves.

The novelty, excitement, and plenty that characterize technological advancement has blinded people to the deeper meanings of life and destroyed our insight into eternal values. The euphoria of getting and spending, and the pace that humanity has adopted in an effort to keep up with machines, have bewitched us and made us tools of our tools. The abandonment of a moral code in favor of amusing and intriguing products enabled technology to develop without ethical restraint. It has been easy to bow to its benefits but ignore its real costs. Many people understand now, however, the urgent need for moral standards that will make us less dangerous to the earth, and ourselves.

Because of the fact that we have little lead time before we are standing amidst the debris of an industrial society that has abused the earth unto revolt, we urgently need a religious attitude toward the earth, one which will infiltrate our actions and institutions.

This is why an earth theology might stand upon its own, outside established religions, and yet be embraced by them as well. There is a leveling effect, a natural ecumenism, in that whether or not one is a member of a creed, we are all inhabitants of the planet. We have a fairly common, long-standing weakness in that the earth is something we take for granted and hardly think about at all. When people sing, "America the Beautiful," or "O Canada," their thoughts are usually patriotic, but they rarely realize that without the land upon which they stand, they would simply not exist.

An earth theology would involve becoming conscious of the earth as an essential part of daily life. Perhaps it has always been a mistake that in addressing envelopes, we do not include "The Earth" as part of the address. Then we might be reminded that nations are part of a single whole, as are religions, and species of living things. Through this realization we would be beginning in an effective way to heal the age old breach of separation, the parent of all other sin. We would comprehend that dumping our wastes in the ocean or in other countries is still dumping them on earth, and in its small way every milligram of toxin adds to the poison in our own bodies and those of the people we love. Loving the earth is a foundation of love for loving anyone else.

Today's prosperity in the Western world stems from gluttonous spending of the irreplaceable natural wealth of the planet. So-called "sustained yield," (better rectified as ruthless exploitation) has led to the systematic destruction of the world's forests, fisheries, mineral and agricultural resources. And this is an attitude that has not sprung up overnight. Franklin Delano Roosevelt noted years ago, for example, that although European nations treated timber as a crop, the timber resources on this continent have been treated as a mine.

Though the spilt milk of past years is irretrievable, we should now realize that enough is enough. While a theology of the earth might seem strange upon first consideration, it would serve to constantly remind us of the sacredness beneath our feet.

The need for religious status to be assigned the planet was recognized by Dr. Walter Clay Lowdermilk, first assistant chief of the U.S. Soil Conservation Service in the first half of the 20th century. Dr. Lowdermilk spent most of his lifetime studying human relationship to the land and the causes of desertification in 28 countries on four continents. He found the same pattern recurred continually. A domino effect was caused by destruction of forests on steep mountainsides. Cutting the forests caused mountain soil, unprotected by vegetation, to wash downhill and cover the fertile valley bottoms. Further rains caused flooding, and landslides, leaving wastelands behind. Syria is a single example of a once heavily forested country devastated by erosion. Lowdermilk concluded that soil erosion in Syria has been so thorough that the country is basically a man-made desert with soils washed away beyond hope of restoration.[10]

In his landmark radio broadcast in Jerusalem in 1939, Walter Clay Lowdermilk expressed belief that if Moses had foreseen the sins of men against the land, he would have been inspired to propose an eleventh commandment to restrain human behavior on earth. According to Lowdermilk the commandment might have said:

> Thou shalt inherit the holy earth as a faithful steward, conserving its resources and productivity from generation to generation. Thou shalt safeguard thy fields from soil erosion, thy living waters from drying up, thy forests from desolation, and protect thy hills from overgrazing by herds, that thy descendants may have abundance forever. If any shall fail in this good stewardship of the earth, thy fruitful fields shall become sterile, stony ground or wasting gullies, and thy descendants shall decrease and live in poverty or perish from off the face of the earth.[11]

In writing this I realize that I have always been more impressed with the works of God/Nature than with the way of life that has stemmed from science and technology. Too many things have been discovered and implemented by science and technology that menace nature and ourselves. While in the long term nature will probably re-cover, our own survival will depend on an awakening spiritual insight.

An enthusiastically supported earth theology could open the door to spiritual renewal. Suddenly we would be able to work at the task of restoring to health and purity the precious earth that we have fouled and desecrated. Our disenchanted young people would be able to identify solid goals that are finally worthwhile. We could work on the side of that which is right and true, and the most visi-ble expression of a deeper meaning beyond life. We could heal the schisms and separations within ourselves and learn the beneficence to being that is gained through dedication of ourselves to something more enduring than the three score and ten commonly associated with our own span of years.

I see a deep love and respect for the earth as rational and realis-tic, and understand that it brings a sense of transcendence that makes us realize that we are in eternity now, at this very moment, and always will be. Our earth is tangible, but mystical as well. We can build our homes upon it, walk upon it, cherish it with our sens-es, thrill to the majesty of a seascape, the beauty of a sunset, or the serenity of an alpine lake nestled between soaring mountain peaks. The sights, sounds, and silences of our homeland are part of the *vis medicatrix naturae*, the healing force of nature, probably the best cure of stress that exists.[12]

Thanksgiving began with the idea of celebrating and appreciat-ing the bounty of the earth. How wonderful is appreciation, and how little time we give to appreciation in today's mad scramble for spir-itually worthless things. Anyone who has knelt at a cold mountain spring after toiling uphill, knows more of appreciation from a refreshing drink of cold water than sophisticated wine-bibbers with rare vintages at their command. Serene simplicity in dusty duds somehow outweighs sartorial splendor and imagined importance. I am glad that I am fortunate enough to recognize the "masterpiece" in which I live, rather than striving to own one.

Frankly, I find it repugnant not to love the real world as distin-guished from the more elaborate but detached improvisations of man. I find that my soul is at home with the soul of the planet, and am pleased that it was attributed a soul and intelligence by the ancients. To live and even to die and to be aware of this masterpiece, this earth, with its mystical ties to the intelligence of the universe is a privilege. Oneness with allness may always be our lot. A new day will dawn, and a benevolent age begin when we develop loyalty to the earth and realize it is a majestic being itself, and a vital cell in the body of the universe.

Endnotes

Chapter I

1. Paul Edwards, Ed. *The Encyclopedia of Philosophy*, Vol.6, (New York: Macmillan, Inc., and The Free Press, 1967), pp.22–31.

2. Ken Wilber, Ed., *Quantum Questions*, (Boston: Shambhala Publications, Inc., 1984), pp.122–125.

3. Ibid, pp.140–146. Note particularly the editor's footnote.

4. Edwards, *Encyclopedia of Philosophy*, Vol. 6, pp.22–23.

5. Peter Tompkins and Christopher Bird, *The Secret Life of Plants*, (New York: Avon Books, 1974), pp.95–205.

6. C.G. Jung, *Synchronicity, an Acausal Connecting Principle*, (N.J.: Princeton University Press, 1973), pp.21–42, suggests interrelation of events not commonly considered related.

7. Michael Talbot, *The Holographic Universe*, (New York: Harper Collins Publishers, Inc., 1991), pp.79–81.

8. Ken Wilber, *Quantum Questions*, pp.184–193.

9. Stephen J. Gould, "This View of Life, The Golden Rule - A Proper Scale for our Environmental Crisis," Natural History Magazine, Sept. 1990, pp.24–30.

Chapter 2

1. Manly P. Hall, *The Secret Teachings of All Ages*, (Los Angeles: The Philosophical Research Society, 1977), pp.29–33.

2. Robert Maynard Hutchins, *Great Books of the Western World*, (Chicago: Encyclopedia Britannica, Inc., 1952), Vol. 12, pp.253–310.

3. Will Durant, *The Age of Faith*, (New York: Simon & Schuster, 1950), pp.255–257.

4. ibid. pp.961–997.

5. John Keats, "Letters to George and Georgiana Keats, Feb. 14–May 3, 1819," in *The Norton Anthology of English Literature*, 4th Ed., (New York: W.W. Norton & Company, Inc., 1979).pp.874–878.

6. Lewis Mumford, *The Conduct of Life*, (New York: Harcourt, Brace, Jovanovich, Inc., 1970), pp.266, 270–275.

7. ibid. p.272.

8. Dr.J. Stan Rowe, personal letter to author

Chapter 3

1. James George, *Asking for the Earth - Waking Up to the Spiritual — Ecological Crisis*, (Shaftesbury, Dorset and Rockport, Mass.: 1995), pp.27–28.

2. Amadeus W. Grabau, *Principles of Stratigraphy*, Vol. 2, (New York: Dover Publications, Inc., 1960). pp.891–900. Reprint, unaltered, of revised edition published in 1924 by A.G. Seiler.

3. Farida A. Wiley, Editor, *John Burroughs' America*, (New York: Devin-Adair Co., 1951), p.275.

4. Walt Whitman, *Leaves of Grass and Selected Prose*, (New York: Random House, Inc., The Modern Library, 1950),p.49.

5. Lewis Mumford, *Technics and Civilization*, (New York: Harcourt, Brace, and World, Inc., 1934), p.391.

Chapter 4

1. C.H Waddington, *The Nature of Life*, (New York: Harper and Rowe, 1962), p.121.

2. James Lovelock, *Gaia, A New Look at Life on Earth*, (Oxford: Oxford University Press, 1979), pp.48, 127–131.

3. New Age Encyclopedia (Lexicon Publications, Inc., 1980), Vol. 14, pp.328–329.

4. "Manas", Los Angeles, Vol. XXXIX, No.10, March 5, 1986, p.6.

5. Lester R. Brown, Hal Kane, & David M. Roodman, *Vital Signs 1994,* (New York: W.W. Norton & Company, 1994), p.78.

6. Thomson King, *Water: Miracle of Nature*, (Collier Books, New York, 1961), p.207.

7. Wendell Berry, *Recollected Essays*, North Point Press, 1981, see essay, "Discipline and Hope," quoted in "Manas", Los Angeles, Vol. XXXIX, No. 6, Feb. 5th, 1986.

8. E.F. Schumacher, in *Roots of Economic Growth*, Raighat, Varanasi, India, Gandhian Institute of Studies, 1967.

9. Herman E. Daly and John B. Cobb, Jr., *For the Common Good*, (Boston: Beacon Press, 1989), p.21.

10. Will Durant, *Our Oriental Heritage*, (New York: Simon and Schuster, 1954), pp.776–780.

11. Paul Edwards, Editor-in-Chief, *The Encyclopedia of Philosophy*, (New York: Macmillan Publishing Co., Inc., & The Free Press, 1967), p.309.

Chapter 5

1. Arthur O. Lovejoy, *The Great Chain of Being, A Study of the History of an Idea*, (Cambridge: Harvard University Press, 1936).

2. ibid., p.119.

3. ibid., p.139.

4. ibid., p.141.

5. Alfred, Lord Tennyson, "Ulysses," Line 70.
6. Lovejoy, p.187.
7. ibid., 190.
8. ibid., p.191.
9. ibid., pp.189–192.
10. ibid., p.197.
11. Robert F. Harrington *To Heal the Earth: The Case for an Earth Ethic*, (Surrey, B.C.: Hancock House, 1990), pp.254–256.
12. J. Stan Rowe, personal letter to the author
13. D. Olive, *Just Reward*, (Toronto: Key Porter Books, 1987), p.23.
14. Lovejoy, pp.210, 252.
15. ibid., p.277.
16. ibid., pp.299–303.
17. ibid., pp.317–326.

Chapter 6

1. Ralph Waldo Emerson, Essay — "Intellect."
2. Albert Schweitzer, *Civilization and Ethics*, (London: Unwin, 1922), pp.234–235.
3. Vinoba Bhave, quoted in "Manas", (Los Angeles: Manas Publishing Co., May 31, 1978), Vol. XXXI, No. 22, p.1.
4. Henry Beston, "Human Events," Aug. 21, 1946, quoted in Manas, Vol. No. 16, April 18, 1979, p.1.
5. Thomas Carlyle, *Sartor Resartus*, (London: J.M. Dent and Sons, Ltd., 1975)

Chapter 7

1. T.C. McLuhan, Compiler, *Touch the Earth*, (New York: Pocket Books, Inc., 1971), p.45.
2. Matthew Fox, *Original Blessing*, (Santa Fe: Bear and Co., 1983), p.49
3. Costa de Loverdo, *Gods with Bronze Swords*, (New York, N.Y., Doubleday, 1970).
4. Will Durant, *The Life of Greece*, (New York: Simon & Schuster, 1939), pp.161-162 & 215–216.
5. "Manas", Vol. 1, Mar. 17th, 1978.
6. Roderick Nash, *Wilderness and the American Mind*, (New Haven, Conn.: Yale University Press, 1967), pp.23–66.
7. Will and Ariel Durant, *The Lessons of History*, (New York: Simon & Schuster, Inc., 1968).
8. Ibid., pp.43–51.
9. Lester Brown, President, Worldwatch Institute, Washington, D.C., Oct. 1998, letter announcing millennial edition of *State of the World, 1999*.
10. Wilfred C. Smith, *Faith and Belief*, (Princeton, N.J.: Princeton University Press, 1979).
11. *Great Books of the Western World*, Vol. VII, "The Republic", p.388.

Chapter 8

1. Quoted in "Manas", (Los Angeles: April 16, 1986), Vol. 39, No.16, p.1–2.

2. "Manas", April 14, 1984, Vol. 37, No. 15, p.2.

3. Ralph Waldo Emerson, Essay "Self-Reliance."

4. "Manas", Vol.27, No. 9, pp.2,7.

5. Manly Palmer Hall, *Pathways to Philosophy*, (Los Angeles: Philosophical Research Society, Inc., 1947), pp.70–99.

6. Lester R. Brown, Hal Kane, David Malin Roodman, *Vital Signs*, (New York: W.W. Norton and Company, 1994,) pp.132–133.

7. Tyron Edwards, D.D. Original Complier, revised and enlarged by Catrevas, Edwards, and Browns, *The New Dictionary of Thoughts*, (Standard Book Company, 1959), p.355.

8. Albert Schweitzer, *The Decay and the Restoration of Civilization*, (London: Unwin Books, 1923).

Chapter 9

1. David Bohm, *Wholeness and the Implicate Order*, (London: Routledge and Kegan Paul, 1980).

2. Plato, *The Republic*, Book V, p.470.

3. Robert Service, "The Men That Don't Fit In," Lines 15–16.

4. Albert Schweitzer, *The Decay and the Restoration of Civilization*, (London: Unwin Books, 1923), p.72.

5. Paul R. Ehrlich, Anne H. Ehrlich, *Population, Resources, Environment*, (San Francisco: W.H. Freeman and Co., 1970), p.324.

6. Hans Selye, *The Stress of Life*, (New York: McGraw Hill Book Co., 1956), pp.273–302.

7. Albert Schweitzer, *Goethe: Five Studies*, (Boston: Beacon Press, 1961), p.111.

8. Edward O. Wilson, *The Diversity of Life*, (Cambridge: Harvard University Press, 1992), p.280.

9. Manas, "The Ethical Sense," June 22, 1988.

Chapter 10

1. Dom. Cuthbert Butler, *Benedictine Monachism*, (Cambridge: Cambridge Speculum Historiale, 1923), pp.319–320.

2. A Monk of Dubai Abbey, Col. *The High History of St. Benedict and His Monks*, (London: Sands and Co., 1945), p.228.

3. Ambrose Bierce, *The Devil's Dictionary*, (New York: Dover Publications, 1958), p.102.

4. Larry Dossey, *Healing Words*, (San Francisco: Harper, 1993), p.205.

5. George Gordon Lord Byron, "Childe Harold's Pilgrimage," Canto IV, Stanza 178.

Chapter 11

1. Lynn White, Jr., *The Historical Roots of our Ecological Crisis* in Francis A. Schaeffer, *Pollution and The Death of Man, The Christian View of Ecology*, (Wheaton, Illinois: Tyndale House Publishers, 1979), pp.97–115.

2. Murray Bodo, OFM, *The Way of St. Francis*, (New York: Doubleday and Co., Inc., 1984), p.145.

Chapter 12

1. Thomas Carlyle, *Sartor Resartus*, Book 2, Chapter 8.

2. Manly P. Hall, *The Secret Teachings of All Ages*, (Los Angeles: The Philosophical Research Society, Inc., 1977), p.CCIV.

3. Lafcadio Hearn, *Gleanings in Buddha-Fields*, (London: Travellers' Library, 1927), p.7–28.

4. Charles S. Elton, *The Ecology of Invasions by Plants and Animals*, (London: Methuen and Co., 1958).

Chapter 13

1. Stewart L. Udall, *The Quiet Crisis*, (New York: Avon, 1963).

2. Linda Starke, Ed., *State of the World 1999*, (New York, London: W.W. Norton & Company, 1999) see foreword. p.XVIII and a newsletter from Worldwatch Institute dated June 1999, p.2.

3. Linda Starke, Ed., *State of the World 1998*, (New York, London: W.W. Norton & Company, 1998), p.62, 205.

4. Lawrence LeShan, *The Medium, The Mystic, and the Physicist*, (New York: Ballantine, 1982), p.11.

5. Richard A. Falk, *The Endangered Planet*, (New York: Random House, 1971).

6. *State of the World 1998*, pp.41–58.

7. Grace Herndon, *Cut and Run*, (Telluride, Co.: Western Eye Press, 1991), p.139.

8. Quoted in Dave McIntosh's, *When the Work's All Done This Fall*, (Toronto: Stoddard Publishing Co. Ltd., 1989), p.194.

9. George Perkins Marsh, *Man and Nature*, (Cambridge, Mass.: The Belknap Press of Harvard University Press, 1965), p.280 (Originally published in 1864).

10. *State of the World 1998*, p.26, p.194.

11. Jonathan Weiner, *The Next One Hundred Years — Shaping the Fate of Our Living Earth*, (New York: Bantam Books, 1990), pp.29,57,67–68.

12. William Shakespeare, *The Merchant of Venice*, Act 1, Sc. 1, Line 88–94.

13. *State of the World 1999*, p.7.

14. Paul R. and Anne H. Ehrlich, *Population, Resources, Environment*, (San Francisco: W.H. Freeman and Co., 1970), p.126–127.

15. James Lovelock, *Healing Gaia, Practical Medicine for the Planet*, (New York: Harmony Books, 1991), pp.153–186.

16. Zoltan P. Rona, MD, "Bugs for Life," *Health Naturally*, April/May, 1998, p.12.

Chapter 14

1. Ken Wilber, *Quantum Questions*, (Boston: Shambala, 1985), p.43.

2. Will Durant, *Our Oriental Heritage*, (New York: Simon and Schuster, 1935), pp.546–549.

3. Lewis Mumford, *The Conduct of Life*, (New York: Harcourt, Brace, Jovanovich, 1951), pp.268–270.

4. Liberty Hyde Bailey, *The Holy Earth*, (New York: Scribner, 1915), Reprint: (Ithaca, N.Y.: New York State College of Agriculture and Life Science, 1980), pp.5–14.

5. Immanuel Kant, *The Critique of Pure Reason*, Vol. 42, *Great Books of the Western World*, (Chicago: Encyclopedia Britannica, Inc., 1952), pp.178–190.

6. Will Durant, *The Life of Greece*, (New York: Simon & Schuster, 1939), pp.650–658.

7. Maxwell Staniforth, *Marcus Aurelius, Meditations*, (Middlesex, England: Penguin Books Ltd, 1964), pp.23–27.

8. Will Durant, *The Age of Faith*, (New York: Simon and Schuster, 1950), pp.820–830.

9. Jean Paradise, *The Encyclopedia of Philosophy*, (New York: Macmillan Company, Inc. & The Free Press, 1967), Vol.II, p.88.

10. Vernon Gill Carter & Tom Dale, *Topsoil and Civilization*, (Norman: University of Oklahoma Press, 1955), pp. 78–87.

11. Inez Marks Lowdermilk, *All in a Lifetime*, (Berkeley, Calif.: Lowdermilk Trust, 1983), pp.198–199.

12. Hans Selye, *The Stress of Life*, (New York: McGraw-Hill, 1956), p.11.

Index

Acknowledgements

We would like to acknowledge the thoughts of the many philosophers, historians, scientists, and other individuals whose works have contributed to the ideas expressed in this book. We also thank the many friends and personal acquaintances with whom we have had conversations that have helped us to clarify our ideas. Thanks especially to the late Dr. J. Stan Rowe who read and made important comments on parts of the manuscript. Thanks also to Dr. David Goranson, and Brian Murdoch for their time and encouragement.

We are particularly grateful to the many hours spent by Roland Sattler in providing computer expertise, which Linda is sadly lacking, and Bob feels he is thankfully lacking! Roland's attention to details and astute comments, especially when our own energy was lagging was greatly appreciated.

Our thanks to Maggie Oliver for use of her beautiful painting on the cover of this book. Our sincere appreciation to the late John A. Livingston for his interest and thoughtful comments on the book, and to Toshie Sumida, Reiki Master, for her unique healing gift.

Special thanks to Dr. David Suzuki for taking the time to read the manuscript and to write a foreword for this edition which we feel greatly enhances the text.

And finally our thanks to all the folks at Hancock House, editor Theresa Laviolette for her excitement over the project and her own great environmental concern. Thanks to Ingrid Luters for her creative help, and to Mia Hancock for her outstanding book and cover design. Special thanks to David Hancock for his encouragement and help over many years.

About the Authors

Linda and Bob Harrington live with their bullmastiff, Shadow, on a forested acreage at Galena Bay, British Columbia. They have also reforested a piece of logged-over land by planting thousands of trees and scattering millions of tree seeds.

Bob is a veteran of WW II, and holds a degree in geology and a master's degree in education. He is the author of several books, and numerous feature articles for newspapers and magazines. His diverse experience includes working as a prospector, as a geologist on dam construction, on the USS *Nautilus* during its construction, and teaching secondary school sciences and university ecology

courses. He was elected selectman and, later, chairman of the Board of Selectman, in a New England town. He served for several years on the editorial committee of the Journal of the Idaho Academy of Science, and he was Western Representative for the Canadian Wildlife Federation for five years.

Working in the 1950s for the USDA as a foreman–supervisor of pesticide spray operations led him to focus on the study of ecology as the overall holistic science. Fellowships in ecology gave him more insight in this field. In 1990 Bob received the British Columbia Environmental Education Award.

Linda has worked with Bob on his books and articles for many years, and shares his passion for Nature. She loves gardening, collecting and sharing wild and traditional garden seeds, and working to ensure their household leaves as small a footprint as possible on the planet.

About the Artist

Maggie Oliver trained as an illustrator at the Art Center College of Design in Los Angeles. She now lives in the village of Procter BC, and specializes in large landscape oil paintings of the West Kootenay area of southeastern British Columbia. Maggie can be contacted at mountainlandscapes@gmail.com